A First Amendment Profile of the Supreme Court

A First Amendment Profile of the Supreme Court

Edited by Craig R. Smith

JOHN CABOT UNIVERSITY PRESS
Distributed by
University of Delaware Press

Published by John Cabot University Press
www.johncabot.edu

Distributed by University of Delaware Press
in partnership with The Rowman & Littlefield Publishing Group, Inc.
4501 Forbes Boulevard, Suite 200, Lanham, Maryland 20706
http://www.rowmanlittlefield.com

Estover Road, Plymouth PL6 7PY, United Kingdom

British Library Cataloguing in Publication Information Available

Library of Congress Cataloging-in-Publication Data

A First Amendment profile of the Supreme Court / edited by Craig R. Smith.
p. cm.
Summary: "A First Amendment Profile of the Supreme Court focuses on the nine justices of the United States Supreme court and determines their frames for assessing First Amendment cases. In each of the chapters, a justice will be profiled in terms of his or her claims during the nomination hearings and the positions they have taken in significant Supreme Court decisions. The object of these chapters it to provide a rhetorical frame that each of these justices would find appealing regarding First Amendment case law"—Provided by the publisher.
Summary: "This book builds on Cicero's foundation by examining the Supreme Court of the United States in terms of how each justice determines his or her position in First Amendment cases. In addition, the profiles drawn in this study can help future Ciceros win their cases before the sitting Court"—Provided by the publisher.
Includes bibliographical references and index.
ISBN 978-1-61149-361-0 (pbk.) — ISBN 978-1-61149-362-7 (ebook)
1. United States Supreme Court. 2. Judicial process—United States. 3. United States Constitution—1st Amendment. I. Smith, Craig R.
KF8742.F567 2011
347.73'26—dc23
2011022054

The paper used in this publication meets the minimum requirements of American National Standard for Information Sciences Permanence of Paper for Printed Library Materials, ANSI/NISO Z39.48-1992.

Printed in the United States of America

This study was made possible by a grant from the Kenneth T. and Eileen I. Norris Foundation.

Contents

Chapter One

Introduction, Methodology, and Overview

Craig R. Smith

Before he became consul of Rome, and before he was unanimously voted pater patriae (father of his country), Cicero achieved fame as a lawyer. For example, his prosecution of the corrupt governor of Sicily led to a meteoric rise in influence in the Senate. Remarkably, Cicero did not come from the patrician class; he was an equite, a knight, from a class created out of successful businessmen and rich farmers. So his success was due not to his lineage but to his rhetorical ability, particularly before the courts of Rome. Cicero understood that adapting to judges and juries—including the Senate when it transformed itself into a jury—was critical to winning his cases. Eventually, Cicero wrote several books on rhetoric which laid out the *stasis* system, a series of questions that produced arguments in any given case and helped lawyers adapt to their audiences.

This book builds on Cicero's foundation by examining the Supreme Court of the United States in terms of how each justice determines his or her position in First Amendment cases. In addition, the profiles drawn in this study can help future Ciceros win their cases before the sitting Court.

Scholarship on the rhetoric of Supreme Court opinions has been important for many years. We have moved from examining lines of argument to the wider frame of rhetorical strategies as we realized that the justices were much less reliant on logic than one might expect in the supreme legal forum of the land.[1] For example, scholars have demonstrated that the use of metaphors often overcomes precedent and/or rationalizes justices' decisions.[2] In First Amendment opinions, these include such well-worn phrases as the "chilling effect," the "slippery slope," or the "pig invited into the parlor." We have also recognized that the rhetorical frame the justices accept has a direct bearing on their decision making.[3] In the extremely controversial *Bush v. Gore* ruling of 2000,[4] the majority accepted the Bush legal team's rhetorical frame that "you can't change the rules in the middle of the game," rejecting the Gore team's rhetorical frame that "every vote should be counted."[5] In this way, the arguments were framed and the dialectic engaged.

We have also seen how persuasion works among the justices themselves. Take the example of William Rehnquist, a man who came to the Supreme Court without any experience as a judge. After the Senate refused to confirm Clement Haynsworth and G. Harold Carswell, Richard Nixon asked his aides in the summer of 1971, "about that clown Renchburg down in the Justice Department?"[6] The nominee, this time by the right name, William Rehnquist, was approved 68 to 22 after some controversy. Rehnquist soon became known as the "lone ranger" of the Supreme Court because he filed 54 single dissents, a Supreme Court record.[7] Most of these opposed judicial activism and relied on a strict reading of the Constitution.

When he became Chief Justice, Rehnquist surprised the media and his critics by forming majorities around many of his opinions. Two factors helped: Reagan appointed more conservatives to the bench and Rehnquist demonstrated social and argumentative skills that produced majorities. Justice John Paul Stevens became so concerned about Rehnquist's influence that he claimed in a public speech that Reagan's attorney general Edwin Meese was conspiring with Rehnquist to advance a conservative agenda.[8]

Eventually, the conservative majority of Rehnquist, Antonin Scalia, Clarence Thomas, Sandra Day O'Connor, and Anthony Kennedy strengthened the sovereign immunity of states, which had been eroded by the Court under Chief Justice Earl Warren. For example, in *Printz v. United States*,[9] the five to four majority struck down portions of the Brady Gun Control Act because it forced state law enforcement officers to conduct background checks. Earlier in 2008, the same five justices that produced the majority in *Bush v. Gore* denied an equal protection claim against a state's treatment of gender-related violence in *United States v. Morrison*.[10] According to the ruling, Congress has no authority under either the commerce clause of the Constitution or the Fourteenth Amendment to enact the Violence Against Women Act, which provided a federal civil remedy for victims of gender-motivated violence. And in *Kimel v. Florida Board of Regents*,[11] a case concerning the use of the gender discrimination clause in the Employment Act, Rehnquist joined Scalia, O'Connor, Thomas, and Kennedy to defend the sovereign immunity of states, arguing that an *imperfection in law is insufficient to justify the application of the Fourteenth Amendment.*

Rehnquist had transformed from a lone dissenter to a majority maker.[12] He has since left the field to younger justices who are no less susceptible to—and capable of—effective rhetoric. It is clear that rhetorical sensitivity to the Supreme Court is important, not only to reading a decision, but to arguing before the justices. The hallmark of rhetoric as an art is that it is audience based. Strategies, proofs, or constraints—call them what you will—arise out of the audience; hence, audience analysis is crucial to effective persuasion. Having filed amicus briefs and sat in on several oral arguments before the Supreme Court, I am regularly astonished at the lack of rhetorical skill evident in presentations before the Court. Lawyers often fail to adjust to the predilections of justices and thereby miss important rhetorical opportunities.

This book focuses on the nine justices of the Supreme Court and determines their frames for assessing First Amendment cases. In the following chapters, each justice will be profiled in terms of his or her claims during the nomination hearings and the positions they have taken in significant Supreme Court decisions. The object of these chapters is to provide a rhetorical frame that each of these justices would find appealing regarding First Amendment case law.

VARIOUS MODALITIES: A DISCUSSION

We ground our profiles of the justices on the theory of Philip Bobbitt. [13] His first major work came in 1982, *Constitutional Fate: Theory of the Constitution*, in which he sought to involve his audience in the dialectical process of constitutional evolution. He abjured external standards and opposed treating the Constitution as a static artifact. He saw constitutional law as a rhetorical practice before the courts and the classroom. His dialectical biography of the Constitution concluded that there were certain "modalities" of argument that emerged over the course of time in Supreme Court rhetoric. These modalities are embedded in arguments found in the opinions and decisions issued by the Supreme Court; thus, meaning can only be properly read in context, and that context has its own rules. He advanced this theory in his 1991 book *Constitutional Interpretation*, which argued that "the law is something we do, not something we have as a consequence of what we do." [14] In that book, he refined his six "modalities" of argument that provide acceptable rationales for Supreme Court rulings, and which Bobbitt ultimately abstracts into a judicial "conscience." [15] Since Bobbitt's modalities are commonly employed in courses on constitutional law, we believe they provide a solid foundation for our analyses in this book. However, since each one of these modalities has rhetorical nuances, we also rely on our own expertise in the field of rhetorical criticism to flesh out the profiles of the justices.

The first modality is the historical; it relies on the intentions of the framers of the Constitution and the ratifiers of its subsequent amendments. [16] Some justices employ this modality only when a plain reading of the Constitution is not possible. Other justices rely on this method in every case in which they believe it is relevant. For example, arguments based on original intent fell on hard times during the reign of Chief Justice Warren; however, they were revived under President Reagan, particularly by his advisor and then attorney general Edwin Meese, and their nominees to the Supreme Court.

Meese was proud to cite many Founders as allies. For example, James Madison, the major author of the Bill of Rights, wrote that the Constitution must be interpreted according to "its true meaning as understood by the nation at the time of its ratification."[17] Fourteen years after his presidency, Thomas Jefferson wrote that we ought to return "to the time when the constitution was adopted, recollect the spirit manifested in the debates, and instead of trying what meaning may be squeezed out of the text, or invented against it, conform to the probable one in which it was passed."[18] Meese endorsed this notion of "original intent" in public, and in the process engaged members of the liberal wing of the Supreme Court in a debate. Speaking before the American Bar Association (ABA) in Washington, D.C., on July 9, 1985, Meese said: "The intended role of the judiciary generally and the Supreme Court in particular was to serve as the 'bulwarks of a limited constitution.' . . . As the 'faithful guardians of the Constitution,' judges were expected to resist any political effort to depart from the literal provisions of the Constitution. The text of the document and the original intention of those who framed it would be the judicial standard in giving effect to the Constitution."[19]

Then Meese zeroed in on his target: "Nowhere else," he said, other than in the decisions of the Supreme Court, "has the principle of federalism been dealt so politically violent and constitutionally suspect a blow. . . . [A] jurisprudence of original intention . . . would produce defensible principles of government that would not be tainted by ideological predilection."[20] He called original intent the "only reliable guide for judgment" and claimed that various rulings hampered state law enforcement, particularly *Miranda v. Arizona*, which established the requirement that law enforcement officers read rights to those they arrest.

On October 12, 1985, at Georgetown University Law School, Justice William Brennan took the very unusual step of publicly responding to the attorney general's criticism. He said that Meese's position would undercut the living and evolving Constitution and reestablish states' rights to a level of influence that preceded the civil rights movement. Brennan argued that original intention was undiscoverable: "But in truth it is little more than arrogance cloaked as humility. It is arrogant to pretend that from our vantage we can gauge accurately the intent of the framers on application of principle to specific, contemporary questions. All too often, sources of potential enlightenment such as records of the ratification debates provide sparse or ambiguous evidence of the original intention."[21] On October 23, 1985, in Chicago, before a Federal Bar luncheon, Justice John Paul Stevens joined Brennan in the attack on the attorney general. Stevens claimed that Meese's argument was incomplete because it overlooked the importance of Civil War amendments to the Constitution. He also claimed that Meese was influencing Justice Rehnquist, who was often a target of Stevens's rhetoric during oral arguments and in written opinions.[22]

Before and after this debate, President Reagan fought for nominees that met Meese's standard, Justice Scalia being the most representative. The result was a conservative turn in the Court that at times seems to have affected even Justice Stevens. In an important First Amendment case regarding the rights of commercial advertisers, Stevens noted a claim from the amicus brief of the Freedom of Expression Foundation, of which I was president: If you take the time to read the newspapers printed in 1791, the year the First Amendment was added to the Constitution, you'll see that the papers the Founders chose to protect from government interference are filled with advertisements for all sorts of products. America's first newspaper, the Boston *News-Letter*, is full of advertising. When the Pennsylvania *Evening Post* printed the first copy of the Declaration of Independence on Saturday, July 6, 1774, it was immediately followed by a full page of advertising. Citizens used these advertisements to determine what to buy and where to buy it; for example, the advertisement often announced when shipment of a given product was arriving and at what wharf. Hence, in the context of the times, one must assume that the original intent of the Founders was to protect commercial speech.

A subissue regarding original intent arises from the framers' commitment to inalienable rights. These rights arise out of natural law, higher law, and the Enlightenment's desire to establish rights for all that previously had only been vested in the ruling class, particularly in Britain through the Magna Carta. Most commonly, these rights are life, liberty, and the pursuit of happiness, which are embedded in the Declaration of Independence, not the Constitution. Natural rights in the Constitution were originally concerned with the common good, domestic tranquility, and national security but were quickly amended to include a bill of rights, the American version of the Enlightenment commitment. During the Civil War, and particularly at Gettysburg, President Abraham Lincoln resurrected the rights embodied in the Declaration. These were enhanced immediately following the Civil War to include equal protection under the law along with due process of the law and voting rights for black men; in 1920, the franchise was extended to women. Natural rights or higher laws have been used to justify everything from a person's right to protect property to same-sex couples being allowed to marry. Thus, what we now see as a natural right might contradict the "original" intent of the Founders, leading to tension in the "originalist position." We shall explore this tension further in the analyses of justices that follow.

The second modality is the "textual"; it focuses on a plain or "strict construction" of the Constitution. Bobbitt claimed this modality or frame relies on words "as they would be interpreted by the average contemporary 'man on street.'"[23] Such readings surface in many obscenity cases. During his confirmation hearings for chief justice, John Roberts claimed that he was not an "originalist"; instead he believed in a "plain reading" of the Constitution in the current context. This modality could rely on close textual reading methods used in the field of rhetorical criticism to ferret out the meanings of the words of the Constitution. However, as most rhetorical scholars can tell you, close textual reading is much more accurate if context is established; that process often throws the interpreter back to "original intent."

This problem was most clearly evident in the recent rulings on the Second Amendment's protection of the right to bear arms. Placing the amendment in context, the Ninth Circuit Court of Appeals ruled that the Second Amendment allows states or the federal government to restrict the possession of guns. The appeals court relied on the standards of "original intent" and "strict construction of the Constitution" to reach a unanimous conclusion. The Second Amendment reads, "A well-regulated militia being necessary to the security of a free state, the right of the people to keep and bear arms shall not be infringed." Judge Reinhardt concluded that "'well-regulated' confirms that 'militia' can only reasonably be construed as referring to a military force established and controlled by a government entity." Reinhardt traces the amendment back through James Madison and the need for some states to protect themselves from disturbances within their borders. Shays's Rebellion in western Massachusetts had frightened many states at that time, hence the need for the right to protect themselves by creating militias. Both the Pennsylvania frame and the Massachusetts constitution argued that the people have the right to keep and bear arms but only for "the common defense." Thus, the Ninth Circuit concluded that the Second Amendment allows states, not individuals, to form militias and thereby confer on individuals of the state the right to bear arms.

However, the Court of Appeals of Washington, D.C., when faced with a similar case, decided to read the amendment word by word rather than contextualizing the amendment into the context of its passage. Using that modality, the court struck down a strict ban on weapon possession in Washington, D.C. Since this ruling established a conflict among the lower courts, the Supreme Court granted certiorari in the D.C. case. The majority refused to contextualize the amendment, and gave it only a plain reading of its words, granting citizens the right to bear arms. The Supreme Court then extended this uncontextualized reading to the states and cities when Chicago's law forbidding the ownership of handguns was struck down.

The third modality focuses on "structural" arguments. These include balancing one amendment against another, state rights versus federal prerogative, and individual rights versus eminent domain. This modality pays attention to crucial relationships. Bobbitt added, "Structuralist arguments are largely factless and depend on deceptively simple logical moves from the entire Constitutional text, rather than from its parts."[24] Justices examine what structures of the Constitution have been established and how to arbitrate among them. In First Amendment law, this modality of argument plays out in many ways. For example, justices often argue that in order to restrict freedom of expression, the restriction must advance a compelling government interest. Freedom of expression is not protected if it defames, is treasonous, or is obscene.

Another example of the structural modality is seen in the way the justices balance the free exercise clause of the First Amendment against the establishment clause. The Court often faces the dilemma of balancing a person's right to freely exercise his or her religion against the prohibition on the state from establishing a religion. Allowing Catholics to practice their faith is not a problem, but it is a problem when the state provides school vouchers to Catholic schools. Native Americans are free to *believe* in traditional ways of the tribe, but they may not *practice* traditional activities if those activities violate the laws of their state.

Bobbitt's fourth modality centers on the role that precedent plays in Supreme Court rulings. In this modality, "doctrinal" rulings (stare decisis) have been established to guide the Court, normally by substantial majorities.[25] I am quick to note that the doctrinal modality is often combined with the structural to help the Court balance one right against another. With regard to the First Amendment, precedents are now clearly established to guarantee that to be declared obscene, expression must be without redeeming social value when taken as a whole, must appeal to prurient interests, *and* must offend community standards.[26] These precedents have created a heavy burden of proof for those who would restrict expression on the grounds that it is obscene.

The same is true for the rulings surrounding libel and slander. The truth is always a defense against collecting damages for alleged defamation. Even when defamatory statements are shown to be false, the plaintiff must show that the expression was harmful, and in the case of public persons, must show that the speaker willfully disregarded the truth; that is, acted with "actual malice."[27] Such precedents protect reporters, who often make inadvertent errors while carrying out their charge.[28]

The fifth modality is the "ethical," which Bobbitt attributed to those who embrace a "living constitution" as opposed to the "limited constitution" of the originalists and strict constructionists. That is, because the context is ever changing for the Constitution, rulings should be derived from "moral com-

mitments of the American ethos that are reflected in the Constitution."[29]
Thus, instead of arguing for a higher law, justices using this modality often
argue that the people, who have formed the union, have matured or have
become sophisticated in terms of their approach to various issues.[30] While a
strict constructionist or an originalist can find no justification for granting a
woman the right to have an abortion, an ethicist can, arguing that our definitions of the right to privacy and unwanted search have evolved. In that way,
ethicists take into account changes in the American ethos. The "separate but
equal" ruling from *Plessy v. Ferguson* (1896) stood for more than half a
century until a unanimous Court in *Brown v. Topeka Board of Education*
struck it down by stretching the equal protection clause of the Fourteenth
Amendment to include educational facilities. *Loving v. Virginia* (1967)[31] and
Palmore v. Sidoti (1984)[32] concerned state laws which discriminated against
blacks; in *Loving* the issue was interracial marriage; in *Palmore* the issue was
child custody. In both cases the Court established that states shouldered a
heavy burden to justify separation of races. In the notorious *Pacifica* case,
the Court ruled that the Federal Communications Commission (FCC) could
impose indecency standards on broadcast speech, arguing in part that the
government could advance social values by restricting certain words.[33]

Another way in which the ethical modality can surface is through arguments that if the framers were alive today they would apply their principles
to new constituencies or developments in the current context. For example,
when the Supreme Court in 1987 upheld the right of the FCC to suspend the
"fairness doctrine," a content control on broadcast speech, they did so in part
because they recognized that broadcast news would have been included in
the framers' definition of press in the First Amendment.

Obviously much good has been done by using this modality. However, it
sometimes smacks of majoritarianism, imposing the values of the many on
the few, as in the case of indecency ruling in *Pacifica*. Further, it rewrites the
Constitution to advance the "American ethos," which is dangerous, whether
done by liberals or conservatives, because then the Constitution becomes
plastic. Thus, it is the ethicists who are most likely to engage the originalists
in confrontations over various issues.

Bobbitt's final modality is the "prudential," which measures costs against
benefits as a basis for a ruling.[34] In this frame a justice "need not treat the
merits of the particular controversy" but instead advance a particular doctrine
according "to the practical wisdom of using the courts in a particular way."[35]
In several rulings on commercial speech, for example, the Supreme Court has
argued that the consumer's need for information, including the prices of
items, is paramount to the state's desire to control the advertising of certain
products.[36] Establishing a test that is used to this day, the Court ruled in
Central Hudson Gas v. Public Service Commission[37] that nonmisleading
speech about legal products could only be restricted if the government

proved it had a substantial interest in doing so and that the restriction was the least restrictive way of advancing that interest. In 2005, in a more controversial decision, the Supreme Court upheld the imposition of eminent domain in a Connecticut case in which a city argued that it had the right to evict low-income housing tenants to allow construction of a shopping mall because it would produce more tax revenue for the city.[38]

CONCLUSIONS

In describing the modalities of argument set out by Bobbitt, I have established a framework for the analysis of each sitting justice on the Supreme Court. What Bobbitt calls a practice-based approach to judicial decision making is actually a rhetorical study of how opinions are framed. Therefore, as we employ Bobbitt's modalities, we will extend them with rhetorical theory to make them more nuanced, and we hope evolutionary, as Bobbitt intended. This will require, as we shall see, revisiting Cicero not only in terms of his theory of argumentation but also in his subtle conjunction of *decorum* and *ornatus*, the use of tropes and figures to fashion a text to meet expectations. Each chapter that follows will focus on a justice using this framework of analysis in the spirit of Bobbitt's dialectical approach to our evolving constitutional law on the First Amendment. Thus, we are not so much interested in what the law is—though that will emerge—as we are interested in how the law is *made*. We reveal which justices use which modalities to create their opinions on First Amendment issues. We hope the study helps those who argue before the Supreme Court to become cognizant of their immediate audience, the nine Supreme Court justices. Above all, we hope to provide the general public with a more accessible understanding of how these justices form their opinions and argue for them.

NOTES

1. See, for example, John L. Lucaites, "Between Rhetoric and 'the Law': Power, Legitimacy, and Social Change," *Quarterly Journal of Speech*, 76 (1990): 435–49. Marouf Hasian, Celeste Condit, and John Lucaites, "The Rhetorical Boundaries of 'the Law': A Consideration of the Rhetorical Culture of Legal Practice and the Case of the 'Separate But Equal' Doctrine," *Quarterly Journal of Speech*, 82 (1996): 323–42. See also Clarke Rountree, "Instantiating 'the Law' and Its Dissents in *Karematsu v. United States*: A Dramatistic Analysis of Judicial Discourse," *Quarterly Journal of Speech*, 87 (2001): 1–24; James Boyd White, "Law as Rhetoric, Rhetoric as Law: The Arts of Cultural and Communal Life," *University of Chicago Law Review*, 52 (1985): 684–702, and *Justice as Translation: An Essay in Cultural and Legal Criticism* (Chicago: University of Chicago Press, 1990).

2. See Richard Boyd, "Metaphor and Theory Change: What Is 'Metaphor' a Metaphor for?" in *Metaphor and Thought*, ed. Anthony Ortony, 2nd ed. (Cambridge: Cambridge University Press, 1993), 481–503.

3. The power of metaphors to produce and use frames was most effectively explored by Max Black in *Models and Metaphors: Studies in Language and Philosophy* (Ithaca, NY: Cornell University Press, 1962). See also Michael J. Reddy, "The Conduit Metaphor: A Case of Frame Conflict in Our Language About Language," in *Metaphor and Thought*, ed. Andrew Ortony. The most recent *Free Speech Yearbook* contains the following essays: Richard A. Parker, "The Case of the Contentious Metaphor: The Marketplace of Ideas as Modernist Mystery," 1–14; Dale A. Herbeck, "Falsely Shouting Fire in a Crowded Theater, a Revolutionary Spark, and Burning the House to Roast the Pig: Fire Metaphors and the First Amendment," 15–26; Joseph J. Hemmer, Jr., "Jefferson's 'Wall of Separation': How Jurisprudential Interpretation Shaped a Secular Polity," 27–40; Susan Balter-Reitz, "Lock Down behind the Schoolhouse Gate: Student Speech from *Tinker* to *Morse*," 41–54; Juliet Dee, "Shedding Light or Casting Shadows? The Penumbra Metaphor, Privacy, and Privileged Communication," 55–64; *Free Speech Yearbook*, 44 (Washington, DC: National Communication Association, 2009–2010).

4. 531 U.S. 98 (2000).

5. Craig R. Smith and Theodore Prosise, "The Supreme Court's Ruling in *Bush v. Gore*: A Rhetoric of Inconsistency," *Rhetoric and Public Affairs*, 4 (2001): 605–32

6. Garrett Epps, *To an Unknown God: Religious Freedom on Trial* (New York: St. Martin's Press, 2001), 159.

7. Perhaps his most famous lone dissent came in the *Bob Jones University* case, in which Rehnquist supported that "university's" right to discriminate among those it admitted.

8. Justice John Paul Stevens, "Remarks before the Federal Bar Association on October 23, 1985," in *The Great Debate: Interpreting Our Written Constitution* (Washington, DC: The Federalist Society, 1986).

9. 521 U.S. 898 (1997).

10. 529 U.S. 598 (2000).

11. 528 U.S. 62 (2000).

12. His most unusual success was in commercial speech case *Posadas v. Tourism Company of Puerto Rico*, 478 U.S. 328 (1986), in which Rehnquist convinced a majority that advertising for Puerto Rican casinos was legal in the states but not in the commonwealth of Puerto Rico. Justice Stevens was outraged by this decision and eventually got it overturned in the *44 Liquormart* ruling of 1996 (see below).

13. If one prefers a deconstructive approach of a more general nature, I recommend the work of J. M. Balkin, particularly "Deconstructive Practice and Legal Theory," *Yale Law Journal*, 96 (1987): 743–65 and "Transcendental Deconstruction, Transcendent Justice," *Michigan Law Review*, 92 (1994): 1131ff.

14. Bobbitt, *Constitutional Interpretation* (Oxford: Basil Blackwell, 1991), 24.

15. Bobbitt, *Constitutional Interpretation*, 163.

16. See Robert M. Howard and Jeffrey A. Segal, "An Original Look at Originalism," *Law and Society Review*, 36 (2002): 113; H. Jefferson Powell, "The Original Understanding of Original Intent," *Harvard Law Review*, 98 (1985): 885–948.

17. As quoted from a letter to G. Jackson, December 27, 1821, in *Letters and Other Writings of James Madison*, vol. 3, 344.

18. Jefferson to William Johnson, June 12, 1823. Library of Congress, http://memory.loc.gov/master/mss/mtj/mtj1/053/1000/1004.jpg.

19. Attorney General Edwin Meese III, speech before the American Bar Association of July 9, 1985, as reprinted in *The Great Debate: Interpreting Our Written Constitution* (Washington, DC: The Federalist Society, 1986), 1.

20. Meese, *The Great Debate*, 8.

21. Justice William J. Brennan, Jr., at Georgetown University, October 12, 1985, in *The Great Debate*, 14.

22. Justice John Paul Stevens, before the Federal Bar Association, on October 23, 1985, in *The Great Debate*, 27.

23. Bobbitt, *Constitutional Interpretation*, 12. Bobbitt's model of a textualist judge is Hugo Black, who often claimed he was simply following what the Constitution plainly said.

24. Philip Bobbitt, "Constitutional Fate," *Texas Law Review*, 58 (1980): 7.

25. Lawrence B. Solum, "The Supreme Court in Bondage: Constitutional Stare Decisis, Legal Formalism, and the Future of Unenumerated Rights," *University of Pennsylvania Journal of Constitutional Law*, 9 (2006): 155–201.

26. Miller v. California, 413 U.S. 15 (1973).

27. New York Times v. Sullivan, 376 U.S. 254 (1964), see particularly 271–72.

28. See, for example, Garrison v. Louisiana, 379 U.S. 64 (1965), which refines New York Times v. Sullivan.

29. Bobbitt, *Constitutional Interpretation*, 12–13.

30. Bruce Ackerman, "The Living Constitution," *Harvard Law Review*, 120 (2007): 1737.

31. 388 U.S. 1 (1967).

32. 466 U.S. 429 (1984).

33. FCC v. Pacifica, 438 U.S. 726 (1978).

34. Cass Sunstein of the University of Chicago is one of the primary advocates of this modality. His books include *Risk and Reason* (2002) and *The Second Bill of Rights* (2004).

35. Bobbitt, "Constitutional Fate," 7. I am reminded of Cicero's theory of *prudentia*.

36. See, for example, Virginia State Board of Pharmacy v. Virginia Citizens Consumer Council, 425 U.S. 748 (1975), or the aforementioned *44 Liquormart* ruling.

37. 447 U.S. 557 (1980).

38. Kelo v. City of New London, 545 U.S. 469 (2005).

Chapter Two

The Nomination Process

Craig R. Smith

In ancient Rome, the senate created the supreme law of the land, judged its own members, and appointed various judges to various levels of adjudication in the Republic. In the United States, the senate acts as a jury only in the cases of an impeached president or ethical violations by its own members. However, it must approve all judges appointed to the federal bench, including members of the Supreme Court. Thus, nominees for the Supreme Court undergo enormous scrutiny; their lives, philosophical positions, and ideological preferences come under the political microscope. In recent times, we have seen this process intensify.[1] The purpose of this chapter is to explore the nomination process and pay special attention to how it has moved from the rhetorical sphere of the Senate into the public sphere. By doing this, I hope to lay a foundation for some of the chapters that follow, which rely on the testimony of the various justices during their nomination hearings. This testimony is particularly important to understanding the bases of judgment that will be used by the most recent nominees to the Supreme Court. Sometimes these statements reveal which modalities the justice-to-be prefers. Sometimes these statements are abandoned once the justice is in place. In either case, they provide an interesting entryway into the justices' thinking.

Let me begin by establishing the difference between the Senate and the public spheres. In 1919 President Woodrow Wilson sent the treaty ending World War I, which required a two-thirds majority, to the Senate for approval. Senator Henry Cabot Lodge, the chair of the Foreign Relations Committee and a historian, gave a speech on the floor of the Senate comparing the treaty's League of Nations to the Holy Alliance of 1812. Lodge circulated a letter opposing the treaty unless it was amended; this "round-robin" was signed by a sufficient number of senators to block the treaty. Wilson announced that he would travel the country to drum up support for his treaty, and particularly its League of Nations provision. In response, Republicans promptly announced that they would send a "truth squad" after Wilson, headed by the progressive Republican senator Hiram Johnson of California. What followed demonstrated that there was a significant difference between the Senate's sphere of argumentation and the public's sphere of persuasion. Johnson, who had been ridiculed in the Senate after Lodge's display of acumen, resonated with crowds across the country using his simpler, more passionate rhetoric, while Wilson, a former college professor, was unable to adapt to the public sphere. At the end of his swing around the country, the president not only lost his treaty but suffered a stroke.

Today, due to the televising of proceedings and other mediation, the U.S. Senate is much less isolated from the public sphere than it was in 1919. Starting with the nomination of sitting justice Abe Fortas for chief justice of the Supreme Court in 1968, the argumentation surrounding some nominations has broadened into the public sphere. This shift was the result of pressure from interest groups, coverage by the media, and/or the behest of senators and the president.

Since 1968, more and more nominations to the Supreme Court have entered the public sphere, to the point where lower court nominations and the Senate's filibuster rule have also engaged the public sphere. After reviewing the controversial nominations between 1968 and the present, this chapter assesses their impact on argumentation in the Senate and public spheres. The chapter relies on Jürgen Habermas's theory of the public sphere in general and his theory of proceduralist law in particular.[2] He argued that "the vacant places of the economic man or welfare-client are occupied by a public of citizens who participate in political communication in order to articulate their wants and needs, to give voice to their violated interests, and, above all, to clarify and settle the contested standards and criteria."[3] Habermas attempted to construct "communicative rationality" based on agreement among the rational citizens in society performing in optimum speaking situations.[4] In such situations, argumentation becomes "a court of appeal that makes it possible to continue communicative action with other means when disagreement can no longer be headed off by everyday routines and yet is not to be settled by the direct or strategic use of force."[5] The model requires speakers who have at their disposal "basic qualifications of speech and symbolic interaction."[6] Furthermore, Habermas maintained that loyalty to the Constitution must transcend cultural and ideological differences if consensus is to be achieved.[7] Thus, if argumentation in the public sphere places more value on interests other than the Constitution, it can lead to fragmentation.

In his book *Between Facts and Norms: Contributions to a Discourse Theory of Law and Democracy*, Habermas extended his theory by acknowledging "offensive" social movements that "bring up issues relevant to the entire society, to define ways of approaching problems, to propose possible solutions, to supply new information, to interpret values differently, to mobilize good reasons, and criticize bad ones."[8] Often it is those outside of government or its normal channels that surface these issues. "Only through their controversial presentation in the media do such topics reach the larger public and subsequently gain a place on the 'political agenda.'"[9]

This chapter attempts to demonstrate that the Senate sphere and the public sphere meet Habermas's paradigm in different ways. The argumentation in the Senate sphere tends to focus on qualifications, constitutional interpretations, and definitions of impropriety. However, because senators play to their constituencies, they often make statements that will gain them access to the media. The more dramatic and controversial the argument, the more likely it is to be covered by the media. Public argumentation tends to focus on the nominees' gender, race, religion, political leanings, and perceived social agenda. This chapter argues that public relations consultants are much more likely to be used in cases where the public sphere is engaged; they, too, seek access to the media. While proponents of direct democracy and democratic renewal welcome such a shift, others concerned about the selection of qualified justices view the public involvement in, and media coverage of, the judicial process as troublesome.

REQUIRING THE ADVICE AND CONSENT OF THE SENATE

Article 2, Section 2 of the United States Constitution reads: "[The president] by and with the advice and consent of the Senate, shall appoint . . . judges of the Supreme Court." This section was the result of intense negotiation during the drafting of the U.S. Constitution and has remained controversial throughout U.S. history.[10] For example, in 1822 former president Thomas Jefferson called for term limits on justices because he was frustrated with how the Federalist judges had dominated the court system.[11] The Supreme Court has recognized this problem in its own decisions. For example, in *Edmunds v. U.S.* in 1997, the Court recognized that "the Framers anticipated that the President would be less vulnerable to interest-group pressure and personal favoritism than" the Senate; however, the Senate's participation "serves both to curb Executive abuses of the appointment power, and 'to promote a judicious choice of [persons] for filling the offices of the union.'"[12]

Section 2 of the Constitution does not require a supermajority in order for a justice to be approved. The U.S. Senate, however, created its own rule that prevents the closing of debate until sixty or more of its one hundred members vote for cloture. Thus, a majority of less than sixty can be stifled by a minority which continues the debate, a tactic known as the filibuster.

Today, even the nominations of judges to lower federal benches and the filibuster have often been thrust into the public sphere. This shift in the nomination process has broad implications for American politics. Thus, implications for public argumentation will be explored in the conclusion of this chapter, since one of the goals of this study is to provide rhetorical advice to those who appear before the Supreme Court.

THE FORTAS CRISIS

President Lyndon Baines Johnson moved Arthur Goldberg, whom John Kennedy had appointed to the Supreme Court, to the United Nations upon the death of Adlai Stevenson in the summer of 1965, and then appointed his friend Abe Fortas to the Court as an associate justice.[13] A memo prepared by the Justice Department's Nicholas Katzenbach in July of 1965 demonstrates how conscious the administration was of various factors that go into the selection process. Fortas was selected not only because he was close to Johnson, but because he was a Democrat, a Jew in the tradition of Brandeis and Frankfurter, between the ages of fifty and sixty, and a judicial liberal.[14] Fortas was approved by acclamation in the Senate.[15]

On June 13, 1967, in a White House Rose Garden ceremony, Johnson took the bold step of nominating the first African American to the Court. Thurgood Marshall had argued for Brown in the *Brown v. Board of Education* case of 1954, which resulted in a unanimous ruling ending public school segregation. The nomination led to a nasty debate in the Senate.[16] Southern senators were particularly vitriolic in their attacks. They hoped to delay Marshall's appointment, as they had when he was appointed to the Second Circuit Court of Appeals in the Kennedy administration.[17] However, as Trevor Parry-Giles makes clear, this debate rarely aroused the public.[18] The controversy was contained "in the Senate," "on the floor of the Senate," and to "floor debate" between "members of the House and Senate."[19] In the end, Marshall's nomination was approved sixty-nine to eleven, with twenty senators not voting. Marshall then began a twenty-four-year tenure on the Court.

At the same time, Fortas counseled Johnson on various matters behind the scenes. In 1968, a bitterly contentious election year because of the Vietnam War, Johnson had the opportunity to appoint Fortas chief justice when the seventy-seven-year-old Earl Warren offered his resignation contingent upon being replaced by a Senate-approved nominee. The nomination immediately fell into contention. Republicans were furious that Warren, the former Republican governor of California, did not wait until after the election. Believing that a Republican would win the White House, many senators claimed they would filibuster any nomination before the next president was selected.

In his acceptance of the nomination in the summer of 1968, Nixon signaled that if elected, he would appoint conservative justices to the Court: "Tonight it's time for some honest talk about the problem of order in the United States. . . . [L]et us recognize that some of our courts in their decisions have gone too far in weakening the peace forces."[20] Hearings revealed that while Fortas had done nothing illegal, he had received twenty thousand dollars a year in consulting fees from the Wolfson Family Foundation and had accepted other gratuities. At that time, a Supreme Court justice made only forty thousand dollars a year. The hearings also revealed Fortas's continuing advisory role to President Johnson. Senator Strom Thurmond led a filibuster on October 2, 1968, that forced the withdrawal of Fortas's nomination for chief justice. The filibuster was also directed at Homer Thornberry, a Johnson protégé whom he had nominated for associate justice to take the Fortas seat. The Fortas controversy spilled into the presidential campaign of 1968 when Nixon linked Fortas to liberal activists on the Supreme Court that had supported disallowing the use of tainted evidence in criminal trials.

HAYNSWORTH AND CARSWELL

In 1969, Richard Nixon's nomination of Warren Burger to replace Earl Warren went well, and may have lulled the president into a false sense of security, particularly when dealing with his own party. Fortas resigned his associate judgeship during Burger's confirmation process, giving Nixon another vacancy. Nixon's nominee for the open associate justice was Clement Haynsworth of South Carolina, who sat on the Fourth Circuit Court of Appeals. A Democrat, Haynsworth had supported Republican presidential candidates since 1964. While Haynsworth had been opposed by civil rights and labor groups in the past, Nixon believed Haynsworth would again prevail and win Nixon more support in the South, a region he divided with George Wallace in the election of 1968. Nixon had carried Haynsworth's state, along with Tennessee, Virginia, Florida, and North Carolina, but he lost the rest of the Deep South. At the behest of Kevin Phillips, a Republican strategist, and Harry Dent, the Republican state chairman from South Carolina, Nixon sought to build a new Republican majority that would include the states of the Deep South.

On August 18, 1969, after a thorough investigation led by Attorney General John Mitchell, Nixon nominated Haynsworth, who ran into opposition almost immediately from liberal groups, who pressured the Senate. While Haynsworth's overall record indicated support for the civil rights of minorities and a flexible reading of the Constitution, in at least six decisions (three of which were overturned by the Supreme Court) he had ruled against minority rights petitions. His labor record was similar. Thus, while civil rights groups opposed Haynsworth, he did not generate enthusiasm among conservative senators who favored strict constructionists on the Supreme Court. In reaction, the White House Congressional Liaison Office began a practice that continues to this day: the creation of ad hoc units to deal with Supreme Court nominees.

While Haynsworth said nothing to justify claims that he was a latent segregationist, he did have conflicts of interest that, in the context of the Fortas crisis, would prove fatal to the nomination.[21] Due to the death of Republican leader Everett Dirksen, Haynsworth's hearing before the Judiciary Committee was postponed until September of 1969. Thus, the opposition forces, which were led by Senator Birch Bayh (D-Indiana), had time to organize a media campaign that would take the debate into the public sphere. It became clear to Bryce Harlow, head of congressional liaison for Nixon, and Attorney General Mitchell that they needed to balance Republican defectors with southern Democratic supporters of the nomination. On October 9, under pressure from the White House, the Judiciary Committee approved the nomination of Haynsworth by a vote of ten to seven.

Until the committee vote, the administration kept a low profile on the nomination. Only Assistant Attorney General William Rehnquist, who was coaching Haynsworth for his hearings, spoke out in favor of the nomination.[22] Rehnquist then complained to Nixon that not enough was being done by his congressional liaison staff and that Mitchell had not provided the president with a proper assessment of the nominee.[23]

Soon after the Judiciary Committee vote, the new Republican minority leader, Bob Griffin, told Harlow that the nomination was doomed. When Harlow recommended to Nixon that he withdraw the nomination,[24] the president demanded that a task force be put together to save it. Nixon believed defecting Republicans could be brought back into line. He told Harlow to activate southern and National Rifle Association (NRA) support. Thus, Nixon rallied groups in the public sphere to counter those activated by Senator Bayh. Nixon's strategy marks a decisive shift in the politics of Supreme Court nominations.

As the battle escalated, Counselor to the President Clark Mollenhoff composed talking points in defense of Haynsworth that were sent to conservative interest groups. In a press conference in his office, Nixon claimed that Haynsworth was a victim of "character assassination" and compared this fight to the one over the nomination of Louis Brandeis, a liberal Jew who was confirmed on a forty-seven to twenty-two vote with twenty-seven abstentions in 1916.[25] Then, in another major shift from the past, the White House, seeking a political advantage, sent the news media a defense of Haynsworth, targeting newspapers in states of swing vote senators.[26] The public was engaged. Patrick Buchanan, then the compiler of the daily news briefings for the president, and Lyn Nofziger, a press aide, were incorporated into the task force; they quickly reinforced the decision to take the fight into the public arena, a step that was offensive to Democrats and Republicans in the Senate. Harry Dent, who had moved into the Political Affairs Office, activated state Republican chairs and contributors across the country. Nixon appointees were urged to support the nomination in the media; the president was personally involved in much of this effort.[27] He instructed Herb Klein to keep pressure on the media; Klein went so far as to appear on *The Tonight Show Starring Johnny Carson*, one of the most popular venues in the public sphere at the time. Like other spokespersons, he pointed out that sixteen former ABA presidents and the Trial Lawyers Association had endorsed Haynsworth.

Senate decorum was soon frayed. Southern Democratic senators supporting Haynsworth resented making the fight a public, partisan one. Republican senators resented the strong-arm tactics of the president's staff, including telephoning wealthy Republican contributors and urging them to lobby their senators. Republican senators John Williams, Hugh Scott, William Saxbe, Charles Percy, Jack Miller, and Bob Griffin eventually voted against Haynsworth's nomination in part because of the tactics of the White House and in part because they had stopped the Fortas nomination on conflict of interest charges and did not want to appear to be hypocritical. These Republican senators felt obligated to apply the same standard to Haynsworth.

Haynsworth lost despite the support of eighteen Democrats because sixteen Republicans voted against him. However, Nixon gained southern sympathy. His next step was to punish the defectors and solidify southern support. He instructed H. R. Haldeman to "destroy" the disloyal senators.[28] To consolidate southern support, on January 19, 1970, Nixon nominated Judge G. Harold Carswell of the Fifth Circuit Court of Appeals in Florida. He also created the Office of Public Liaison and put Charles Colson in charge. In this way, the White House clearly signaled that it would appeal to the public sphere to support its nominee, who had the blessings of Attorney General Mitchell, Chief Justice Warren Burger, and Secretary of State William Rogers.[29] A new cycle of media wars and public engagement began, with Nixon unaware of past statements by Carswell that would further engage the public arena.

The ad hoc group in charge of the Carswell nomination met each morning at eight,[30] a meeting in which various tasks were assigned. Clark MacGregor ran congressional relations with Bill Timmons; Dick Moore and Bill Safire ran the press operation; Colson generated public support. Again Nixon was intimately involved in the nomination campaign, using his power of patronage and presidential prestige to try to persuade senators.[31]

Carswell owned no stocks or bonds; he was financially clean. However, the opposition found a quotation from 1948 in which, when running for public office in Georgia, Carswell said, "Segregation of the races is proper and the only practical and correct way of life in our states. I have always so believed and I shall always so act."[32] Carswell immediately renounced the statement as a youthful indiscretion.

Next, the opposition added the label of "mediocre" to Carswell's list of sins, which was confirmed when Senator Roman Hruska (R-Nebraska) foolishly claimed that the mediocre had a right to be represented on the Court. The nomination was defeated fifty-one to forty-five on April 8, 1970. Nixon wrote in his memoirs, "I was determined that [the opposition] would at least pay a political price for it in the South."[33] Nixon claimed in a press conference that Carswell was defeated because he came from the South. Nixon then nominated moderate Republican Harry A. Blackmun of Minnesota, who was unanimously confirmed by the Senate on May 12, 1970, and later disappointed conservatives by supporting the majority decision in *Roe v. Wade*. In the fall of 1970, Nixon entered into the ensuing congressional election campaign armed with a wedge issue: crime, the reduction of which he connected to strict constructionist judges. He also campaigned across the South seeking converts to the Republican Party.

It is important to note that while the Haynsworth and Carswell nominations had been thrust into the public arena, neither man was criticized for his ideology or his methods of constitutional interpretation. While Nixon tried to put a political face on the attacks, they consisted of either the appearance of impropriety or racism. As we shall see, the notion of ideological assessment for the public debate did not emerge until the 1980s.

NIXON'S LATER APPOINTMENTS

In September of 1971, justices Hugo Black and John Harlan resigned. Black, formerly of Alabama, became a civil liberties advocate and an originalist, who believed in a close reading of the language of the Constitution alone as a basis for making decisions. Harlan was one of the most conservative judges on the Court, and had regularly opposed the Warren agenda. Thus, Nixon would have the opportunity of a lifetime; he could now appoint a third and fourth justice to the Court, remaking it in his image.

His first choice was attorney Lewis Powell of Virginia, who was easily confirmed; the process was contained between the Senate and the White House. His second choice was William Rehnquist, who proved to be more controversial. Rehnquist had written a memo in 1952, when he was clerking for Justice Jackson, which defended the "separate but equal" decision in

Plessy v. Ferguson. Under questioning Rehnquist claimed he had written the memo at the behest of Jackson to present one side of the issue for a debate among Jackson's staff. Other witnesses disputed Rehnquist's version of the context of his memo. However, the charges against Rehnquist failed to ignite public controversy, and he was confirmed sixty-eight to twenty-six. Nonetheless, the public battles over Haynsworth and Carswell would haunt the selection process in the future.[34]

THE NOMINATION OF ROBERT BORK

President Reagan was successful in getting his nominees appointed to the federal courts because he had a Senate majority when he came into office and remained popular with the public until publicity surrounding the Iran-Contra affair damaged his reputation late in his second term. Official records show that he appointed about fifty federal judges a year during his two terms, leaving an indelible mark on the judiciary.[35] One reason for this success was the fact that the Justice Department was given more authority in the Office of Legal Policy with regard to the selection of nominees. The Office was ideologically driven by presidential counselor, and eventual attorney general, Edwin Meese III, who, as we have seen, was a firm believer in the precept of original intent.[36]

Before Meese came to full power, however, the Justice Department reported to William French Smith, who believed it was time a woman was appointed to the Court. The selection of Sandra Day O'Connor proved felicitous. She was easily approved even though her ABA rating was only "qualified." When it came to selecting Supreme Court justices under Meese's direction, the going was more difficult. As we saw in the previous chapter, Meese had taken his notion of "original intent" public and in the process engaged members of the liberal wing of the Supreme Court to debate him.

This rare public exchange educated the news media, but did not engage the public. However, it was a prelude to the battle that would follow over Meese's recommendations to the president regarding appointments to the federal bench. Meese put Charles J. Cooper in charge of the Office of Legal Counsel and consulted with William Bradford Reynolds of the Justice Department when appointments became available. In the Nixon administration, Reynolds had been in the Justice Department, where he worked closely with Solicitor General Robert Bork. Reynolds had led the fight to roll back affirmative action programs.[37] Denied a promotion by the Senate, Reynolds continued to pursue his own course. For example, he intervened in four employment discrimination cases seeking to alter consent decrees that required racial or gender quotas. In 1985, he suggested what the ideal Supreme Court justice would look like. This internal memo decried judicial activism and endorsed federalism, meaning state's rights. The memo called for "commitment to strict principles of 'nondiscrimination'" and an end to affirmative action and racial prejudice. [38]

In 1986, when Chief Justice Burger retired to coordinate the celebration of the bicentennial of the Constitution, Reagan announced that he would nominate Rehnquist for chief justice and Antonin Scalia from the D.C. Circuit Court of Appeals to take Rehnquist's associate seat. Scalia was not well known, nor well published. His affable and humorous testimony before the Judiciary Committee carried the day. He won appointment unanimously on the same day that Rehnquist was moved up to chief justice by a divided Senate. Scalia was a textualist who some suspected would be in favor of reversing *Roe v. Wade*, a move that would also be favored by an originalist like Rehnquist. Thus, when Reagan nominated Robert Bork on July 1, 1987, to replace the retiring Powell, a wave of lobbying overwhelmed the Capitol. As acting attorney general, Bork had fired Watergate prosecutor Archibald Cox when no one else would do it. As a Yale professor, he had defended strict construction and close reading of the Constitution and attacked judicial activism. As a member of the D.C. Circuit Court of Appeals, he had put his philosophy into his rulings. The ABA divided on the Bork nomination, with the majority declaring him "well qualified" and the minority claiming he was "not qualified." In contrast, in the cases of Rehnquist and Scalia, the "well qualified" designation had been unanimous. The ABA majority report claimed that Bork's rulings had been "balanced" and "fair." [39] Bork's essays and books, however, revealed that he did not believe the Constitution should be interpreted liberally. He drew the most attention for his 1963 article in *New Republic* and his lectures that were published in the *Indiana Law Journal*. In the former, he implied that the 1964 Civil Rights Act violated the rights of white owners; in the latter, he made clear that only explicit language in the Constitution gives Congress power to act. Furthermore, he often ignored legislative intent to give legislation a literal reading, which worked against the interpretations put in place by the Warren court in general and *Roe v. Wade* in particular.

Since Bork was not tainted by any financial or other kinds of scandals, he would have to be attacked on ideological grounds if his nomination was to be stopped. [40] There were many reasons to believe that the Bork nomination would be contained in the Senate's sphere. The Democrats had regained control of the Senate. In the wake of the Iran-Contra scandal, Howard Baker, a moderate, had become Reagan's chief of staff. With Reagan's popularity slipping, Baker decided that Reagan should stay in the background during this nomination process. [41] However, Baker was not the only person who had Reagan's ear, nor were the Democrats eager to keep the fight in the Senate.

President Reagan included Bork's nomination as the third item in a speech to the nation in August. Reagan was responding to the fact that Democratic senators Edward Kennedy and Joseph Biden had gone public on the nomination.[42] In an appearance on *Face the Nation*, Biden, the chair of the Judiciary Committee, had warned that if the president nominated someone like Bork, the Senate would resist because Bork had an unacceptable "predisposition" on all major issues.[43] The day after the nomination, on the floor of the Senate, Kennedy played to the media by proclaiming that "Robert Bork's America is a land in which women would be forced into back alley abortions, blacks would sit at segregated lunch counters, rogue police could break down citizens' doors in midnight raids, school children could not be taught about evolution."[44] A week later, Biden claimed that the public needed to become much more active in this struggle because the administration was moving the Supreme Court back in time to the age of strict constructionism and conservative judicial activism. Kennedy and Biden made clear that an ideological litmus test would be applied to Bork, as opposed to a financial, criminal, or competency-based test, and that these issues would be taken public. This combination of argumentative moves by the opposition was unique in the annals of the appointment process.

By the time Bork's nomination became official, a coalition of civil libertarian groups had coalesced to fight him. The coalition was led by Ralph Neas of the Leadership Conference on Civil Rights[45] and included Kate Michelman of the National Abortion Rights Action League, Estelle Rogers of the Federation of Women Lawyers, and many more. Michelman's press release claimed, "We're going to wage an all-out frontal assault like you've never seen before on this nomination."[46] Her rhetoric invited a conservative response. Columnist George Will, for example, launched an attack on Senator Biden "because groups were jerking his leash."[47] When Biden continued to assure civil rights groups that he would oppose the Bork nomination, even the *Washington Post* faulted him: "While claiming that Judge Bork will have a full and fair hearing, Sen. Joseph Biden this week pledged to civil rights groups that he will lead the opposition to the confirmation. As the Queen of Hearts said to Alice, 'sentence first—verdict afterwards.'"[48]

To begin what ended up being twelve days of hearings, former president Ford, Republican senators Dole and Danforth, and Congressman Hamilton Fish introduced Bork to the Senate Committee, while his family sat behind him. In his opening statement as a member of the committee, Republican Senator Alan Simpson anticipated the "high drama" of the process.[49] However, in his opening statement, Bork sought to avoid controversy by dodging some issues: "I cannot, of course, commit myself as to how I might vote on any particular case and I know you would not wish me to do that."[50] Bork gave testimony or answered questions on five of the twelve days of the hearing; he retracted several of his previous statements, rationalized others, and gave rather boring discourses on case law. Biden pointed out that Bork's scholarship indicated that he would overturn *Griswold v. Connecticut*, a 1965 ruling striking down a state's prohibition on the use of contraceptives;[51] *Skinner v. Oklahoma*, a 1942 ruling that stopped involuntary sterilization of criminals; *Shelly v. Kraemer*, a 1948 ruling forbidding state courts from enforcing racially restrictive covenants; and the cases on one person, one vote. Bork responded that his opinions of 1971 were not his opinions in 1987. When Democratic senator Patrick Leahy asked Bork just how far he had moved from his 1971 article, Bork's answer seemed disingenuous: "About to where the Supreme Court currently is."[52] Under further questioning from Leahy, Bork reversed his previous opposition to *Brandenburg v. Ohio*, a 1969 ruling protecting speech that did not pose "a true threat."

Humorlessly, he engaged Republican senator Arlen Specter in a long philosophical debate on the Constitution. He claimed to have changed his mind about *Hess v. Indiana*, another free speech case. He said that he would not overturn *Roe v. Wade*, and that commercial and broadcast speech probably deserved more First Amendment protection than he had previously thought. However, Bork was dismissive of the Ninth Amendment, which reads, "The enumeration in the Constitution, of certain rights, shall not be construed to deny or disparage others retained by the people." Moderate Republican senators were angered by his attitude on this point.[53] They also felt uneasy with the number of times Bork had claimed to have changed his mind on landmark cases. They suspected what Senator Leahy would claim was a "confirmation conversion."[54]

In the hearing room and behind the scenes, administration operatives provided conservative Republican senators with material to refute the attacks of the Democrats and to help Bork reestablish his credibility. Nonetheless, Bork often failed to take advantage of softball questions from his supporters. Bork left Senator Orrin Hatch stranded on the issue of literacy tests.[55] When Senator Gordon Humphrey encouraged Bork to comment on rulings related to crime, he dodged the question with a jaw-dropping response: "I'm not an expert on criminal law."[56]

Witnesses on both sides came before the committee; many of these drew national media attention. Congresswoman Barbara Jordan and Atlanta's mayor Andrew Young attacked Bork's opposition to such "one man, one vote" decisions. Judge Shirley Hufstedler and constitutional expert Philip Kurland claimed Bork would undercut unenumerated rights. Chief Justice Berger defended Bork's interpretation of the Ninth Amendment, though with some hesitation. Cabinet member Carla Hills from the Ford administration and Griffin Bell, Carter's attorney general, were more helpful to Bork. Nonetheless the committee voted five to nine against the nomination. No single nomination had ever taken up so much time; even Clarence Thomas's two sets of hearings would not last as long. Bork's wife, Mary Ellen, met with

Republican senators the day after the committee vote to complain about how her husband had been treated. At a meeting with White House Communications Director Tommy Griscom, Bork demanded that President Reagan give a speech to the nation backing a full Senate vote on the nomination. Griscom denied the request.[57] Three weeks later after a meeting with Reagan, Bork walked to the White House press room and challenged the Senate to hold a vote on his nomination. He claimed that his record had been distorted and he wanted the full Senate on record.

At the same time, the White House gained an advantage when press reports of plagiarism eliminated Senator Biden from the ongoing Democratic presidential nomination process. President Reagan went on the offensive; eventually, he would make more than thirty public statements in support of Bork—some on national television to the viewing public.[58] This was another major turning point in the nomination process, because from that moment on, presidents would make public statements supporting their nominees, a practice that was quite rare prior to Reagan.[59]

Courting the public, Bork continued to engage the press to his advantage. Tom Korologos, a Washington lobbyist with influence in Republican circles, arranged interviews and coached his client on tough questions.[60] The White House Office of Communications set up fifteen radio interviews a week to support Bork.[61] In the South many radio stations played Jesse Jackson's condemnation of Bork.[62] Griscom coordinated the newspaper opinion page efforts of administration officials, resulting in at least twenty being published. The conservative Washington Legal Foundation, founded as a counterweight to the liberal ABA, rallied support, as did Secretary of Education William Bennett.

Expanding the public arena, the women's movement mobilized its largest letter-writing and phone call campaign ever. Members led a "media task force" dedicated to stopping the nomination. For the first time, advertisements against a Supreme Court nominee appeared on television; one was narrated by the actor Gregory Peck and paid for by television producer Norman Lear's People for the American Way. Peck stated, "Robert Bork could have the last word on your rights as citizens, but the Senate has the last word on him. Please urge your senators to vote against the Bork nomination, because if Bork wins a seat on the Supreme Court, it will be for life—his life and yours."[63] Ralph Nader's Public Citizen Litigation Group released a detailed study of Bork's fifty-six most controversial rulings, ignoring over four hundred others that were uncontroversial and generally had unanimous support from Bork's colleagues on the bench. The White House counted almost three hundred special interest groups that opposed Bork. These groups were successful in getting the news media to turn negative on Bork's nomination in the crucial July 1 to October 9 period.[64] For example, the *Washington Post* and the *New York Times* editorialized against Bork's nomination.[65]

The public and media pressure forced the full Senate to take up the nomination. After three days of dramatic debate, six moderate Republicans voted against Bork.[66] The nomination was defeated fifty-eight to forty-two on October 23, 1987. The White House public relations machine and congressional liaison office could not overcome Bork's rhetorical inadequacies, change of positions on important cases, and record on political issues and the major media opinion leaders turning against him.

Bork's nomination marked a major sea change in the confirmation process. As Yalof has written, "Robert Bork's ill-fated Supreme Court bid in 1987 fundamentally changed the nature of public discourse that would surround all future Supreme Court appointments. By their persistent attacks on Bork's academic writing, Democratic senators established a precedent for challenging future nominees on strictly ideological grounds."[67] And, one might add, by doing so in the public arena.

Matters went from bad to worse for the administration when Reagan nominated Douglas Ginsburg, who then confessed to smoking marijuana with his law students at Harvard. His nomination was withdrawn on November 11, 1987. Reagan then turned to Anthony Kennedy, who was approved unanimously after a noncontroversial hearing.

THE THOMAS NOMINATION

If anyone believed that Bork's adventure in the public sphere was a fluke, they were disabused of the notion when Clarence Thomas, an African American, was nominated to the Supreme Court by President George H. W. Bush. There would be significant differences between the two events. Aside from the fact that Thomas was approved, Thomas's backers used narrative to great effect, and Thomas himself broke through media screeners to appeal to the public directly, something Bork failed to do.

To replace Thurgood Marshall, President George H. W. Bush nominated Thomas on July 1, 1991. Born in the segregated South, and raised in Pin Point, Georgia, Thomas was a product of poverty, Catholic boarding schools, and hard work. He eventually entered and left two seminaries, as a result of being the victim of racism. After graduating from Holy Cross College with honors, Thomas attended Yale Law School. From there he went to work for moderate senator John Danforth of Missouri and changed his voter registration to Republican.

Thomas's early life provided a potent narrative that President Bush and his advisors used to influence the nomination process by taking the story to the public.[68] In fact, soon after the announcement of the nomination, Bush touted Thomas's accomplishments in a series of venues. On July 8, 1991,

Bush claimed that Thomas offered a "stirring testament to what people can do."[69] On August 6, the president said he was "deeply moved" by Thomas's life story.[70] The president continued his unprecedented prehearings campaign of persuasion in mid-August by claiming that "his personal story cannot help but move people."[71] The same strategy was used in a teleconference with the National Governors Association on August 18, in a speech to the National Association of Towns and Townships and a speech to the nation, both on September 6, and at a fund-raising dinner in Philadelphia on September 12, 1991. No president prior to Bush had made as many statements in support of a nominee before his or her hearings as Bush did for Thomas. Using the Justice Department's strategy, Bush clearly sought to replace questions about ideology with the narrative of Thomas's life, which was much more accessible to the public than theoretical considerations. The press was quick to take up the same theme.[72] Thus, even before Anita Hill's charges of sexual harassment, Thomas was in the public eye. The charges would serve to widen the public forum. However, the initial round of hearings came first.

In 1981 and 1982, Thomas served as assistant secretary for civil rights in the Department of Education. Subsequently, President Reagan chose Thomas to head the Equal Employment Opportunity Commission (EEOC), which supported most affirmative action programs. While the Civil Rights Commission was critical of the Reagan administration in many areas, it singled Thomas out for praise. In fact, Thomas's EEOC was critical of the Reagan Justice Department, deciding not to file amicus briefs opposing it only after major pressure from the White House. In 1983 the EEOC resolved over seventy-four thousand complaints, compared with less than fifty-eight thousand in 1980 under Carter. Only after 1984 did Thomas openly begin to question the hiring regulations of the EEOC in particular, and the use of quotas for reparation or past abuses in general.[73]

Thomas's sixteen months of noncontroversial service on the D.C. Circuit Court of Appeals, his conversion on the issue of affirmative action, and his support of natural rights made him attractive to the Bush administration, particularly to White House Counsel C. Boyden Gray, who helped usher the nominee through the process. The media generally reported favorably on Thomas; however, a red flag went up when the ABA gave Thomas only a "qualified" designation, the same designation applied to O'Connor and Carswell.

During his first set of hearings, Thomas refused to speculate on how he might vote on various cases. His opening statement read, "A judge must not bring to his job, to the court, the baggage of preconceived notions, of ideology, and certainly not an agenda."[74] While his performance was not brilliant, Thomas dodged enough questions to pass muster. For example, when confronted with inconsistencies in his record, Thomas explained that it was one thing to be part of an administration and quite another to be a judge, the same rationale later used by John Roberts when he was nominated for chief justice in 2005. Thomas asked the members of the Judiciary Committee to assess him in his role as a member of the D.C. Circuit Court of Appeals. He also relied on the narrative of his upbringing to defuse criticism.[75]

Thomas was followed by three days of testimony from various witnesses opposing or favoring his nomination. Some revealed that, contrary to what he said in his statement, Thomas had indicated his displeasure with the *Roe v. Wade* decision. On September 27, the committee voted seven to seven on the nomination. President Bush immediately urged the public to contact their senators to support Thomas's nomination.[76] Bush also brought the Christian Coalition and the NRA on board. In response, the board of the NAACP voted against the nomination forty-nine to one and the National Bar Association and the National Council of Black Lawyers, both African American groups, opposed the nomination. The battle was escalating.

Just as the Senate was about to vote on Thomas, National Public Radio broke a story: Anita Hill, an African American former employee of Thomas at the Department of Education and a professor of law at the University of Oklahoma, claimed in testimony to the FBI that he had sexually harassed her. Due to a staff error, committee chair Biden had failed to provide the information to the other committee members.

A second round of hearings, in which Thomas angrily denied the charges, began on October 11, 1991. Then Hill repeated her reluctant FBI testimony about intimate sexual innuendos.[77] That evening, Thomas's testimony in reply drew huge television ratings.[78] An electric moment came when viewers saw Thomas accuse the panel of conducting a "high-tech lynching of an uppity black man."[79] Thomas's indignation and passionate delivery stood in marked contrast to his previous testimony. ABC's *Nightline* ran three programs on the hearings; ABC, NBC, and CBS provided live coverage of the second hearing.

Over the next forty-eight hours, Hill returned and new witnesses were called on the specific charge of sexual harassment. Republican senators accused Hill of lying, or of being part of a conspiracy to stop the nomination.[80] Thomas returned one more time to protest how he was being treated and refused to withdraw his name.[81] Throughout the two sets of hearings over eleven days, the committee heard from fifty different interest groups, most of which opposed the nomination. After more media coverage and debate in the Senate, Thomas was confirmed on a vote of fifty-two to forty-eight, the closest confirmation vote in the twentieth century. Thomas's nomination battle was won not only because of the rhetorical strategies of President Bush and his Justice Department, but also because of Thomas's own ability to manipulate the media at a live, very public hearing.[82]

Since Thomas's explosion, most Supreme Court nominations have been rather peaceful, in part because the nominees were not extremists and proved facile at dodging tough questions. Ninety-six senators approved of Clinton's nomination of Ruth Bader Ginsburg; only three voted against. Eighty-seven senators approved his nomination of Stephen Breyer; only nine voted against. After Thomas, presidents seem to have learned that low-key nominations are better than high-profile ones. Presidential staffs are leery about what potential nominees have written and said. They are cautious about financial dealings, past indiscretions, and publications.[83] The result is safe nominations such as that of John Roberts, whom President George W. Bush endorsed in a public speech. The news media quickly noted that Roberts and his wife were Catholics, and that she was a leader in the antiabortion movement. Conservative interest groups, such as Operation Rescue, endorsed Roberts; liberal groups, such the National Organization of Women (NOW), labeled Roberts an extremist. Despite being opposed by Senate minority leader Reid, Roberts was endorsed by the ranking Democrat on the Judiciary Committee, Senator Patrick Leahy, which ensured that the nomination would be approved. After the unsuccessful nomination of Harriet Miers, the president's lawyer, the president quickly nominated Samuel A. Alito for the opening and publicly supported him with a call for an up or down vote on the nomination.[84] Senators contained the nomination within their sphere by invoking cloture on a vote of seventy-five to twenty-two and then confirming the nomination mainly along partisan lines.[85]

President Obama's nomination of Sonia Sotomayor followed the same pattern, as did the nomination of Elena Kagan.

CONCLUSIONS

In his theory, Habermas promoted a public sphere of universal assent induced by practical, rational argument. He provided a standard against which we can measure the argumentation in the public and Senate spheres, but he did not provide a theory that specifically explains what happens when the nomination process enters the public sphere. That must be left to inductive studies like the one completed in this chapter. It shows that engaging the public sphere can lead to a media circus, but can also mean that the public has more access to information about the nominees, thereby empowering them to make better arguments in terms of Habermas's paradigm. From presidential news conferences to appearances on the *Tonight Show*, mediation of the nomination process opens it to the public. When the public sphere is engaged, there are many more venues available for the debaters involved in the controversy. Furthermore, initial attacks on the nominee by one side, whether ideological or political, engender responses by the other side that escalate the debate and often attract the attention of the public. These heated exchanges are carried on the national news and opinion programs to the public, who become further involved in the battle. However, as anyone who has been a guest on so-called interview programs can tell you, interviewers seek drama through polarization. They pit guests against one another in a way that is deleterious to the argumentative process.

Such an arena contrasts starkly to what happened after the Thomas hearings and confirmation. The Senate sphere became more closed. The Senate Judiciary Committee conducted questioning on private matters in closed executive session, locking the public out of the Ruth Bader Ginsburg and Stephen Breyer hearings. Surprisingly, prior to his theory of procedural law, Habermas's work might be read to support the Senate's approach. He questioned the value of debate that is mediated: "The public sphere in the world of letters was replaced by the pseudo-public or sham-private world of culture consumption. . . . The world fashioned by the mass media is a public sphere in appearance only."[86] The public sphere has been so invaded by the public media that sensible debate is marginalized, and instead of becoming involved and empowered, the public has become passive consumers to whom special interests pander. Thus, senators are not actually engaging in public sphere debate; they are entering the mediated sphere of publicity to advance their position and gain support in future elections.

The shift to ideological concerns with Bork and sexual matters with Thomas created a tendency to move nomination debates into the public sphere if they are at all controversial. The result is a longer nomination process. Unless nominees, their backers, and their attackers understand how decisions are made in the public sphere, they are likely to fail to achieve their goals, particularly if they are naive about how the public arena operates.

This chapter analyzed the impact on public persuasion when the debate over court nominees is taken into the public sphere. First, arguments in the public sphere do not provide the kind of rational completeness Habermas sought when he called for public reflection on the implication of court decisions.[87] These arguments tend to focus on social issues, the rules of the game, and the gender, race, or religion of the nominee, in contrast to the focus on constitutional interpretation, qualifications, ethics, and alleged wrongdoing of the nominee in the Senate sphere. While the public is not engaged by explanations of the incorporation doctrine, or the precept of original intent, they are much more passionate about abortion, drug use, sexual misconduct, and racism. Thus, argumentation shifts from qualifications and constitutional theory in the Senate sphere to social and political issues in the public sphere. As such, the argumentation is less likely to be "civil" in the sense in which Habermas used the word for his rational democracy.[88]

Second, if nominations are delayed, opponents of the nominee have a much better chance of gathering evidence and arguments in opposition that they can use to generate public debate on the nominee. Fortas and Bork were disadvantaged by delays that occurred in their nomination process, allowing public opposition to coalesce. However, because their nominations had a full debate in the public and Senate spheres, it is fair to assume that Habermas would have endorsed such delays to allow enough time in the nomination process for public argument.

Third, once the public sphere is engaged, it can be used for political advantage in a way that the Senate sphere cannot. President Johnson claimed that Fortas had been rejected on political grounds, which excited loyal Democrats; Nixon claimed that Fortas would be soft on criminals, which excited loyal Republicans. In Haynsworth's case, Nixon injected the nomination into the congressional campaign, using Johnson's strategy when he claimed that Haynsworth was rejected for political, regional, and ideological grounds. President Nixon lost his nominations of Carswell and Haynsworth but succeeded in advancing his political agenda and winning over southern voters. Thus, Johnson and Nixon shifted the nomination process to the public sphere by including it in campaigns that focused on different issues than those that engaged the Senate. If these campaign arguments were disingenuous—and they certainly appear to be—then they violated Habermas's standards.

As a corollary, the public relations operation in the White House has expanded greatly in terms of its size and involvement in federal court nominations. There is a new emphasis on checking scholarly writing of nominees, as well as legal opinions; that move has provided a different kind of evidence for the arguments that are developed. Some writings, as in the case of Bork, may be used to argue that the nominee is out of touch, ideologically unacceptable, or theoretically flawed. Under Nixon, the public relations divisions began to do polling when a nomination got in trouble. As we have learned, interest groups now do polling to determine the best way to attack or defend a nominee. Thus, public sphere argumentation has become poll driven.

Fourth, engaging the public sphere has promoted a tit-for-tat mentality that smacks of political revenge instead of civil debate.[89] Republicans had to sacrifice Haynsworth because of what they had done to Fortas; Thomas was nominated in response to what happened to Bork. The Democrats filibustered George W. Bush's federal nominees because Republicans had filibustered Clinton nominees. Such an atmosphere does not contribute to a refined, rational, and well-argued nomination process recommended by Habermas's consensual model.[90] He was particularly concerned about the disregard for integrity in civic debate, a characteristic quite common when nomination enters the public sphere in America.

Fifth, engaging the public sphere has led to an escalation in presidential involvement in the public debate over nominees. Presidents have become advocates of their nominees to an extent unheard of before the Bork nomination. They present their nominees to the public and then endorse their nominees in public speeches. They regularly engaged the media and interest groups to rally support for their candidates.

Sixth, Thomas's nomination indicates that when the public sphere is engaged, argumentation can change in at least two ways other than those mentioned above. First, narratives seem to capture the attention of the media and move the public. Second, a nominee can break through media screens by making an effective, and usually passionate, rhetorical appeal. Neither of these tactics is likely to move members of the Senate sphere. And these tactics appear to be outside the realm of what Habermas recognized as the normative sphere of rational argumentation.

Seventh, the argumentative roles that senators play during the hearings often define how or why they engage the public. Watson and Stookey identified at least four roles that senators perform: evaluator, validator, partisan, and advocate.[91] Senators will shift roles and even combine them depending on partisan and ideological variables. An Orrin Hatch will try to validate the nomination of a Robert Bork, while at times playing his advocate. However, that same senator might become an evaluator of a Ruth Bader Ginsburg. The senator's adopted role shapes the argumentation the senator uses in public forums. Senator Arlen Specter's prosecutorial role in his questioning of Anita Hill on live television nearly resulted in his defeat at the polls because Pennsylvania viewers were incensed at the aggressive nature of his questions.[92]

As Ronald Reagan once opined, the selection of nominees to the Supreme Court has become a partisan, and often ideological, struggle.[93] The president has at his disposal several loci of argumentation to win the day. These include the White House Congressional Liaison Office and Communication Center, the Justice Department (particularly the Office of Legal Counsel), interest groups, and the party's national political committees. All of these can act in concert through various ad hoc groups to pressure the Senate to confirm a nominee. They also clash with opposing interest groups and the opposing party's apparatus.

Because the number of players has grown and because the media focuses on it, the nomination process has become increasingly public. Thus, when a nominee is chosen, the screening process is crucial, not only because it can generate evidence and arguments in favor of the nominee but also because it can discover an Achilles heel. If the results of the screening are favorable, the White House liaison office then must decide how to use the arguments in favor of the nominee. At first, such arguments are directed at members of the Senate Judiciary Committee, and then to the whole Senate. However, should the nomination run into trouble, the appeals may be expanded beyond normative Senate argumentation and to the public sphere. The liaison office may also expand the involvement of the administration to the Justice Department and the political wing of the White House.

The same pattern with some modification is true of the opposition. Initially, those groups opposing the nomination, usually special interest groups, focus their attention and testimony on the senators on the Judiciary Committee. If these groups are successful, they need not expand the scope of the controversy. However, should they fail, they then expand the scope first to the Senate at large and then to the public, having nowhere else to turn.

The role the U.S. Supreme Court played in the selection of the president in 2000 increased the stakes in the nomination process because those who sit on the Court were seen by many to have chosen the president. For that reason, nomination to the Supreme Court will continue to engage the attention and scrutiny of the media and the public.[94] Unless nominees are carefully screened, they are likely to face intensive media campaigns for and against them in a mediated public sphere.

NOTES

1. See Lee Epstein, Andrew D. Martin, Kevin M. Quinn, and Jeffrey A. Segal, "Ideological Drift among Supreme Court Justices: Who, When, and How Important?" *Northwestern University Law Review*, 101 (2007): 1483–97.

2. See Jürgen Habermas, "Paradigms of Law," in *Habermas on Law and Democracy: Critical Exchanges*, ed. Michel Rosenfeld and Andrew Arato (Berkeley: University of California Press, 1998). Habermas writes, "an economic society institutionalized in the form of private law (above all through property rights and contractual freedom) was separated from the sphere of the common good and the state," 14.

3. Habermas, "Paradigms of Law," 18.

4. Habermas has admitted that this model of the "public sphere" in his early work tended to exclude minorities and other marginalized groups. See his "Further Reflections on the Public Sphere," in *Habermas and the Public Sphere*, ed. Craig Calhoun (Cambridge, MA: MIT Press, 1992), 466–68

5. Jürgen Habermas, *The Theory of Communicative Action*, trans. T. McCarthy (Boston: Beacon Press, 1984), vol. 1, 17–18.

6. Jürgen Habermas, "Toward a Theory of Communicative Competence," *Inquiry*, 13 (1970): 367.

7. Jürgen Habermas, "Citizenship and National Identity: Some Reflections on the Future of Europe," *Praxis International*, 12 (1992): 7.

8. Jürgen Habermas, *Between Facts and Norms: Contributions to a Discourse Theory of Law and Democracy*, trans. William Regh (Cambridge, MA: MIT Press, 1996), 370.

9. Habermas, *Between Facts and Norms*, 381.

10. See Michael J. Gerhardt, *The Federal Appointments Process: A Constitutional and Historical Analysis* (Durham, NC: Duke University Press, 2000). Theodore Y. Blumoff, "Separation of Powers and the Origins of the Appointments Clause," *Syracuse Law Review*, 37 (1987): 1037; James E. Gauch, "The Intended Role of the Senate in Supreme Court Appointments," *University of Chicago Law Review*, 56 (1989): 337; Matthew D. Marcotte, "Advice

and Consent: A Historical Argument for Substantive Senatorial Involvement in Judicial Nominations," *New York University Journal of Legislation and Public Policy*, 5 (2001–2002): 519–62.

11. Letter from Thomas Jefferson to William T. Berry, July 2, 1822, in *The Writing of Thomas Jefferson* (H. A. Washington edition, 1859), vol. 7, 256.

12. Edmunds v. U.S., 520 U.S. 651, 659–60 (1997).

13. Some have argued that Goldberg transferred because his decisions were badly written and poorly reasoned. See L. Marvin Overby, Beth M. Henschen, Julie Strauss, and Michael H. Walsh, "African-American Constituents and Supreme Court Nominees: An Examination of the Senate Confirmation of Thurgood Marshall," *Political Research Quarterly*, 47 (1994): 839–41.

14. David Alistair Yalof, *Pursuit of Justices: Presidential Politics and the Selection of Supreme Court Nominees* (Chicago: University of Chicago Press, 1999), 83.

15. It is important to note that Dwight Eisenhower's nominees were approved easily and seemed bipartisan. They included Earl Warren, John Harlan, William Brennan, and Potter Stewart. Eisenhower is said to have later regretted the appointment of Warren, the former conservative Republican governor of California, who became a liberal activist on the Court. Harlan remained true to his strict constructionist roots by opposing Warren's agenda. Brennan supported it fully, and Stewart was ambiguous about it.

16. For a full account, see Linda S. Greene, "The Confirmation of Thurgood Marshall to the Supreme Court," *Harvard Blackletter Journal*, 6 (1989): 27–50.

17. Strom Thurmond led the filibuster that delayed the appointment for a year.

18. Trevor Parry-Giles, "Character, the Constitution, and the Ideological Embodiment of 'Civil Rights' in the 1967 Nomination of Thurgood Marshall to the Supreme Court," *Quarterly Journal of Speech*, 82 (1996): 364–82.

19. Parry-Giles, "Character, the Constitution," 371–74. See also Stephen L. Carter, *The Confirmation Mess: Cleaning Up the Federal Appointments Process* (New York: Basic Books, 1994), 6–12.

20. Richard M. Nixon, "Acceptance of the Republican Nomination," *Vital Speeches of the Day*, 34 (1968): 674–78.

21. The conflict of interest was very small. Though Haynsworth had resigned as a director of Vend-A-Matic, he voted in a case for a company that held 3 percent of Vend-A-Matic's stock.

22. John Anthony Maltese, *The Selling of Supreme Court Nominees* (Baltimore, MD: John Hopkins University Press, 1995), 74.

23. Yalof, *Pursuit of Justices*, 108.

24. Maltese, *The Selling*, 75.

25. *Public Papers of the Presidents of the United States: Richard Nixon* (Washington, DC: U.S. Government Printing Office, 1969), 815, 818; Richard Nixon, *The Memoirs of Richard Nixon* (New York: Grosset and Dunlap, 1978), 420–21. It is interesting to note that there were few hearings concerning Supreme Court nominations before the controversy surrounding Brandeis. But it was the 1937 nomination of Hugo Black that led to of regular hearings.

26. Maltese, *The Selling*, 75.

27. Maltese, *The Selling*, 79.

28. H. R. Haldeman, *The Haldeman Diaries: Inside the Nixon White House* (New York: Putnam, 1994), 95.

29. Yalof, *Pursuit of Justices*, 109.

30. Maltese, *The Selling*, 132. The group drafted senators Dole and Baker, and included Charles Colson, Herb Klein, Jeb Magruder, Bryce Harlow, William Rehnquist, and John Dean.

31. Maltese, *The Selling*, 134.

32. Nixon, *The Memoirs*, 422.

33. Nixon, *The Memoirs*, 422.

34. For example, in reaction to the way southern nominees had been treated, President Jimmy Carter created the Circuit Court Nominating Commission by executive order. He encouraged the states to follow suit, which about half did. The Commission would prescreen nominees before they came to the U.S. Senate for approval. President Ronald Reagan abolished

the Commission and substituted his own President's Committee on Federal Judicial Selection, which was retained by Bush, but abolished by Clinton, who turned the authority over to Office of Policy Development in the Justice Department.

35. David G. Savage, "Vacancy Rate on Federal Bench Is at a 13-Year Low," *Los Angeles Times*, November 6, 2003: A14.

36. Ethan Bronner, *Battle for Justice: How the Bork Nomination Shook America* (New York: W. W. Norton, 1989), 42.

37. When William Bradford Reynolds was nominated for associate attorney general, he was savaged by civil rights leaders. Benjamin Hooks, executive director of the NAACP, claimed Reynolds was trying to turn back two decades of progress on civil rights. Bronner, *Battle for Justice*, 48. Reynolds's condemnation of busing and racial quotas led to the defeat of the nomination. It also foreshadowed Bork's troubles because the same moderate Republican senators who made the difference with Reynolds would make the difference in the case of Bork.

38. As printed in Yalof, *Pursuit of Justices*, 143.

39. Harold Tyler to Senator Joseph Biden, September 21, 1987, in U.S. Senate Committee on the Judiciary, *Nomination of Robert H. Bork to Be Associate Justice of the Supreme Court of the United States*, 100th Congress, 1st session (Washington, DC: U.S. Government Printing Office, October 1987), 1232.

40. See Mary Katherine Boyte, "The Supreme Court Confirmation Process in Crisis: Is the System Defective, or Merely the Participants?" *Whittier Law Review*, 14 (1993): 517–47; Frank Guliuzza III, Daniel J. Reagan, and David M. Barrett, "Character, Competency, and Constitutionalism: Did the Bork Nomination Represent a Fundamental Shift in Confirmation Criteria?" *Marquette Law Review*, 75 (1992): 409–37; Mark Silverstein, *Judicious Choices: The New Politics of Supreme Court Confirmations* (New York: Norton, 1994).

41. Mark Gitenstein, *Matters of Principle: An Insider's Account of America's Rejection of Robert Bork's Nomination to the Supreme Court* (New York: Simon and Schuster, 1992), 11. Gitenstein was the chief counsel for the Democrat-controlled Senate Judiciary Committee.

42. Bronner (50) claims there were 180 groups in the coalition that opposed Bork.

43. Gitenstein, *Matters of Principle*, 30.

44. Bronner, *Battle for Justice*, 98.

45. In 2004, Neas became the head of Norman Lear's People for the American Way, which also fought the Bork nomination. As we shall see, Neas was among the first in 2005 to oppose President Bush's renomination of candidates to the federal bench who had been stopped earlier by Democratic filibusters in the Senate.

46. Gitenstein, *Matters of Principle*, 57.

47. Gitenstein, *Matters of Principle*, 58.

48. Gitenstein, *Matters of Principle*, 64.

49. Gitenstein, *Matters of Principle*, 222.

50. *Nomination of Robert H. Bork*, 105.

51. Bork had been critical of Justice William O. Douglas's use of "penumbras" of the Constitution in which the right to privacy "emanated."

52. Gitenstein, *Matters of Principle*, 232.

53. The present author served as the director of senate services for the Republican Conference of the U.S. Senate from 1979 to 1980, and was a consultant to several Republican senators and Vice President Bush during the Bork nomination. He witnessed the frustration of Republican senators with the Bork nomination.

54. There is strong evidence that they were right, especially when, in 1990, Bork claimed that the "only" legitimate way to read the Constitution was in the context of its original meaning. See Robert H. Bork, *The Tempting of America: The Political Seduction of the Law* (New York: Free Press, 1990), 143.

55. Bronner, *Battle for Justice*, 234.

56. Bronner, *Battle for Justice*, 234.

57. Gitenstein, *Matters of Principle*, 12.

58. By comparison, Reagan only made two public statements for Sandra Day O'Connor, five for Scalia, four for Rehnquist, three for Douglas Ginsburg, and none for Kennedy. Maltese, *The Selling*, 88, 114–15.

59. Maltese, *The Selling*, 114. Certainly, Franklin Roosevelt had challenged the Supreme Court in 1937, when he tried to add members to it. But that fight was about the direction of the Court, not a single nominee. Roosevelt fought for his nominees behind the scenes. Andrew Jackson was more public about his desire to place Roger Taney on the Court, especially after his first nomination was blocked by the Whigs.

60. Korologos had been close to Senator Howard Baker and had worked in the Nixon and Ford White Houses as a congressional liaison officer.

61. Maltese, *The Selling*, 130.

62. Bronner, *Battle for Justice*, 146.

63. Bronner, *Battle for Justice*, 155.

64. Bronner, *Battle for Justice*, 151.

65. Ironically, the *Post* admitted that Bork had suffered a "lynching" by special interest groups (Bronner, 312). One can only speculate as to whether this language inspired Clarence Thomas's complaint of suffering a "high-tech lynching" during his hearings (see below).

66. Each of the six was heavily lobbied by women's groups and each had received campaign contributions from them. However, some had also received contributions from the NRA.

67. Yalof, *Pursuit of Justices*, 189. See also Norman Vieira and Leonard E. Gross, "The Appointments Clause: Judge Bork and the Role of Ideology in Judicial Confirmations," *Journal of Legal History*, 11 (1990): 311–52; Albert P. Melone, "The Senate's Confirmation Role in Supreme Court Nominations and the Politics of Ideology versus Impartiality," *Judicature*, 75 (1991): 68–79. The point here is not that previous justices had been subjected to ideological scrutiny. Certainly presidents from Adams and Jefferson regularly populated the court with justices who reflected their own ideologies. The point is that an attack on the ideology of the candidate had not been used in the public sphere in any significant way before Bork.

68. Jane Mayer and Jill Abramson point out that the Justice Department sought to "bury ideology and sell biography" using the "Pin Point story." *Strange Justice: The Selling of Clarence Thomas* (Boston: Houghton Mifflin, 1994), 30.

69. "Remarks Announcing the New American Schools Development Corporation Board, July 8, 1991," *Public Papers of the Presidents of the United States: George Bush, 1991*, Book II (Washington, DC: U.S. Government Printing Office, 1992), 830.

70. "Remarks at the Annual Convention of the National Fraternal Order of Police in Pittsburgh, Pennsylvania, August 14, 1991," *Public Papers of the Presidents of the United States: George Bush, 1991*, Book II (Washington, DC: U.S. Government Printing Office, 1992), 1041.

71. "Remarks at a Kickoff Ceremony for the Eighth Annual National Night Out against Crime in Arlington, Virginia, August 6, 1991," *Public Papers of the Presidents of the United States: George Bush, 1991*, Book II (Washington, DC: U.S. Government Printing Office, 1992), 1119.

72. Trevor Parry-Giles, "Celebritized Justice, Civil Rights, and the Clarence Thomas Nomination," in *The White House and Civil Rights Policy*, ed. James Aune (College Station, TX: Texas A and M University Press, 2004), 268–300.

73. Parry-Giles, "Celebritized Justice."

74. *Nomination of Judge Clarence Thomas to Be Associate Justice of the Supreme Court of the United States: Hearings before the Committee on the Judiciary, United States Senate*, 102nd Congress, 1st session, pt. 1, October 10–15 (Washington, DC: U.S. Government Printing Office, October 1991), 110.

75. See Nancy Fraser, "Sex, Lies and the Public Sphere: Some Reflections on the Confirmation of Clarence Thomas," *Critical Inquiry*, 18 (1992): 595–612.

76. "Remarks at a Kickoff Ceremony for the Eighth Annual National Night Out against Crime in Arlington, Virginia, August 6, 1991," *Public Papers of the Presidents of the United States: George Bush, 1991*, Book II (Washington, DC: U.S. Government Printing Office, 1992), 1119.

77. Her argument was that references to pornographic videos, pubic hair, and the like were tantamount to sexual harassment.

78. Maltese, *The Selling*, 93.

79. *Nomination of Judge Clarence Thomas*, 157–58. Like Hugo Black's radio address of 1937, when he was in trouble for his past association with the Ku Klux Klan, Thomas's outburst broke through the mediating screen of news reporters and commentators. Earlier, Thomas had previewed this strategy when he said, "I have been able . . . to defy poverty, avoid prison, overcome segregation, bigotry, racism, and obtain one of the finest educations available in this country. But I have not been able to overcome this process. . . . I will not provide the rope for my own lynching." *Nomination of Judge Clarence Thomas*, 8–10.

80. Vanessa Bowles Beasley, "The Logic of Power in the Hill-Thomas Hearings: A Rhetorical Analysis," *Political Communication*, 11 (1994): 287–97.

81. For a full analysis, see William L. Benoit and Dawn M. Nill, "A Critical Analysis of Judge Clarence Thomas' Statement Before the Senate Judiciary Committee," *Communication Studies*, 49 (1998): 179–95; Michael J. Gerhardt, "Divided Justice: A Commentary on the Nomination and Confirmation of Justice Thomas," *George Washington Law Review*, 60 (1992): 969–96.

82. See Joseph Faria and David Markey, "Supreme Court Appointments after the Thomas Nomination: Reforming the Confirmation Process," *Journal of Legal Commentary*, 7 (1991): 389–416; John Massaro, "President Bush's Management of the Thomas Nomination," *Presidential Studies Quarterly*, 26 (1996): 816–27.

83. See Susan Low Bloch and Thomas G. Krattenmaker, *Supreme Court Politics: The Institution and Its Procedures* (Minneapolis: West Law, 1994); Henry J. Abraham, *Justices and Presidents: A Political History of Appointments to the Supreme Court*, 4th ed. (New York: Oxford University Press, 1999).

84. See, for example, the president's national Saturday radio address of January 28, 2006.

85. Alito's most controversial decision came in *Planned Parenthood v. Casey* (1991), in which Alito voted to uphold a section of a Pennsylvania law requiring that the father of the fetus be notified about the intention to have it aborted. He voted with the majority in all other cases in which they voted to strike down provisions of the law. In a five to four ruling in 1992, with O'Connor in the majority, the Supreme Court overturned the entire law, including the provision that Alito had supported. This decision was a major reaffirmation of *Roe v. Wade*. In his first ruling on the Court, Alito broke with the most conservative justices, Rehnquist, Thomas, and Scalia, and supported a stay of execution in a Florida case.

86. Jürgen Habermas, *The Structural Transformation of the Public Sphere* (Cambridge, MA: MIT Press, 1999), 160, 171.

87. See Habermas, *Between Facts and Norms: Contributions to a Discourse Theory of Law and Democracy*, 440–41. In this section, Habermas calls for public hearings to monitor administrative decisions.

88. Habermas, *Between Facts and Norms*, 370ff.

89. Brent Wible argues that "filibustering judicial nominees has proven a problematic, polarizing tactic that entrenches partisanship in the appointment process." "Filibuster vs. Supermajority Rule: From Polarization to a Consensus- and Moderation-Forcing Mechanism for Judicial Confirmations," *William and Mary Bill of Rights Journal*, 13 (2005): 937.

90. Jürgen Habermas, "Struggles for Recognition in Constitutional States," *European Journal of Philosophy*, 1 (1993): 128.

91. George L. Watson and John A. Stookey, *Shaping America: The Politics of Supreme Court Appointments* (New York: HarperCollins, 1995), 149–55.

92. S. Ashley Armstrong, "Arlen Specter and the Construction of Adversarial Discourse: Selective Representation in the Clarence Thomas–Anita Hill Hearings," *Argumentation and Advocacy*, 32 (1995): 75–89; Donald Grier Stephenson, Jr., *Campaigns and the Court: The U.S. Supreme Court in Presidential Elections* (New York: Columbia University Press, 1999), 214–17.

93. PBS, *MacNeil/Lehrer NewsHour*, October 1, 1987.

94. Theodore Prosise and Craig R. Smith, "The Supreme Court's Ruling in Bush v. Gore: A Rhetoric of Inconsistency," *Rhetoric and Public Affairs*, 4 (2001): 605–32.

Chapter Three

Chief Justice Roberts

Tim West

> Judges and Justices are servants of the law, not the other way around. Judges
> are like umpires. Umpires don't make the rules, they apply them. The role of
> an umpire and a judge is critical. They make sure everybody plays by the rules,
> but it is a limited role. Nobody ever went to a ball game to see the umpire.
> —Chief Justice John Roberts, hearing before the Senate Judiciary Committee [1]

President George W. Bush nominated John G. Roberts, Jr., to the Supreme
Court on July 19, 2005. [2] Originally intending to replace the retiring Justice
Sandra Day O'Connor with Judge Roberts, President Bush altered Roberts's
nomination from associate justice to chief justice on September 6, 2005, due
to the death of Chief Justice William Rehnquist two days earlier. [3] Because of
Roberts's extensive experience in front of the Supreme Court (Roberts
argued thirty-nine cases before the Supreme Court as an attorney), his clerk-
ship with Justice Rehnquist from 1980 to 1981, and his stint on the Court of
Appeals for the D.C. Circuit from 2003 to 2005, Bush was very confident
about Roberts's ability to lead the high court. [4] In order to fill the chief justice
vacancy before the upcoming court session in October, President Bush
pressed the Senate to accelerate their confirmation schedule.

The Republican-controlled Senate complied with Bush's request and began the confirmation hearings for Roberts on September 6, 2005. Initially
there were questions regarding Roberts's judicial philosophy. [5] Even though
many judicial scholars recognized that Roberts typically adjudicated "between the lines" of precedent, critics predicted that Roberts would align
himself with the conservative members of the Supreme Court and rule accordingly. [6] Most senators echoed the sentiments voiced by Arlen Specter
(then R-Pennsylvania) when he stated, "I think we have a man . . . who is a
nonactivist judge which everybody is looking for." [7]

On September 22, 2005, the Senate Judiciary Committee approved the nomination of Roberts on a thirteen to five vote. This vote was significant because it indicated that Roberts had sufficient support to be filibuster-proof during the full Senate votes. Additionally, Roberts gained Democratic support from Senator Patrick J. Leahy, the ranking Democrat on the Committee (Vermont), Senator Herb Kohl (D-Wisconsin), and Senator Russell D. Feingold (D-Wisconsin), which increased the momentum of his nomination. Senator Kohl explained his endorsement of Roberts by remarking, "Judge Roberts came before this committee as a very well-respected judge with a sterling academic record and a remarkable legal career. He leaves this committee with that reputation intact, if not enhanced."[8]

One week later, the success that Roberts experienced in front of the Senate Judiciary Committee was replicated on the Senate floor. On September 29, 2005, the Senate voted seventy-eight to twenty-two to confirm Roberts. Senator Bill Frist (R-Tennessee), the Republican majority leader at the time, underscored Roberts's successful appointment by stating: "With the confirmation of John Roberts, the Supreme Court will embark upon a new era in its history, the Roberts era. . . . For many years to come, long after many of us have left public service, the Roberts court will be deliberating on some of the most difficult and fundamental questions of U.S. law."[9] Roberts assumed his role on the Court on October 3, 2005.[10] During his first few terms as chief justice, Roberts's opinions reshaped jurisprudence in America, including First Amendment law. Over the course of his first four years on the Court, Chief Justice Roberts has been integral in molding the freedoms of speech, press, and religion in the twenty-first century.

Judges use various strategies to frame their interpretation of legal questions.[11] Modalities, as defined by Phillip Bobbitt, encompass the rationales for these strategies and construct judicial conscience.[12] This chapter will examine the framing employed by Roberts during First Amendment cases argued before the Supreme Court. By observing the modalities Roberts used, this chapter hopes to reveal what rhetorical frames appeal to him. In dissecting the modalities used in Roberts's nomination hearings; observing the modalities utilized during two of Roberts's most significant First Amendment opinions, *Morse v. Frederick* (2007)[13] and *Federal Election Commission v. Wisconsin Right to Life, Inc.* (2007);[14] and addressing the rhetorical implications of the modalities used by Justice Roberts, this chapter will enable advocates to make more compelling arguments to Chief Justice Roberts in the future.

CONFIRMATION HEARINGS

Confirmation hearings before the Senate Judiciary Committee are crucial to the nomination process. They can be trying and controversial; however, during Roberts's confirmation hearings, the highly polarized opinions reminiscent of the confirmation hearings of Louis D. Brandeis, John J. Parker, Robert Bork, and Clarence Thomas were held to a minimum. Amid early threats of Democratic opposition to the appointment of John Roberts, such as the one made by Senator Ted Kennedy (D-Massachusetts), President George W. Bush and several key Republican senators quickly launched a campaign of persuasion to squelch opposition to Roberts. Nonetheless, his hearings allowed the public to understand his judicial philosophy, which provided insight into his thought process on the bench. Simultaneously, Roberts's confirmation hearings shed light on his interpretation of the First Amendment and how he planned to frame his rulings.

At the hearings, Senator Specter asked the first question of Roberts concerning the Fourth Amendment. Specifically, Senator Specter asked Roberts if he believed that the right to privacy exists within the Constitution. Roberts responded by eliding the First and Fourth amendments:

> I do. The right to privacy is protected under the Constitution in various ways. It's protected by the Fourth Amendment, which provides that the right of people to be secure in their persons, houses, effects and papers is protected. It's protected under the First Amendment, dealing with prohibition on establishment of a religion and guarantee of free exercise, protects privacy in matters of conscience. It was protected by the Framers in areas that were of particular concern to them that may not seem so significant today, the Third Amendment, protecting their homes against the quartering of troops.[15]

Roberts's response illuminated his opinion of the First Amendment. His comment reflected a strict interpretation of the Constitution. Phillip Bobbitt explained that the reliance on the "strict construction" of the Constitution is a "textual" modality.[16] This plain reading of the Constitution relies on the "average" or "rational" person's understanding of the law. This reading is buttressed by the structural modality and uses warrants from the Fourth, First, and Third amendments. Moreover, this statement also introduced Roberts's perceptions of the establishment clause and freedom of expression that were developed in more depth later in the hearings.

Senator Mark DeWine (R-Ohio) pressed Roberts on his strict textual philosophy of the Constitution by asking him if he believed that the First Amendment was flexible enough to exist in 2005 during the "digital age." DeWine's insightful question forced Roberts to employ a different modality to construct his judicial analysis because there is obviously no textual grounding on the Internet and other "e-technologies" in the Constitution. Roberts responded to DeWine's question by retorting:

> I appreciate the point, and I do know that even in the analysis in this particular area, one of the factors that the Court considers is the availability of alternative avenues for expression, and a concern, if they are cutting off a particular mode of expression, a particular avenue, [we ask] are there alternatives available? And I think that's a very important consideration. I think you're quite right that this is one of those areas in which technology is going to figure in a very prominent way, and the question of whether this type of analysis that grew up when you're talking about a public square or a town hall type thing, applies in the Internet situation, and whether there's changes that do need to be made in the analysis.[17]

The comment illustrates that Roberts was willing to use alternative analysis to make decisions. His characterization of doing what is "right" or prudent suggested that Roberts could use the prudential modality when no textual justifications exist for such an analysis. Bobbitt characterized the "prudential" modality as "the particular wisdom of using the courts in a particular way."[18] This type of logic acts as a "cost-beneficial" rationale, which justifies a given decision through the implications of such a decision.

The final modality that appeared in the confirmation hearings of John Roberts was the doctrinal modality. This rhetorical framing is essentially the reliance on past precedent to guide future rulings. Logically, this modality appeals to previous courts' rationales that have been tempered with time and legal fortitude.

Judge Roberts embraced the doctrinal modality in response to questions posed by Senator Dianne Feinstein (D-California), in which she sought Roberts's opinion on freedom of religion in addition to his ability to adjudicate a case without interjecting his religious convictions. Roberts, a Catholic, answered Feinstein's query by stating:

> I would have to confront that case with an open mind in light of the arguments presented, in light of the precedents of the Court, and the litigants in those cases are entitled to have judges that haven't expressed views on that particular case. . . . What the courts have to do is make sure they provide a level playing field in which people disputing the impact of the Constitution, on whose right prevails, have judges who will decide that case according to the rule of law, and not according to whether they think one right should prevail or another.[19]

Roberts's statement not only reflected his ability to apply doctrinal or precedential logic. By telling Senator Feinstein, the Senate Judiciary Committee, and the public that he was willing to adjudicate fairly based on prior Supreme Court decisions, Roberts created a judicial conscience that appeared to be bound to the history of law.

During his tenure leading the Supreme Court, Roberts's opinions have played a critical role in several important First Amendment cases. In the next section of this chapter, I will examine two of Chief Justice Roberts's most significant decisions and discuss the ways in which his rhetorical tactics utilize different modalities.

MORSE V. FREDERICK

Before the Olympics begin, a torch lit with the fire of Mount Olympia must travel through the host country to signify the upcoming games. This time-tested tradition set the stage for one of the recent landmark First Amendment Supreme Court cases. *Morse v. Frederick* (2007),[20] also known as "Bong Hits 4 Jesus," pitted Juneau, Alaska, high school senior Joseph Frederick against his high school principal, Deborah Morse, over her decision to stifle Frederick's speech.[21] In 2002, during the Olympic torch celebrations, Frederick planned on achieving brief national fame thanks to a homemade banner. As the torch neared, Frederick, with the help of a few friends, unveiled his fourteen-foot banner, which read "Bong Hits 4 Jesus." While catching the attention of his peers and television cameras, Frederick also caught the attention of Morse, who forced Frederick to remove the sign before suspending him for ten days due to the sign's inappropriate, allegedly drug-endorsing message.[22]

Frederick quickly filed suit against Morse and the school because, as articulated in *Tinker v. Des Moines Independent Community School District* (1969), "students [do not] shed their constitutional rights to freedom of speech or expression at the schoolhouse gate."[23] Frederick's argument was that the school violated his freedom of speech due to its overly broad restriction on behavior, a standard that led to his suspension.

Morse, on the other hand, contended that Frederick's suspension was justified because his sign endorsed marijuana use, a practice that was incompatible with the school's policy on drugs.[24] Morse and the school district believed that their decision to punish Frederick was fair and reasonable because their fundamental obligation was to provide a safe and educational environment for all students, even if that was at the expense of one student's ability to speak freely.

Oral arguments before the Supreme Court in *Morse v. Frederick* began on March 19, 2007, and the outcome was issued on June 25, 2007. The split decision had Roberts, Scalia, Kennedy, Thomas, and Alito in the majority ruling that Frederick's First Amendment claims were invalid. Roberts's majority opinion stunned Frederick and his proponents because Roberts's decision eroded the precedent set by *Tinker* , which had expanded the rights of high school students.[25]

Morse v. Frederick clearly revealed Roberts's judicial philosophy. Multiple modalities appeared within this opinion. Roberts began his opinion by referencing several previous court cases. He also commenced his decision with the doctrinal rationale because it was constrained by written and applied law. While the chief justice used this approach to introduce his ruling, he also used a doctrinal-prudential synthesis to frame his opinion. This hybrid modality was expressed when Roberts stated, "Consistent with these principles, we hold that schools may take steps to safeguard those entrusted to their care from speech that can reasonably be regarded as encouraging illegal drug use."[26] Roberts's use of precedent and principles, as well as the prudential term "reasonably," introduced an argument with one modality (doctrinal) and synthesized it with another modality (prudential). Roberts ultimately crafted an opinion that justified the narrowing of student speech rights by adhering to doctrinal and prudential strategies.

We should note that despite Roberts's continual use of precedent throughout his decision, there was substantial precedent that contradicted Roberts's opinion. That may be why, ultimately, Roberts's decision in *Morse* rested on prudential logic, not precedent. Using cost-benefit analysis, Roberts made the case for a compelling government interest by remarking, "The problem remains serious today . . . About half of American 12th graders have used an illicit drug, as have more than a third of 10th graders and about one-fifth of 8th graders . . . Nearly one in four 12th graders has used an illicit drug in the past month . . . Some 25% of high schoolers say that they have been offered, sold, or given an illegal drug on school property within the past year."[27] Even though the facts about teenage drug use in America were compelling, Roberts's opinion had moved away from doctrinal framing. Instead, Roberts continued to rely on prudential logic by arguing that:

> Thousands of school boards throughout the country—including JDHS—have adopted policies aimed at effectuating this message. . . . Those school boards know that peer pressure is perhaps "the single most important factor leading school children to take drugs," and that students are more likely to use drugs when the norms in school appear to tolerate such behavior. . . . Student speech celebrating illegal drug use at a school event, in the presence of school administrators and teachers, thus poses a particular challenge for school officials working to protect those entrusted to their care from the dangers of drug abuse.[28]

Roberts engaged in cost-beneficial calculus in order to gauge the potential ramifications of not ruling in favor of Morse and the school district. This instance of calculative logic suggested that prudential reasoning was the most important modality in Roberts's decision in *Morse v. Frederick*.

FEDERAL ELECTION COMMISSION V. WISCONSIN RIGHT TO LIFE, INC.

The Bipartisan Campaign Reform Act (BCRA) of 2002 attempted to level the American political field by eliminating the appearance of corruption during federal elections.[29] One provision of the far-reaching BCRA was its desire to regulate "issue ads." All political candidates were to avoid the undue influence of corporate and union political action committees (PACs) and special interest groups; the issue ads provision (Section 203) of the BCRA prohibited the airing of ads that endorsed and attacked politicians within the sixty days of a general election and thirty days of a primary election. Ultimately this provision tried to prevent ad blitzes from interest groups and PACs the week or even the night before elections. However, in order to achieve these legislative goals, BCRA may have jeopardized constitutional rights.[30] Wisconsin Right to Life (WRTL), Inc., was one of the groups who believed this provision eroded its right to speak freely.

In 2004 WRTL intended to run several political ads before the 2004 general election. However, invoking BCRA, the Federal Elections Commission (FEC) prohibited WRTL from airing their ads. WRTL was surprised because they believed their ads, which only suggested that voters tell their congresspersons to avoid filibustering judicial nominees, were completely within the bounds of the BCRA. WRTL filed suit against the FEC because they were certain their First Amendment rights were being violated.

Oral arguments in *FEC v. WRTL* (2007)[31] began on April 25, 2007, and the ruling was announced June 25, 2007. With Roberts, Scalia, Kennedy, Thomas, and Alito again comprising the majority, the Court ruled that WRTL's First Amendment claims were valid. Chief Justice Roberts read the opinion and announced that the so-called sham ads were indeed constitutionally protected.

Roberts's opinion in this case was rhetorically significant because it clarified Roberts's judicial framing. Roberts began by employing the doctrinal modality to establish the distinction between issue ads and nonissue ads:

> We have long recognized that the distinction between campaign advocacy and issue advocacy "may often dissolve in practical application. Candidates, especially incumbents, are intimately tied to public issues involving legislative proposals and governmental actions." *Buckley v. Valeo* , 424 U. S. 1, 42 (1976)

(per curiam). Our development of the law in this area requires us, however, to draw such a line, because we have recognized that the interests held to justify the regulation of campaign speech and its "functional equivalent" "might not apply" to the regulation of issue advocacy.[32]

Roberts grounded his decision on the precedent set in *Buckley*. This strategy was particularly important for Roberts in this trial because the Court had the burden of closely mirroring the decision-making calculus used in *McConnell v. FEC* (2003) [33] or the Court would risk damaging the legitimacy of its earlier precedent in campaign finance rulings. Roberts used the doctrinal modality in this ruling to remove any appearance of personal bias from the decision.

Roberts also employed the textual modality in his decision. Near the conclusion of the majority opinion, he noted that:

> Yet, as is often the case in this Court's First Amendment opinions, we have gotten this far in the analysis without quoting the Amendment itself: "Congress shall make no law . . . abridging the freedom of speech." The Framers' actual words put these cases in proper perspective. Our jurisprudence over the past 216 years has rejected an absolutist interpretation of those words, but when it comes to drawing difficult lines in the area of pure political speech— between what is protected and what the Government may ban—it is worth recalling the language we are applying. McConnell held that express advocacy of a candidate or his opponent by a corporation shortly before an election may be prohibited, along with the functional equivalent of such express advocacy. We have no occasion to revisit that determination today. But when it comes to defining what speech qualifies as the functional equivalent of express advocacy subject to such a ban—the issue we do have to decide—we give the benefit of the doubt to speech, not censorship. The First Amendment's command that "Congress shall make no law . . . abridging the freedom of speech" demands at least that.[34]

Roberts's concluding remarks reiterated how important the textual modality was to his judicial conscience, and potentially foreshadowed his perspective on future cases regarding freedom of expression. This decision is important because Justice Roberts utilized multiple modalities, but, more importantly, displayed a precise order in which modalities should be used. By beginning a decision with a doctrinal modality and then shifting to textual strategies, Roberts's opinions reflected two ends of a spectrum that he will most likely continue to use for the remainder of his time on the Court.

Further, Roberts's calculus in *FEC v. WRTL* foreshadowed his concurring ruling in *Citizens United v. Federal Election Commission* (2010).[35] Decided in January 2010, this split decision overturned parts of McCain-Feingold BCRA that had prevented unions and corporations from "electioneering communication"; the Court held that those laws impede freedom of speech.

In his decision, the chief justice drew from his logic in *FEC v. WRTL* (2007) by arguing, "The restrictions thus function as the equivalent of a prior restraint, giving the FEC power analogous to the type of government practices that the First Amendment was drawn to prohibit. The ongoing chill on speech makes it necessary to invoke the earlier precedents that a statute that chills speech can and must be invalidated where its facial invalidity has been demonstrated."[36] Roberts's opinion in *Citizens United v. Federal Election Commission* (2010) mirrored his reliance upon the doctrinal modality by "invoking the earlier precedents," and importantly revealed the utility of precedent to persuade Chief Justice Roberts.

CONCLUSIONS

President Bush's nomination of Judge Roberts as chief justice may have been initially controversial, but Roberts cannot be criticized for altering his judicial conscience postnomination. He has consistently utilized conservative methods, with a plain reading of the Constitution serving as his guide when evaluating cases before him. His paradigm, which consists of textual, prudential, and doctrinal modalities, summarizes Justice Roberts's process of adjudication. From his nomination hearings to his Supreme Court rulings, Roberts may not please everyone with his decisions; however, his decisions are predictable and consistent. Due to his consistent reliance on his judicial philosophy, it is clear that advocates should employ certain tactics to successfully persuade Roberts.

It is easy to see that arguments that appeal to Roberts are parallel to arguments that typically appeal to other conservative justices. Above all, arguments require logical explanations for granting First Amendment protection to individuals claiming that their rights have been hindered. It is a practice that Roberts has in common with several members of the Court, and more importantly is what advocates must be aware of when speaking before the chief justice.

When arguing before Chief Justice Roberts, advocates should focus their argumentation on textual and doctrinal lines of reasoning. As Roberts's opinions illustrated, he has shown a tendency to construct the foundation of his argumentation along textual and precedential lines. For example, this tendency was pronounced in his recent ruling in *Snyder v. Phelps* wherein despite a lower district court's ruling that Snyder had suffered extreme emotional stress due to Phelps rhetoric, Roberts held that the First Amendment protected Phelps's speech. This means that an advocate should diligently incorporate textual and doctrinal warrants into his or her arguments in order to persuade Roberts.

Another strategy that advocates should use before Roberts is prudential logic to reinforce argumentation. After using textual or precedential logic, Roberts commonly ends his rationales by examining the costs and benefits of a given ruling. Advocates should replicate his strategy in order to appeal to the chief justice. Ultimately, Roberts makes his decisions accessible to a wide array of people through the use of various modalities by perceiving himself as an umpire for the rule of law. As this chapter has explained, Roberts assesses the law from the perspective of his judicial conscience, which relies on textual, doctrinal, and prudential modalities. Those who argue before the chief justice might consider using the same tactic.

NOTES

1. *Confirmation Hearing on the Nomination of Justice John G. Roberts to Be Chief Justice of the United States* before the Committee on the Judiciary, United States Senate , 109th Congress, 1st session, September 12–15 (Washington: U.S. Government Printing Office, 2005), 67.

2. William Kristol, "Bush Rises to the Occasion," *Weekly Standard*, July 19, 2005, http://www.weeklystandard.com/Content/Public/Articles/000/000/005/853sknln.asp (accessed September 4, 2009).

3. Julie Hirschfeld, "Bush Picks Roberts for Chief Justice," *Baltimore Sun*, September 6, 2005, http://www.sun-sentinel.com/news/nationworld/bal-te.roberts06sep06,0,1626128.story (accessed September 4, 2009).

4. Todd S. Purdum, Jodi Wilgoren, and Pam Belluck, "Court Nominee's Life Is Rooted in Faith and Respect for Law," *New York Times*, July 21, 2005, http://www.nytimes.com/2005/07/21/politics/21nominee.html?ei=5090&en=c055515d290a3215&ex=1279598400&partner=rssuserland&emc=rss&pagewanted=all (accessed September 6, 2009).

5. Warren Richey, "Would Roberts Practice the Restraint He Preaches?" *Christian Science Monitor*, September 1, 2005: 3.

6. Warren Richey, "Roberts Court Faces First Abortion Cases," *Christian Science Monitor*, November 8, 2006: 1.

7. "Roberts Is a 'Nonactivist Judge,' Panel Chair Says," *St. Petersburg Times*, July 22, 2005: 3A.

8. Charles Hurt, " Judiciary Committee Approves Roberts; Enough Support Gained to Avoid Senate Filibuster," *Washington Times* , September 23, 2005: A01.

9. David Stout, "Roberts Confirmed on 78-to-22 Senate Vote," *International Herald Tribune* (September 30, 2005): 5.

10. Tom Ichniowski, "Observers Look for Clues to 'Roberts Court'; Supreme Court Could Receive Petitions to Hear Clean Water and Labor Cases During Its Current Term," *Engineering News-Record*, October 10, 2005: 9.

11. See Craig R. Smith and Theodore Prosise, "The Supreme Court's Ruling in Bush v. Gore: A Rhetoric of Inconsistency," *Rhetoric and Public Affairs*, 4 (2001); John L. Lucaites, "Between Rhetoric and 'the Law': Power, Legitimacy, and Social Change," *Quarterly Journal of Speech*, 76 (1990); Bobbitt, *Constitutional Interpretation*.

12. Craig R. Smith, "Introduction, Methodology, and Overview," chapter 1 of this book.

13. Morse v. Frederick, 393 U.S. 503 (2007).

14. Federal Election Commission v. Wisconsin Right to Life, Inc., 551 U.S. 449 (2007).

15. *Confirmation Hearing on the Nomination of Justice John G. Roberts*, 146.

16. Bobbitt, *Constitutional Interpretation*, 12.

17. *Confirmation Hearing on the Nomination of Justice John G. Roberts*, 228.

18. Bobbitt, "Constitutional Fate," 7.

19. *Confirmation Hearing on the Nomination of Justice John G. Roberts*, 240.

20. Morse v. Frederick, 393 U.S. 503 (2007)

21. Jonathan Zimmerman, "School 4 Free Thinkers," *Christian Science Monitor*, March 22, 2007: 9.

22. Robert Barnes, "Justices to Hear Landmark Free-Speech Case; Defiant Message Spurs Most Significant Student 1st Amendment Test in Decades," *Washington Post*, March 13, 2007: A03.

23. Tinker v. Des Moines Independent Community School District, 393 U.S. 503, 506 (1969).

24. Robert Barnes, "Justices Consider Rights Issues; Decisions on Speech, Property Limits Could Be Far-Reaching," *Washington Post*, March 20, 2007: A03

25. "Ruling in Alaska Banner Case Tightens Limits on Students' Speech Rights," *USA Today*, June 26, 2007: 2A.

26. *Morse v. Frederick*, 393 U.S. 503, 505 (2007).

27. *Morse v. Frederick*, 393 U.S. 503, 516 (2007).

28. *Morse v. Frederick*, 393 U.S. 503, 516 (2007).

29. "FEC: Follow the Law," *Washington Post*, April 4, 2005: A22.

30. Stephen Dinan, "Issue Ads Allowed in Election Run-Up; Panel OKs Naming Candidates," *Washington Times*, December 26, 2006: A01.

31. Federal Election Commission v. Wisconsin Right to Life, Inc., 551 U.S. 449 (2007).

32. Federal Election Commission v. Wisconsin Right to Life, Inc., 551 U.S. 449, 457 (2007).

33. McConnell v. Federal Election Commission, 540 U.S. 93 (2003).

34. Federal Election Commission v. Wisconsin Right to Life, Inc., 551 U.S. 449, 478 (2007).

35. Citizens United v. Federal Election Commission, 558 U.S. ___ (2010). Slip op. 50.

36. Citizens United v. Federal Election Commission, 558 U.S. ___ (2010). Slip op. 50, 53.

Chapter Four

Associate Justice Stevens

R. Brandon Anderson

Justice John Paul Stevens played an integral part in the decision-making processes of the United States Supreme Court for thirty-four years. President Gerald Ford nominated Stevens to the Court, having been impressed with staff reports. The Senate enthusiastically agreed, by a vote of ninety-eight to zero.[1] Throughout Stevens's time on the bench, many argued that his conscience has shifted from the conservative wing to which he was nominated to the liberal bloc. Stevens is quick to counter that it is not he that has changed, but that the Court has made a distinct shift to the right. Throughout his years on the bench, Stevens utilizes his rhetorical prowess and pragmatism to his advantage. He regularly formed coalitions with his colleagues, particularly Justice Kennedy, to maximize the chances of winning the key vote for a majority (see chapter 6). In some instances when they were both in the majority against the chief justice, Stevens assigned majority opinions to Kennedy to secure his vote. Conversely, he wrote some majority opinions in ways that persuaded Kennedy to join him.[2] Stevens examined the details of every case with great care, deciding each one based on the best judgment he could apply to competing sides and explaining his reasons as fully as possible. In order to be as pragmatic as possible, Stevens often relied on the historical context of the case at bar. In fact, Stevens believed his role was to interpret the Constitution with fidelity to the legal traditions that had evolved in America.[3] In an interview with the *New York Times* Stevens argued "that the court has an obligation to protect ideals of equality and liberty in light of the nation's entire history, rather than legalistically parsing the original understanding of the Constitution."[4] He continued by saying that "Originalism is perfectly sensible. I always try to figure out what the original intent was, but to say that's the Bible and nothing else counts seems to me quite wrong."[5] This sentiment was an important aspect of Stevens's decision mak-

51

ing because he understood that there is an important history behind the text of the Constitution. However, he realized that it could do as much harm to make decisions by being an originalist as it could to dismiss original intent altogether.

This chapter provides a thematic analysis of a collection of Stevens's First Amendment dissents and concurrences, while also examining his 1975 confirmation hearings. To provide a better understanding of Steven's decision-making processes, this chapter is divided into five sections that delve into the approaches the justice utilizes. The first section examines Stevens's writings on symbolic speech, the second explores his decisions on political speech, the third investigates the justice's views concerning obscenity, and the fourth looks at one final case. The final section offers insight into gaining adherence from the modalities that Stevens employs throughout his First Amendment decisions.

SYMBOLIC SPEECH

The term symbolic speech applies to a wide range of nonverbal communication. Many expressive activities, including marching, wearing armbands, and displaying or destroying the U.S. flag, are considered forms of symbolic expression. The First Amendment of the Constitution has granted protection to these forms of symbolic speech through the Supreme Court; however, the scope of that protection varies greatly within the opinions of each justice. Justice Stevens's jurisprudence concerning symbolic speech is pragmatic and spans the modalities of ethical and doctrinal decision making. In order to gain a better understanding of Stevens's jurisprudence, I begin with his dissent in *Texas v. Johnson*, which involved the burning of the American flag by a protestor at the 1984 Republican convention in Dallas, Texas.

In his dissent in *Texas v Johnson*,[6] Stevens revealed his use of the ethical modality. In Bobbitt's words, the ethical modality of constitutional argument derives "rules from those moral commitments of the American ethos that are reflected in the Constitution."[7] This type of constitutional thinking can be described as philosophical, aspirational, or moral. In his dissent in *Texas v. Johnson*, Stevens appealed to an established American ethos by vigorously arguing that the government may ban the burning of the American flag. The flag, unlike other emblems, "uniquely symbolizes" the nation's ideals of "liberty and equality" and is "worthy of protection from unnecessary desecration."[8] Moreover, Stevens concluded that the case had nothing to do with "disagreeable ideas." It involved disagreeable conduct that diminishes the value of an important national asset; Johnson was punished only for the means by which he expressed his opinion, not the opinion itself. Johnson's expression, if protected, would have a disastrous effect on the national morale because it undermined the symbolism carried by the flag. In his opinion, Stevens linked the flag to many saints in the American pantheon of civil religion, including Patrick Henry, Susan B. Anthony, Abraham Lincoln, Nathan Hale, Booker T. Washington, and the men and women who fought in World War II. In so doing, he argued that the flag deserved to be protected from desecration and that that interest trumped any claim for protecting symbolic speech.

A year later, Justice Stevens reasserted his ethical beliefs in *U.S. v. Eichman.*[9] In another dissent concerning flag desecration, he stated that "the freedom of expression protected by the First Amendment embraces not only the freedom to communicate particular ideas but also the right to communicate them effectively. However, that right is not absolute." Stevens continued with a powerful analogy to illustrate these beliefs: "The communicative value of a well-placed bomb in the Capitol does not entitle it to the protection of the First Amendment."[10] In Stevens's dissents in these two cases, he supported the beliefs of the public, a position roughly akin to those who justify censorship of obscene and indecent material. Stevens, a World War II veteran, believed that tarnishing a valued symbol would have a negative effect on the American psyche; to protect those who burn the flag would harm the patriotism that flows from the Constitution and the Founders.

In 2007, the Supreme Court reexamined precedents that were set in the 1969 *Tinker v. Des Moines* decision, which declared that students do not lose their First Amendment rights when they pass through the schoolhouse door. As seen in the previous chapter, in *Morse v. Frederick*[11] the Court decided whether the First Amendment allows public schools to prohibit students from displaying messages that may have promoted the use of illegal drugs at school-supervised events. In his dissent, Stevens employed the doctrinal and ethical modalities. The doctrinal modality "reflects the common law approach to the development of legal norms through the gradual accumulation of case law."[12] This approach compels justices to search out past interpretations as they relate to the specific problem at hand and then try to organize them into a coherent whole.

Unlike in *Johnson*, where Stevens joined the conservatives, his dissent in *Morse* places him in the liberal camp. He argued that "the Court does serious violence to the First Amendment in upholding—indeed, lauding—a school's decision to punish Frederick for expressing a view with which it disagreed."[13] Stevens criticized the majority decision as one that trivializes the two cardinal principles upon which *Tinker* rests. First, the government may not prohibit the expression of an idea simply because society finds the idea itself offensive or disagreeable.[14] Second, promoting illegal drug use is not a proscribable incitement to imminent lawless action.[15] The majority's decision upholds a punishment handed out on the basis of a listener's disagreement with her (the principal's) understanding (or, more likely, misunder-standing) of the speaker's viewpoint.[16] Moreover, he noted, "Encouraging drug use might well increase the likelihood that a listener will try an illegal drug, but that hardly justifies censorship."[17] In this decision, Stevens empha-sized the importance of adherence to the rules and principles of the *Tinker* decision. However, he seemed to contradict his position in *Texas v. Johnson.* Perhaps in an attempt to overcome this difficulty, Stevens returned to the ethical modality to demonstrate the effects of the majority's argument that the banner was an incitement to drug use.

Stevens wrote, "Admittedly, some high school students (including those who use drugs) are dumb. Most students, however, do not shed their brains at the schoolhouse gate, and most students know dumb advocacy when they see it."[18] The notion that the message on this banner would actually persuade either the average student or even the dumbest one to change his or her behavior is implausible. Stevens "schoolhouse" reference not only rekindles images of Vietnam protesters in *Tinker*, it also implies that ridiculous postu-lating does not persuade anyone. Thus, overbroad punishment was not neces-sary. Stevens claimed that it would be "profoundly unwise to create special rules for speech about drug and alcohol use," pointing to the historical exam-ples of both opposition to the Vietnam War and resistance to Prohibition in the 1920s.[19] Again, Stevens invoked his own personal history to illustrate the narrative arc of the American experience in hopes of protecting his vision of the true meaning of our American ethos.

POLITICAL SPEECH

The second section of this chapter examines Justice Stevens's jurisprudence regarding political speech. This highly protected form of speech is important to a functioning democracy. When examining political speech cases, Stevens combined prudential, ethical, and doctrinal reasoning. The result is pragmatic argumentation that seeks to balance the costs and benefits of a particular rule.

In 2006, *Randall v. Sorrell*[20] reached the Supreme Court. It investigated the constitutionality of a Vermont campaign-spending statute. In a six to three decision, the majority held that the Buckley precedent should stand, including its ban of expenditure limits. The Court affirmed that some limits on political contributions are constitutional, but perceived "danger signs" indicating that Vermont's exceptionally low limits could prevent candidates from campaigning effectively.[21] Justice Stevens dissented, arguing that Buckley should be overruled as it pertains to expenditure limits. Stevens embraced a doctrinal approach and composed an attack on the precedent of *Buckley v. Valeo.*[22] He argued that in the sixty-five years prior to *Buckley*, some congressional races had been subject to limits on expenditures and contributions. The earlier jurisprudence treated limits as permissible regulations of conduct, rather than speech.[23] In Stevens's view, the Court had abandoned tradition and precedent, and thereby weakened the First Amendment in the second half of *Buckley*. Ultimately, Stevens believed that a reexamination of *Buckley* would allow for reasonable limitations on campaign expenditures; he did not believe that money equals symbolic speech, a position he would reinforce in 2010's *Citizens United v. Federal Election Commission*. Imposing spending limits would free candidates and their staffs from the perpetual burden of fundraising. Thus, even though Stevens utilized the doctrinal modality to illustrate the harms in the *Buckley* prohibition on campaign spending, he ultimately summarized the dissent through prudential reasoning. He argued that the continual campaigning and constant need for campaign funds to be competitive would negatively affect politicians' overall effectiveness in their jobs. Thus, the positives of limiting expenditures would greatly outweigh the negatives.

Stevens eventually turned to an ethical modality to summarize his arguments against *Buckley*'s protection of campaign spending. He again used historical anecdotes by invoking the names of William Jennings Bryant, William McKinley, Abraham Lincoln, and John F. Kennedy in his attempt to speak to the values of the American ethos. Stevens contended that a modest budget would do little to preclude a candidate from effectively communicating with the electorate.[24] Moreover, in his final statement, the justice directly referenced the framers' intent. Stevens claimed that "the framers would have been appalled by the impact of modern fundraising practices on the ability of elected officials to perform their public responsibilities. . . . They would have found statutes limiting funding within congress's authority."[25] Stevens used the original ideals of the Founders not as an originalist would, but instead to show that their Constitution is living and ultimately provides a transcendent value for the current context. The framers' morality encouraged civic service and that, for Stevens, is an ethical standard to which we should hold our political leaders.

In 1998 the Supreme Court heard *Arkansas Educational Television Commission v. Forbes*,[26] which raised the question: Is the exclusion of a ballot-qualified candidate from a debate sponsored by a state-owned public television broadcaster a violation of the candidate's First Amendment right to freedom of speech? The Court's majority held that public broadcasters could selectively exclude participants from their sponsored debates so long as these were not designed as "public forums." Justice Stevens dissented, utilizing the prudential modality.

He asserted that state-owned broadcasters take on a greater burden when planning and managing political debates. Thus, the government must adhere to the First Amendment's guarantee of openness in public forums, especially when dealing with campaigns for political office. The majority opened the door to censorship or marginalization of minority positions. Stevens asserted that there is a drastic need for preestablished objective criteria for state agencies to use when determining who may participate. Such criteria would also offer the public some assurance that the decisions on eligibility are not arbitrary. Stevens was concerned about the negative effects of the majority's ruling on political debates.

Finally, in 2010 the Supreme Court issued a landmark decision that could dramatically affect political campaign speech. In *Citizens United v. Federal Elections Commission*, the Court held that corporate and union funding of independent political broadcasts cannot be limited under the First Amendment. The five to four decision resulted from a dispute over whether, during a federal campaign, a nonprofit corporation named Citizens United could air via cable a film that was critical of Hillary Clinton, and whether the group could advertise the film in broadcast ads featuring Clinton's image, in apparent violation of the 2002 Bipartisan Campaign Reform Act.[27] The majority opinion, written by Justice Kennedy, found that the appellate court's decision[28] to prohibit independent expenditures by corporations and unions was invalid and could not be applied to spending such as that for *Hillary: The Movie*. Furthermore, Kennedy wrote, "If the First Amendment has any force, it prohibits Congress from fining or jailing citizens, or associations of citizens, for simply engaging in political speech."[29] In other words, Kennedy and the majority held that a corporation or union is nothing less than an association of citizens whose speech is protected by First Amendment.

However, the majority's decision provoked a ninety-page dissent from Stevens, who reaffirmed his beliefs about campaign electioneering and the First Amendment. He penned his dissent utilizing the prudential, doctrinal, and ethical modalities. He began by examining the framers' understanding of political campaigns when drafting the Constitution. He contended that the majority misinterpreted what the framers had in mind when they constructed the document. In fact, Stevens wrote, "the framers thus took it as a given that corporations could be comprehensively regulated in the service of the public welfare. . . . They had little trouble distinguishing corporations from human beings, and when they constitutionalized the right to free speech in the First Amendment, it was the free speech of individual Americans that they had in mind." Stevens's pragmatic inclination limits the scope of the First Amendment to only those who have the ability to speak for themselves. Moreover, he condemned the majority's decision by arguing that "corporations were conceived of as artificial entities and do not have the technical capacity to 'speak.'" Proving that the framers and ratifiers understood "the freedom of speech to encompass corporate speech is, I believe, a far heavier burden than the majority believes."[30] Thus, it is clear that the historical framework that

Stevens utilized differs from the framework of Kennedy, Roberts, and Scalia. Moreover, a close reading of his dissent reveals that Stevens's framework grounds three other modalities.

His dissent moved through three stages: (1) the procedural history of the case, (2) stare decisis, and (3) the ethical implications of the case. During this disquisition, Stevens revealed his dependence on the prudential, doctrinal, and ethical modalities. Often, he harshly chastised the justices on the other side of the decision for not thoroughly examining each component of the case. Stevens wrote that the majority fails to see the future implication of their sweeping decision. He wrote, "The fact that a Court can hypothesize situations in which a statute might, at some point down the line, pose some unforeseen [danger] as applied, does not come close to meeting the standards for a facial challenge."[31] The majority, which could have issued a narrow, limited ruling in this case, instead used the occasion to overstep normal bounds and reverse a century of legal opinion.

Even though Stevens frequently utilizes prior case law and precedent within his dissent, the doctrinal modality is overshadowed by the prudential and ethical modalities. The ethical modality flows from Stevens's anxiety about future implications that shine through the doctrinal modality. Throughout the dissent, a concern about the effect of constant electioneering/campaigning becomes evident. Within this case, his pragmatism focuses on a greater concern with the effects on the morality of politics.[32]

OBSCENITY

In *Miller v. California*,[33] the Supreme Court established a three-pronged test for determining whether a "work" (for example, written material or a performance) is obscene and therefore unprotected by the First Amendment. Thus, when examining obscenity cases, justices can turn to this precedent to support their decisions. However, when Justice Stevens wrote on obscenity, he often utilized prudential reasoning in conjunction with the doctrinal modality. In 1997 the Court addressed the issue of how much protection the First Amendment affords the Internet. *Reno v. American Civil Liberties Union*[34] was the first major Supreme Court ruling regarding the regulation of materials distributed via Internet, and it examined whether the Communications Decency Act (CDA) was overbroad and therefore violated the First Amendment since it extended obscenity standards to a new form of media.

Writing for a unanimous court, Justice Stevens outlined the rationale for holding that the Act violated the First Amendment because its regulations amounted to a content-based blanket restriction of free speech. Stevens revealed his prowess for doctrinal reasoning in this fifty-two-page decision.

Stevens gave narrow readings to the decisions in *Red Lion Broadcasting v. FCC*,[35] *Pacifica Foundation v. FCC*,[36] *Sable v. FCC*,[37] and *Miller v. California*[38] to make his case against the CDA. Stevens intertwined precedent from each case in his effort to demonstrate the weaknesses of the congressional statute. The technical way that Stevens applied the three prongs of the Miller test illustrates his dependence on the method. He wrote, "in contrast to *Miller*, the CDA presents a greater threat of censoring speech that falls outside the statute's scope. Given the vague contours of the coverage of the statute, it unquestionably silences some speakers whose messages would be entitled to constitutional protection."[39] Through the use of prior precedents, Stevens effectively illustrated how the doctrinal modality can form a majority. Within this decision, precedent supports the unanimous position that there is no compelling government interest advanced by the statute that would justify curtailing freedom of expression.

In 2004, the issue of Internet restrictions again came before the justices of the Supreme Court. In *Ashcroft v. American Civil Liberties Union*[40] the Court ruled five to four that Congress's Child Online Protection Act (COPA) violated the First Amendment. The majority held that Congress had not met its burden to show that the COPA requirements were more effective than other methods of preventing minors from viewing questionable material. Justice Stevens concurred with the decision and exhibited a prudential interpretation to support his opinion. He drew upon his opinion in *Reno v. ACLU*[41] in weighing the pros and cons of the COPA statute. Stevens argued that "the government may not penalize speakers for making available to the general world wide web that which the least tolerant communities deem unfit for their children's consumption."[42] Thus, Stevens believed that the statute was overbroad and therefore chilled speech because the statute employed a vague community standard.

Moreover, Justice Stevens referenced the effects that such a statute could have, including an abuse of power and a negative impact on the family dynamic. In a very candid section of his concurrence, Stevens revealed that COPA's criminal penalties are ultimately overbearing and hazardous. He continued, "As a parent, grandparent and great-grandparent, I endorse the goal without reservation. As a judge, however, I must confess to a growing sense of unease when the interest in protecting children from prurient materials is invoked as a justification for using criminal regulation of speech as a substitute for, or a simple backdrop to, adult oversight of children's viewing habits."[43] Thus, Stevens showed his prudential reasoning in an attempt to come up with a decision that would cover present and future needs. He argued that COPA could have had far-reaching, negative effects for years to come. Not only did Stevens endorse the First Amendment, he also weighed the cost of giving parents a free pass in terms of censoring what their children experience. It was their job to parent, not the job of the federal government.

OTHER FIRST AMENDMENT CASES

One final case that deserves examination is *Boy Scouts of America et al. v. Dale.*[44] This case examined whether the application of a New Jersey law violated the Boy Scouts' First Amendments rights of expressive association. The Boy Scouts claimed they had a right to bar homosexuals from serving as troop leaders. In a five to four opinion delivered by Chief Justice Rehnquist, the Court held that "New Jersey's public accommodations law to require the Boy Scouts to admit Dale violated the Boy Scouts' First Amendment right of expressive association."[45] In other words, the Court gave the Boy Scouts of America (BSA) a constitutional right to bar homosexuals from serving as troop leaders because the Scouts' freedom of assembly rights include deciding with whom not to associate.

Justice Stevens's dissent called upon all three modalities addressed above. First, Stevens argued that the New Jersey law does not impose any serious burden on the Scouts' collective effort on behalf of its shared goals, nor does it force them to communicate any message they do not wish to endorse.[46] Thus, the law abridges no constitutional right of the Boy Scouts. The pragmatic approach that Stevens utilized in this decision begins with a doctrinal application of BSA evidence and Supreme Court decisions. First, Stevens examined the BSA *Scoutmaster's Handbook*, which established the Scouts' central tenets; it stated that a Scout is "morally straight" and "clean."[47] Following a detailed examination of myriad definitions of moral, straight, and clean, Stevens determined, "it is plain as the light of day that neither one of these principles—'morally straight' and 'clean'—says the slightest thing about homosexuality. Indeed, neither term in the *Boy Scout Handbook* expresses any position whatsoever on sexual matters."[48] Thus, the Boy Scouts did not have any precedential standing in their bylaws to prohibit members based on sexual preference.

Furthermore, Justice Stevens scrutinized prior precedents dealing with discrimination. He determined that "organizations that attempt to foster a belief at odds with antidiscrimination laws will have a First Amendment right to association that precludes forced compliance with those laws." However, he argued that this protection does not give the group carte blanche to discriminate at will, or out of fear of what the public reaction will be if group membership is opened to homosexuals. Stevens's use of doctrine allowed him to offer a detailed criticism of the majority's decision.[49]

In his summary, Justice Stevens took advantage of the prudential and ethical modalities to ground his arguments. He appealed to the humanism in the American conscience in writing that "unfavorable opinions about homosexuals have ancient roots, which have been nourished by sectarian doctrine."[50] He continued, "Interaction with real people rather than adherence to

traditional ways of thinking about members of unfamiliar classes has modified these opinions." Stevens used prudential reasoning, arguing that decisions like this one lead to uninformed and traditionalist ways of thinking,
which do not allow for a growth of the nation. In fact, he stated that "the
decision made by the Court creates a constitutional shield for a policy that is
itself the product of a habitual way of thinking about strangers."[51] Again,
Stevens referenced the negative effects that could come from a precedent of
this nature. Conversely, Stevens's final sentence in his opinion is an appeal
to ethical reasoning. The justice borrowed a sentence from Justice Brandeis
to complete his opinion: "We must be ever on our guard, lest we erect our
prejudices into legal principles."[52] This final appeal by Stevens again reveals
his belief in the need for morals and virtues.

CONCLUSIONS

The analysis in this chapter reveals that Justice Stevens's rhetorical choices
shape his pragmatic decision making. He methodically employs the doctrinal, ethical, and prudential modalities, presenting himself as concerned with
the pragmatics of law and how it affects the day-to-day lives of the American
citizenry. However, that is not to say that Stevens is bound by these modalities. His understanding and appreciation of the Constitution and law compel
him to examine every aspect of the case he is deciding. In Stevens's view, the
framers of the Constitution "made no attempt to fashion a Napoleonic Code
that would provide detailed answers to the many questions that would inevi-
tably confront future generations."[53] Instead, they often used general language with the expectation that "the vast open spaces in our charter of
government" would be interpreted incrementally "by the common-law process of step-by-step adjudication that was largely responsible for the development of the law at the time this nation was conceived."[54] By recognizing
how Stevens views the framers' intentions, we can begin to build a technique
for appealing to his pragmatism.

Though Stevens left the Court in the summer of 2010 and his replace-
ment, Elena Kagan, has been confirmed, it might serve as an object lesson to
attempt to figure out how to appeal to a pragmatic justice. In such a case, an
advocate would be wise to begin by appealing to the doctrinal modality.
Throughout this chapter, we have seen that Stevens depended heavily on the
prior case law. Stevens held that precedents laid out before offer a starting
point for the decision-making process. It is evident when reviewing Stevens's decisions that he methodically searched out past interpretations as
they relate to the specific case in question. He then tried to organize them
into a coherent whole and fit the solution of current problems into that whole.

Thus, if advocates can begin to build a tight case using prior doctrine, they may have a solid foundation when appealing to pragmatists, because they may use the doctrinal modality to lay the groundwork for their prudential reasoning.

When utilizing prudential reasoning, Stevens also revealed his pragmatic foundation. He commonly reviews all of the facts of a case, then proceeds to weigh the consequences of the decision. Therefore, it would be wise for advocates before a pragmatist to consider the possible outcomes of any given ruling.

After examining Justice Stevens's First Amendment opinions, it becomes clear that he is not always pragmatic. He also draws upon the ethical modality to reinforce his opinions. Bobbitt explained that the force of ethical argument relies on a characterization of American institutions and the role within them of the American people, or the character or ethos of the American polity.[55] Stevens clearly adhered to this belief system. Moreover, Stevens's decisions reveal that he believed that the morality of the country must be maintained and that the Supreme Court has a heavy burden of responsibility to not only protect that morality but create an environment in which it can develop. Moreover, Stevens often cited personal experiences in an attempt to appeal to shared patriotic American values, which he believes will help safeguard the vision that the framers had for this country. Thus, when attempting to persuade a justice like Stevens, advocates must examine impact their arguments have on the American ethos. Second, advocates must present their cases within the framework of morality and values of that ethos. Finally, it may be wise to be aware of a justice's own personal history as justices often frame their decisions by relying on life experiences.

While sitting on the bench, Stevens witnessed a shift in the ideologies of his counterparts. However, he claimed that he had been consistent in his understanding of the Constitution. Stevens contended that his jurisprudence was determined by his confidence in the ability of judges to resolve difficult issues. Thus, it is not simply personal ideologies that should guide a judge's decision, but trust in the process of making those decisions. Nonetheless, his pragmatic use of the doctrinal, prudential, and ethical modalities leaves an important legacy that both advocates and future justices should turn to when examining the constitutionality of First Amendment cases.

As Justice Stevens's final session on the bench came to a close, President Barack Obama nominated Solicitor General Elena Kagan to fill the vacant position. The May 10, 2010, nomination of Kagan revealed that the former Harvard Law School dean had no prior judicial experience on the bench.[56] Nonetheless, she had amassed an impressive resume. Prior to the nomination, Elena Kagan dedicated her life to politics and the study of law. Following an academic career that included a master of philosophy from Oxford and a juris doctor from Harvard, Kagan became a law clerk for Circuit Judge Abner

Mikva, and then Associate Justice Thurgood Marshall, both liberal judges. Kagan joined the faculty at the Law School of the University of Chicago in 1991. Her time in Chicago eventually led her to the deanship at the Harvard Law School, where she served for five years as the first woman dean at Harvard. Along the way, Kagan frequently found high-profile positions within Democratic administrations. From 1995 to 1999, Kagan served as President Bill Clinton's associate White House counsel and was eventually nominated for the U.S. court of appeals for the District of Columbia.[57] Kagan was nominated and later confirmed as solicitor general by President Barack Obama.

As the confirmation hearing began, much of the criticism surrounding Kagan was that she had no judicial experience, nor had she written much. There was little or no record of her ideological point of view. That makes it difficult to examine the nominee through Bobbitt's modalities. Nevertheless, throughout the hearings, she frequently fielded questions concerning the First Amendment, which may offer insight into her decision-making process.

Senators Klobuchar, Franken, Leahy, Hatch, Schumer, and Coburn all pressed the nominee on her interpretation of the First Amendment. Kagan fielded the questions eloquently and answered them with a calculated confidence.[58] As the three days of questioning concluded, a theme emerged that may lead to a better understanding of her constitutional position. Kagan frequently deferred to prior case law. In fact, throughout the hearings, Kagan often called upon precedent when addressing difficult issues. When Senator Durbin (D-Illinois) inquired about her beliefs on the death penalty, Kagan deferred to precedent. She stated, "The constitutionality of the death penalty generally is established law and entitled to precedential weight." When pressed further by Durbin, she continued, "I do think that the constitutionality of the death penalty generally is settled precedent. I think even Justice Stevens agreed with that."[59] Furthermore, Kagan's utilization of prior cases throughout the hearings worked to demonstrate a breadth of knowledge about precedential standing and its effect on the courts today.

This chapter revealed Justice Stevens to be a staunch pragmatist that prefers to examine each case with respect and precision. As Elena Kagan progressed through her confirmation hearings, she positioned herself as a pragmatist centered within Bobbitt's doctrinal modality. When asked whether she identifies herself closer to Justice Scalia's constitutional interpretation or Justice Souter's, she insisted that cases are often decided on a case-to-case basis and that it is not an either/or decision. However, in terms of First Amendment cases, she stated:

> In many circumstances, precedent is the most important thing. One good example of this is an interpretation of the First Amendment where the court very rarely, actually, says, you know, What did the framers think about this? The

framers actually had a much more constricted view of free speech principles than anybody does in the current time. And when you read free speech decisions of the court, they're packed with reference to prior cases, rather than reference to some original history.[60]

In this statement, Kagan reinforced her doctrinal inclinations when examining the First Amendment. However, similar to Stevens, she seemed to understand the importance of contextualizing the decision-making process through a historical viewpoint.[61] She stated "that courts appropriately look to both kinds of constitutional interpretation, courts appropriately look to original intent, courts appropriately look to precedent, and that it depends on the provision of the Constitution, it depends on the case, it depends on the issue as to whether which will be effective."[62] It may be this understanding that will guide her into a pragmatic use of the modalities, similar to Justice Stevens.

As President Obama introduced Solicitor General Kagan as his choice for the Supreme Court, he spoke very highly of her pragmatism and her ability to think clearly about each case presented to her. President Obama claimed to be seeking a person that would be able to cross ideological lines and build majorities, as the pragmatic Stevens had. When Elena Kagan replaced the iconic Stevens in October 2010, she faced the arduous task of filling the shoes of a great and influential Supreme Court thinker that utilized a pragmatic mix of constitutional interpretation that represented a devotion to the Court and a commitment to fair rule of the law.

NOTES

1. *Hearings before the Committee on the Judiciary United States Senate Ninety-Fourth Congress First Session on the Nomination of John Paul Stevens to Be an Associate Justice of the Supreme Court of the United States,* December 1975 (Washington, DC: U.S. Government Printing Office, 1975).
2. Jeffrey Rosen, "The Dissenter," *New York Times Magazine,* September 23, 2007: 6.
3. Justice John Paul Stevens, "Remarks before the Federal Bar Association on October 23, 1985," in *The Great Debate: Interpreting Our Written Constitution* (Washington, DC: The Federalist Society, 1986).
4. Jeffrey Rosen, "The Dissenter": 3, 6.
5. Jeffrey Rosen, "The Dissenter": 3.
6. 491 U.S. 397 (1989).
7. Philip Bobbitt, *Constitutional Interpretation,* 18.
8. 491 U.S. 397 (1989).
9. 496 U.S. 310 (1990).
10. 496 U.S. 310 (1990).
11. 393 U.S. 503 (2007).
12. Bobbitt, *Constitutional Interpretation.*
13. 393 U.S. 503 (2007).
14. 393 U.S. 503 (2007).
15. 395 U. S. 444 (1969).

16. 551 U.S. 393 (2007).

17. 551 U. S. 393 (2007).

18. 551 U. S. 393 (2007).

19. Justice Stevens noted: "The current dominant opinion supporting the war on drugs in general and our anti-marijuana laws in particular, is reminiscent of the opinion that supported the nationwide ban on alcohol consumption when I was a student." He then compared the questioning of the government's prohibition of alcohol consumption with contemporary questioning of marijuana policy. Just as prohibition in the 1920s and early 1930s was secretly questioned by thousands of otherwise law-abiding citizens," he continued, "so opponents of the war on drugs today may express their views only silently for fear of majority disapproval."

20. 548 U.S. 230 (2006).

21. 548 U.S. 230 (2006).

22. 424 U.S. 1 (1976).

23. 548 U.S. 230 (2006).

24. 548 U.S. 230 (2006).

25. 548 U.S. 230 (2006).

26. 523 U.S. 666 (1998).

27. 558 U.S. ___ (2010).

28. 2 U.S.C. §441b.

29. 558 U.S. ___ (2010).

30. 558 U.S. ___ (2010).

31. Stevens recognized the facial challenge in the First Amendment context under which a law may be overturned as impermissibly overbroad because a substantial number of its applications are unconstitutional. He argued that Citizens United had not made a case for overbreadth. Moreover, the Court never addresses these issues unless they are brought about by the litigants.

32. Stevens writes, "In my judgment, such limitations may be justified to the extent they are tailored to improving the quality of the exposition of ideas that voters receive."

33. 413 U.S. 15 (1973).

34. 521 U.S. 844 (1997).

35. 395 U.S. 367 (1969).

36. 438 U.S. 726 (1978).

37. 492 U.S. 115 (1989).

38. 413 U.S. 15 (1973).

39. 521 U.S. 844 (1997).

40. 542 U.S. 656 (2004).

41. 521 U.S. 844 (1997).

42. 542 U.S. 656 (2004).

43. 542 U.S. 656 (2004).

44. 530 U.S. 640 (2000).

45. 530 U.S. 640 (2000).

46. 530 U.S. 640 (2000).

47. 530 U.S. 640 (2000).

48. 530 U.S. 640 (2000).

49. Stevens takes issue with the majority decision because it "rests entirely on the statements in BSA's brief." He continues by stating, "this is an astounding view of the law, I am unaware of any previous instance in which our analysis of the scope of constitutional right was determined by looking at what a litigant asserts in his or her brief and inquiring no further."

50. 530 U.S. 640 (2000).

51. 530 U.S. 640 (2000).

52. 530 U.S. 640 (2000).

53. John Paul Stevens, "The Freedom of Speech," *Yale Law Journal*, 102 (1993): 1293, 1297.

54. Stevens, "The Freedom of Speech," 1293, 1297.

55. Bobbitt, *Constitutional Interpretation*, 11.

56. Justices who had no judicial experience include William Rehnquist, Lewis Powell, Earl Warren, and Louis Brandeis.

57. However, Kagan's nomination process ended following Senator Orrin Hatch's failure to schedule a new hearing. David G. Savage, "Little Light Shed on Bush Judicial Pick," *Los Angeles Times* (September 27, 2002): A-18 .

58. It is important to remember that in a 1995 book review, Kagan stated that the confirmation hearings had become "hollow and vapid." She continued by stating that "Senators effectively have accepted the limits on inquiry." She said the process had become one where "repetition of platitudes has replaced discussion of viewpoints and personal anecdotes have supplanted legal analysis."

59. Elena Kagan, *Hearing before the Senate Committee on the Judiciary*, 111th Congress (2010), n.p.

60. Elena Kagan, *Hearing* (2010), n.p.

61. Kagan stated, "The framers could have given, like, a whole primer on police practices. . . . But they didn't do that. And I think that they didn't do that because of this incredible wisdom that they had; that they knew that the world was going to change . . . sometimes they laid down very specific rules. Sometimes they laid down broad principles. Either way, we apply what they say, what they meant to do. So in that sense, we are all originalists." Elena Kagan, *Hearing* (2010), n.p.

62. Elena Kagan, *Hearing* (2010), n.p.

Chapter Five

Associate Justice Scalia

Jennifer J. Asenas

Antonin Gregory Scalia, known as "Nino" by friends and family, was nominated by President Ronald Reagan and confirmed by the Senate to the Supreme Court in 1986. Justice Scalia satisfied three Reagan administration criteria: "He appeared to be at least as conservative as Warren Burger, he wrote in a more forceful prose than did Burger, and he was from a group of ethnic Catholics important to the electoral success of the Republican Party."[1] His nomination passed unanimously in part because the promotion of Justice William H. Rehnquist to chief justice distracted attention from Scalia, who was affable and witty and breezed through his confirmation hearings.

Justice Scalia is one of the Court's most interesting characters; he makes his opinions known both in and outside of the courtroom. When he is not "busy haranguing some hapless advocate,"[2] Justice Scalia uses public forums to display his charm as well as his judicial philosophy. In a 2008 interview with Leslie Stahl on *60 Minutes*, he displayed his good-humored nature by making jokes and offering interesting anecdotes. Stahl stated that his writing, an element of his judicial duties at which he works hard with the hope that it will encourage people to read the Court's decisions, is known for its "bold and colorful style." However, some of that "color" is directed toward his colleagues. Justice Ruth Bader Ginsberg, also interviewed during the story, has been the recipient of Justice Scalia's "zingers." He has called some of her opinions "'absurd,' another 'implausible speculation,' and another 'self-righteous.'"[3] Yet Justice Ginsburg says that Justice Scalia is "so utterly charming, so amusing, so sometimes outrageous, you can't help but say 'I'm glad that he's my friend' or 'he's my colleague.'"[4]

Justice Scalia also uses his public appearances to explain his judicial philosophy. In a speech he delivered to the Catholic University of America, Justice Scalia stated that he is a part of "a small but hardy school, called 'textualists' or 'originalists.'"[5] Originalism "treats a constitution like a statute, and gives it the meaning that its words were understood to bear at the time they were promulgated."[6] However, he is also a textualist, which means that his commitment to originalism is not bound by the original intent of the framers. Textualists, explains Scalia, "don't care about the intent, and I don't care if the framers of the Constitution had some secret meaning in mind when they adopted its words. I take the words as they were promulgated to the people of the United States, and what is the fairly understood meaning of those words."[7]

To better understand how Justice Scalia's judicial philosophy influences how he makes sense of the law, this chapter will analyze his decisions on First Amendment cases using Philip Bobbitt's six modalities, outlined in chapter 1. Although each kind of reasoning may be found in his opinions, Justice Scalia primarily relies on historical, precedential, and structural modes to justify his positions. Analysis of these categories suggests that consistency with American political praxis and tradition is Justice Scalia's primary rhetorical strategy. This chapter will analyze Justice Scalia's opinions and dissents on the First Amendment in terms of historical, precedential, and structural reasoning in turn. It will then analyze Justice Scalia's rhetorical style and suggest ways in which potential interlocutors might adapt to Justice Scalia.

HISTORICAL

The historical modality relies on arguments based on the "original understanding of the constitutional provision" that "*bound* government and that the People had therefore devised a construction which they could enforce its limits and rules."[8] Bobbitt claimed that we do not know and cannot know what the framers intended by the words they inscribed in the Constitution.[9] Justice Scalia agrees that intent cannot be known. He is interested in the original meaning of the words and finds definition in praxis, or practical application. For example, he argues that the establishment clause is "enshrined in the Constitution's text" but analysis of official actions "show *what it meant*."[10] The difference is not trivial and reflects the way in which Justice Scalia provides evidence for his interpretation of the Constitution. For Justice Scalia, there are two distinct trajectories under the historical modality. The first relies on the beliefs and practices of the framers at the time the Constitution was written and adopted. The second references the traditions of Americans as historical justification for his interpretation.

Justice Scalia's reliance on historical evidence was most evident in *McCreary County v. the American Civil Liberties Union of Kentucky* (2005). In this case, two Kentucky courthouses mounted a display on the evolution of law, which included the Ten Commandments. The American Civil Liberties Union (ACLU) sued, arguing that the display of the Ten Commandments violated the establishment clause. Justice Scalia dissented from the majority ruling, citing multiple examples from "official acts and official proclamations of the United States or of the component branches of its Government"[11] which include the use of prayer and invocation of God at various governmental functions and "Washington's prayer at the opening of his Presidency and his Farewell Address, President John Adams's letter to the Massachusetts Militia, and Jefferson's and Madison's inaugural addresses." The model adopted by America in the political and judicial system was one where:

> George Washington added to the form of Presidential oath prescribed by Art. II, §1, cl. 8, of the Constitution, the concluding words "so help me God." . . . The Supreme Court under John Marshall opened its sessions with the prayer, "God save the United States and this Honorable Court." . . . The First Congress instituted the practice of beginning its legislative sessions with a prayer. . . . The same week that Congress submitted the Establishment Clause as part of the Bill of Rights for ratification by the States, it enacted legislation providing for paid chaplains in the House and Senate. . . . The day after the First Amendment was proposed, the same Congress that had proposed it requested the President to proclaim "a day of public thanksgiving and prayer, to be observed, by acknowledging, with grateful hearts, the many and signal favours of Almighty God." . . . President Washington offered the first Thanksgiving Proclamation shortly thereafter, devoting November 26, 1789 on behalf of the American people "to the service of that great and glorious Being who is the beneficent author of all the good that is, that was, or that will be," . . . thus beginning a tradition of offering gratitude to God that continues today.[12]

Therefore, he argues that "it is entirely clear from our Nation's historical practices that the Establishment Clause permits this disregard of polytheists and believers in unconcerned deities, just as it permits the disregard of devout atheists."[13]

Justice Scalia reasserts the historical significance of the Ten Commandments in *Pleasant Grove City v. Summum* (2009).[14] Summum is a spiritual group which wanted to erect a stone monument to display the Seven Aphorisms of Summum. The mayor of Pleasant Grove City denied the group's request. The Summum group sought an injunction citing a violation of their freedom of speech, especially since there was a display of the Ten Commandments in the park. The Court ruled that the city did not have to accept the monument because it constituted government, not personal, speech and therefore was not subject to strict scrutiny of the First Amendment. In his concurring opinion, Justice Scalia writes to calm the fears of Pleasant Grove

City, which might worry that its "victory has propelled it from the Free Speech Clause frying pan into the Establishment Clause fire." He argued that in 2005, the Court ruled in *Van Orden v. Perry* (2005) that the Ten Commandments "have an undeniable historical meaning" in addition to their "religious significance," thus the Ten Commandments are exempt from violating the establishment clause because they are a historical document. [15]

In another case about a state's endorsement of a religion, Justice Scalia appeals to tradition. In *Lamb's Chapel v. Center Moriches School District* (1993), the Center Moriches School District repeatedly denied requests by Lamb's Chapel to use the school's facilities for an after-hours religiously oriented film series. New York's attorney general argued that the school justifiably denied Lamb's Chapel because "Religious advocacy . . . serves the community only in the eyes of its adherents, and yields a benefit only to those who already believe." [16] Justice Scalia responded by arguing that while the framers were drafting the First Amendment, "Congress enacted the Northwest Territory Ordinance that the Confederation Congress had adopted in 1787—Article III of which provides: 'Religion, morality, and knowledge, being necessary to good government and the happiness of mankind, schools and the means of education shall forever be encouraged.'" [17]

In the *City of Boerne v. P. F. Flores, Archbishop of San Antonio, and United States* (1997), the Court decided that the city of Boerne violated the 1993 Religious Freedom Restoration Act by denying the archbishop the ability to expand his church. Justice Scalia wrote a concurring opinion primarily to refute the dissenting opinion of Justice O'Connor and her interpretation of the free exercise clause based on historical materials. He counters using his own historical materials to support the decision in *Employment Division v. Smith* (1990), which argued that the free exercise clause gave individuals the right to believe, but not practice, parts of his or her religion when that practice violated federal or state laws. [18] He states:

> Religious exercise shall be permitted so long as it does not violate general laws governing conduct. The "provisos" in the enactments negate a license to act in a manner "unfaithfull to the Lord Proprietary" (Maryland Act Concerning Religion of 1649), or "behav[e]" in other than a "peaceabl[e] and quie[t]" manner (Rhode Island Charter of 1663), or "disturb the public peace" (New Hampshire Constitution), or interfere with the "peace [and] safety of th[e] State" (New York, Maryland, and Georgia Constitutions), or "demea[n]" oneself in other than a "peaceable and orderly manner" (Northwest Ordinance of 1787). . . . At the time these provisos were enacted, keeping "peace" and "order" seems to have meant, precisely, obeying the laws. "[E]very breach of law is against the peace." Queen v. Lane, 6 Mod. 128, 87 Eng. Rep. 884, 885 (Q. B. 1704). Even as late as 1828, when Noah Webster published his American Dictionary of the English Language, he gave as one of the meanings of "peace": "8. Public tranquility; that quiet, order and security which is guaranteed by the laws; as, to keep the peace; to break the peace." An American

> Dictionary of the English Language 31 (1828). This limitation upon the scope of religious exercise would have been in accord with the background political philosophy of the age (associated most prominently with John Locke), which regarded freedom as the right "to do only what was not lawfully prohibited."[19]

In this way, Justice Scalia defends his interpretations by using older (and in his mind more legitimate) and very detailed documentation for a proper reading of the free exercise clause.

The First Amendment issue at hand in *Board of Education of Kiryas Joel Village School District v. Grumet* (1994) was whether or not a 1989 New York statute intentionally drew its boundaries in accordance with the boundaries of the village of Kiryas Joel, a religious enclave of Satmar Hasidim, who practice a strict form of Judaism. The problem was that only Satmars attended the state-funded school. Taxpayers and state school associations filed a lawsuit claiming that the school zoning violated the establishment clause. The Court ruled six to three that the statutes did indeed exclude everyone but the Satmars.

Justice Scalia disagreed with the majority. He begins his dissent by stating that the "Founding Fathers would be astonished to find that the Establishment Clause . . . has been employed to prohibit characteristically and admirably American accommodation of the religious practices . . . of a tiny minority sect."[20] He argues that it would be better to adopt James Madison's view that the state could not "'punish a religious profession with the privation of a civil right.'"[21] He later argues that the "populating of North America is in no small measure the story of groups of people sharing a common religious and cultural heritage striking out to form their own communities."[22] To deny Kiryas Joel the ability to educate their handicapped children in an all-Satmar school is to "believe that large portions of the civil authority exercised during most of our history were unconstitutional."[23]

Justice Scalia also uses the lack of historical praxis as evidence. In *City of Boerne v. Flores* (1997), he wrote a concurring opinion responding to Justice O'Connor's dissent "that historical materials support a result contrary to the one reached in *Employment Division, Department of Human Resources of Oregon v. Smith* (1990)."[24] Justice Scalia points out that "the most telling point made by the dissent is to be found, not in what it says, but in what it fails to say. Had the understanding in the period surrounding the ratification of the Bill of Rights been that the various forms of accommodation discussed by the dissent were constitutionally required . . . it would be surprising not to find a single state or federal case refusing to enforce a generally applicable statute because of its failure to make accommodation. Yet the dissent cites none."[25] Another example of the lack of historical evidence as evidence is in *New York State Board of Elections v. Lopez Torres* (2008). In this case the Court considered whether or not New York's system of allowing parties to choose nominees for state Supreme Court justices violates the challengers' First Amendment rights because they did not have a "fair shot" at election. Denying the petitioners' request, writing for the Court, Justice Scalia argues that "None of our cases establishes an individual's constitutional right to have a 'fair shot' at winning the party's nomination."[26] In fact, historical practice proves the opposite: that "Party conventions, with their attendant 'smoke-filled rooms' and domination by party leaders, have long been an accepted manner of selecting party candidates."[27]

Justice Scalia relies essentially on what is in the Constitution; when in doubt he relies on the intent of the framers. In his concurring opinion in *Citizens United v. Federal Election Commission* (2010), Justice Scalia addresses Justice Stevens's "original understandings" position using historical evidence about the presence of corporations in the eighteenth century. The case under consideration evaluated whether or not Citizens United, a non-profit corporation, could create and distribute a documentary critical of Senator Hillary Clinton during her campaign for the presidential nomination in 2008. In a five to four decision, the Court ruled that barring corporate financial support for independent broadcasts violated the First Amendment.

In his concurring opinion, Justice Scalia makes a comparative argument—his "proper analysis" of historical evidence versus Justice Stevens's lack of evidence. Justice Scalia bases his reasoning not on the framers' "personal affection or disaffection for corporations" but on the "understood meaning of the text they enacted."[28] He begins by asking if the framers and Americans of the 1800s hated corporations so much "how came there to be so many of them?" He then argues that even if the Founders disliked corporations, it was because they disliked state-granted corporations that had monopoly privileges, not the kind of corporations we have today. Moreover, the "lack of a textual exception for speech by corporations cannot be explained on the ground that such organizations did not exist or did not speak. To the contrary, colleges, towns and cities, religious institutions, and guilds had long been organized as corporations at common law and under the King's charter."[29] Given the historical presence of corporations and that the First Amendment "offers no foothold for excluding any category of speaker, from single individuals to partnerships of individuals, to unincorporated associations of individuals, to incorporated associations of individuals."[30] Against this "proper" reading, the "dissent offers no evidence about the original meaning of the text to support any such exclusion."[31]

By appealing to the praxis of the framers and American tradition, Justice Scalia uses history to provide the evidence and rationale for his interpretation of the Constitution and decisions. Consistent with Justice Scalia's appeals to tradition and history is his use of precedent to make First Amendment decisions.

PRECEDENTIAL

Bobbitt's fourth modality centers on the role that precedent plays in Supreme Court rulings. In this modality, "doctrinal" rulings have been established to guide the Court, normally by substantial majorities. As his interpretation is bound by the tradition of the framers and U.S. citizens at that time, so are Justice Scalia's decisions bound by previous rulings of the Court. At his confirmation hearings, Justice Scalia stated that he believes the Court is "bound to its earlier decisions by the doctrine of *stare decisis.*"[32] Indeed, Justice Scalia often appeals to the ethos of the Court.

In keeping with his appeals to the past, Justice Scalia also relies on Supreme Court precedent to ground his decisions. In his confirmation hearings, Justice Scalia suggested he would be faithful to these rulings by stating his belief in stare decisis, to stand by that which is decided. This mode of reasoning finds legitimacy in the legal process.[33] Justice Scalia seems to rely heavily on past Court decision on the issue of pornography, as the framers did not directly comment or act on such matters.[34]

In 2008, Justice Scalia wrote the opinion for the Court in the *United States v. Williams* case. Michael Williams was convicted of pandering child pornography. The issue at hand was whether the PROTECT Act, which prohibits pandering any material that intends to or would make people believe it is child pornography, is overbroad under the First Amendment. The majority of the Court did not find that the statute was overbroad. Writing for the Court, Justice Scalia begins the decision by stating, "We have long held that obscene speech—sexually explicit material that violates fundamental notions of decency—is not protected by the First Amendment."[35] He then cites *Roth v. United States* (1957), a landmark case that redefined the Constitutional test for obscene material. However, Justice Scalia takes care to mention two important cases that limit the use of obscenity to proscribe sexually explicit material: *Miller v. California* (1973), a decision that produced a test for what constitutes obscenity by reinforcing community standards, and *Jenkins v. Georgia* (1974), which clarified *Miller*; the Supreme Court argued that only "hard core sexual conduct" is obscene. Justice Scalia then uses more case law to establish the link between obscenity and child pornography. He cites *Osborne v. Ohio* (1990) and *New York v. Ferber* (1982), both of which make illegal the possession and distribution of child pornography. To answer the claims of the U.S. Court of Appeals for the Eleventh Circuit, which argued that the PROTECT Act was constitutionally overbroad, Justice Scalia also uses the ethos of the legal process by stating, "All courts are in agreement that what is usually referred to as 'factual impossibility' is no defense to a charge of attempt."[36]

In *Federal Election Commission v. Wisconsin Right to Life* (2007), the Supreme Court considered whether or not three advertisements that asked constituents to contact two U.S. senators and tell them to oppose filibusters of judicial nominees sponsored by the Wisconsin Right to Life, a nonprofit political advocacy corporation, violated the Bipartisan Campaign Reform Act of 2002. The Act prohibited corporate funds from being used for certain political advertisements in the sixty-day period prior to an election. In his concurring opinion, Justice Scalia relies heavily on and begins with the "seminal case of *Buckley* v. *Valeo.*"[37] He argues that "*Buckley* might well have been the last word on limitations on independent expenditures."[38] The tests since *Buckley* "fall short of the clarity that the First Amendment demands,"[39] but in *Buckley*, the Court "narrowed the ambiguous phrase 'any expenditure . . . relative to a clearly identified candidate' to mean any expenditure 'advocating the election or defeat of a candidate.'"[40] Moreover, if there is ambiguity as to whether the advocacy is express advocacy, which directly calls for the election or defeat of a candidate, or issue advocacy, to be consistent with the First Amendment is either to "eliminate restrictions on independent expenditures altogether or to *confine* them to one side of the *traditional* line—the express-advocacy line, set in concrete on a calm day by *Buckley*, several decades ago."[41]

Justice Scalia's heavy use of *Buckley* reinforces his stated commitment to stare decisis. However, one might argue that *Buckley*, which does not limit campaign expenditures, is inconsistent with *Austin v. Michigan Chamber of Commerce* (1990), where the Supreme Court decided in favor of the Michigan Campaign Finance Act, which prohibited corporations from using treasury money for independent expenditures to support or oppose candidates in elections for state offices. Furthermore, in *McConnell v. Federal Election Commission* (2003), bans on soft money were upheld to avoid "both the actual corruption threatened by large financial contributions and . . . the appearance of corruption" that might result from those contributions.[42] In *McConnell*, Justice Scalia argues that there is no need to defer to precedent when "an erroneous 'governing decisio[n]' has created an 'unworkable' legal regime."[43] Here Justice Scalia mixes historical argument with precedent to make the argument for the correctness of *Buckley*. He argues:

> It is not as though *McConnell* produced a settled body of law. Indeed, it is far more accurate to say that *McConnell* unsettled a body of law. Not until 1947, with the enactment of the Taft-Hartley amendments to the Federal Corrupt Practices Act, 1925, did Congress even purport to regulate campaign-related expenditures of corporations and unions. . . . When the Court finally did turn to that question, it struck them down. . . . Our subsequent pre-McConnell decisions, with the lone exception of Austin, disapproved limits on independent

expenditures. The modest medicine of restoring First Amendment protection to nonexpress advocacy—speech that was protected until three Terms ago—does not unsettle an established body of law.

Moreover, "McConnell's §203 holding has assuredly not become 'embedded' in our 'national culture.'" In this way, Justice Scalia recognizes the intermingling of history and precedent and uses the combination to argue against particular Supreme Court decisions. And in *Citizens United* in 2010, he would side with the narrow majority allowing corporate and union funding of independent advertising, overturning the ruling in *Austin* (see above).

Sometimes the questions that come before the Court do not have a direct practice or tradition that Justice Scalia can draw upon to make his decisions. Many of these cases have competing interests and involve the freedom of expression. In these cases, Justice Scalia almost always protects political speech, in part because that is what that freedom has meant.

STRUCTURAL

Bobbitt's third modality focuses on "structural" arguments. These arguments are "inferences from the existence of constitutional structures and the relationships which the Constitution ordains among these structures."[44] Moreover, as Smith explains in chapter 1 of this book, justices also use structural arguments as a means of balancing between competing interests, such as the First Amendment and the establishment clause.

Justice Scalia makes two kinds of structural arguments. The first has to do with the kinds of power a justice has in the American political system. He is adamant that his job is to apply the laws as understood by those who first implemented them, not to "write a new Constitution" from the bench.[45] Justice Scalia seeks to "preserve a bright line between the judicial and legislative branches of government."[46] In *Federal Election Commission v. Wisconsin Right to Life, Inc.* (2007), Justice Scalia writes that the First Amendment "was not designed to facilitate legislation, even wise legislation."[47] Therefore, the balance between what the legislature should do and what the Court should do is clear: legislators should pay attention to the will of the people and make laws that reflect their standards and morality. Judges should apply the law based on the original meaning of the Constitution without regard for the political implications. For example, in *New York State Board of Elections et al. v. Lopez Torres* (2008), Justice Scalia writes that what constitutes a "fair shot" for winning an election is "a reasonable enough question for legislative judgment. . . . But it is hardly a manageable constitutional question for judges—especially for judges in our legal system, where traditional electoral practice gives no hint of even the existence, much less the content, of a constitutional requirement for a 'fair shot' at party nomination."

The other kind of structural argument Justice Scalia makes has to do primarily with expression. It is important to note that he is suspicious of laws that "regulate political speech because he views protection of such speech to be the main purpose of the First Amendment."[48] However, he is also reticent to trigger First Amendment analysis unless the issue at hand directly prohibits speech. For example, in *Barnes v. Glen Theater, Inc.* (1991), Justice Scalia agreed that a law prohibiting nude dancing did not violate the First Amendment.[49] His explanation relied on the distinction between conduct and expression. He wrote that "the challenged regulation must be upheld, not because it survives some lower level of First Amendment scrutiny, but because, as a general law regulating conduct and not specifically directed at expression, it is not subject to First Amendment scrutiny at all."[50] Child pornography, however, elicits First Amendment analysis when weighed against competing constitutional interest. In *United States v. Williams* (2008), Justice Scalia finds that:

> Over the last 25 years, we have confronted a related and overlapping category of proscribable speech: child pornography. . . . We have held that a statute which proscribes the distribution of all child pornography, even material that does not qualify as obscenity, does not on its face violate the First Amendment. . . . The broad authority to proscribe child pornography is not, however, unlimited. Four Terms ago, we held facially overbroad two provisions of the federal Child Pornography Protection Act of 1996.[51]

After reviewing the facts of the case, Justice Scalia begins his analysis by stating:

> According to our First Amendment overbreadth doctrine, a statute is facially invalid if it prohibits a substantial amount of protected speech. The doctrine seeks to strike a balance between competing social costs. On the one hand, the threat of enforcement of an overbroad law deters people from engaging in constitutionally protected speech, inhibiting the free exchange of ideas. On the other hand, invalidating a law that in some of its applications is perfectly constitutional—particularly a law directed at conduct so antisocial that it has been made criminal—has obvious harmful effects. In order to maintain an appropriate balance, we have vigorously enforced the requirement that a statute's overbreadth be substantial, not only in an absolute sense, but also relative to the statute's plainly legitimate sweep.[52]

In the end, the social cost of child pornography which "harms and debases the most defenseless of our citizens" is greater than the need to protect an individual's right to expression, and a law that made the pandering or requesting of child pornography illegal was not overbroad.

On questions of political speech, Justice Scalia paints with a broader stroke. In *RAV v. St. Paul* (1992), "St. Paul and its *amici* defend the conclusion of the Minnesota Supreme Court that, even if the ordinance regulates expression based on hostility towards its protected ideological content, this discrimination is nonetheless justified because it is narrowly tailored to serve compelling state interests."[53] Regardless of the desired outcome, the question before the Court, as Justice Scalia sees it, is "whether content discrimination is reasonably necessary to achieve St. Paul's compelling interests." For Justice Scalia, the short answer is no. He writes, "[w]here the government does not target conduct on the basis of its expressive content, acts are not shielded from regulation merely because they express a discriminatory idea or philosophy. . . . The First Amendment does not permit St. Paul to impose special prohibitions on those speakers who express views on disfavored subjects."[54] Moreover, "In its practical operation, the ordinance goes even beyond mere content discrimination to actual viewpoint discrimination."[55]

In 2004, the state of Washington initiated a "modified blanket primary" system where each candidate on the ballot could affiliate with the party of his or her choosing regardless of whether the party approved of his or her candidacy. Washington's justification was that the electorate would benefit from this small amount of information: which party the candidate identifies with (even though that party may not endorse her or him). The question before the Court in *Washington State Grange v. Washington State Republican Party* (2008) was: Does an individual's right to associate him or herself with a party outweigh a party's right to control their support and endorsement? In his dissenting opinion, Justice Scalia argues that such a system would only be acceptable if there were a compelling state interest. In his mind, however, "Washington's law imposes a severe burden on political parties' associational rights" and does not advance "a compelling state interest."[56] For him, a party's endorsement "for the election of candidates is fundamental to the operation of our political system, and state action impairing that association bears a heavy burden of justification. Washington's electoral system permits individuals to appropriate the parties' trademarks, so to speak, at the most crucial stage of election, thereby distorting the parties' messages and impairing their endorsement of candidates."[57] Therefore, political parties must be allowed to grant and withhold their names on ballots for the overall good of the electoral process.

Finally, in *Federal Election Commission v. Wisconsin Right to Life, Inc.* (2007), Justice Scalia uses both kinds of structural arguments. In his concurring opinion, Justice Scalia argues that in questions concerning healthy campaigns and freedom of speech, "it is pretty clear which side of the equation *this institution* is primarily responsible for. It is perhaps our most important constitutional task to assure freedom of political speech. And when a statute creates a regime as unworkable and unconstitutional as today's effort at as-applied review proves to be, it is our responsibility to decline enforcement."[58] Justice Scalia restates his position that the Supreme Court should concern itself only with constitutional issues and that the protection of individuals' and corporations' right to political speech should be unwavering.

APPEALING TO JUSTICE SCALIA

Justice Scalia's opinions on the First Amendment and his understanding of the role of the Supreme Court have significant implications for the would-be advocate before the Court. Basic tips on how to prepare and present arguments to judges can be found in Justice Scalia and Bryan A. Garner's *Making Your Case: The Art of Persuading Judges*. The book outlines important elements of persuasion, such as "Always start with a statement of the main issue before fully stating the facts" and make eye contact.[59] These are sound pieces of advice drawn from a variety of sources including rhetorical theory developed by classical Roman rhetoricians Quintilian and Cicero, but I would argue that Cicero's most important insights on how to appeal to Justice Scalia specifically are neglected in his book. Cicero's discussion of *ornatus*, as both a stylistic and a structural rhetorical resource, may be an effective approach to appealing to Justice Scalia's sense of *decorum*. We've already seen that to persuade Justice Scalia, one should foreground arguments against a backdrop of originalism. However, it would also be helpful to understand the connection between *decorum* and *ornatus* and how they can be used to persuade Scalia.

Ornatus is a subset of *decorum*, the most basic definition of which is "the use of language to adapt to the expectations of the audience."[60] *Ornatus* uses "rhythm, tropes, and figures to . . . arouse proper decorum."[61] The term refers to a linguistic strategy used to "attain and retain the hearer's state of mind" and "unsettle the emotion" as well as an intellectual pursuit that "actually belongs to *inventio*."[62] In this sense, ornatus not only fashions a speech through language choices, but also "cast[s] light upon things" and "reveal[s] things and, through that, receive[s] place," which implies its connection to *kosmos*, the Greek word referring to order.[63]

In his theories on rhetoric, Cicero combines both emotional arousal and the pleasure of order to bring attention to a message. As Per Fjelstad has argued, "Cicero's theory of *ornatus* insists an orator display emotions relevant to the performance while responding to the need of listeners to hear emotional expression against a backdrop of relative calm."[64] This advice combines the linguistic and structural elements of *ornatus*. Both components bring about the "intensification of our basic linguistic orientation to reality."[65] This may seem like rather vague advice, but an analysis of Scalia's First Amendment decisions offers an effective case study.

The backdrop of relative calm is particularly important for Justice Scalia. The preceding analysis of his First Amendment decisions demonstrates that his use of historical, precedential, and structural arguments all stem from his interpretation of what the framers and Americans at the time meant when the Constitution was written and adopted. This is the fundamental order that is Justice Scalia's relative calm. Thus, the underlying structure of any argument made to appeal to Justice Scalia must be based in the political practices of Americans at the time the Constitution was written. This may seem rather confining; however, given the diversity among the states at the time, there would be a multitude of traditions that could rightly be called "American." In this way, the interlocutor would shed new light on what originalism could mean, thereby expanding rhetorical possibilities.

The second element of *ornatus* is emotional expression. Understanding how to handle emotional expression when addressing Scalia requires an analysis of his own creative expression in his First Amendment decisions. His written decisions on the First Amendment reveal his penchant for drama. He has written biting criticisms of his colleagues, indulges in hyperbole, and uses aggressive metaphors to make his position memorable.

Most particularly in his dissent, Justice Scalia admonishes his colleagues while also detailing his disagreement with the Court's decision. Christopher E. Smith argues that Justice Scalia "launches verbal assaults to wound his colleagues and tarnish their judicial reputations rather than to persuade them and the public of the correctness of his views."[66] He sometimes offers entire dissenting and concurring opinions to refute other justices, opinions in which he belittles other justices' logic and questions their evidence. For example, in his concurring opinion in *Good News Club v. Milford Central School* (2001), Justice Scalia mocks the dissenters when he writes, "Justice Stevens fears without support in the record . . . its actions may prove (shudder!) divisive."[67] In *Board of Education of Kiryas Joel Village School District v. Grumet* (1994), Justice Scalia writes, "I turn, next, to Justice Souter's second justification for finding an establishment of religion: his facile conclusion that the New York Legislature's creation of the Kiryas Joel School District was religiously motivated. But in the Land of the Free, democratically adopted laws are not so easily impeached by unelected judges."[68] Thus, in one fell swoop, Justice Scalia refutes his opposition, questions his intellect, and mocks him. However, Justice Scalia does not limit his attacks to one-liners or to his dissents. In *City of Boerne v. Flores*, he writes an entire concurring opinion to refute Justice O'Connor's dissenting opinion, questioning her use and understanding of historical evidence.[69]

Hyperbole is also one of Justice Scalia's favorite rhetorical tools. In *Federal Election Commission v. Wisconsin Right to Life* (2007), Justice Scalia argues that the decision in *Austin* "was a significant departure from *ancient* First Amendment principles."[70] In *Good News Club v. Milford Central School* (2001), Justice Scalia begins his decision by stating that the consistency between his reading and the Court's reasoning of the establishment clause as it is relevant in this case is "zero."[71] But perhaps his most amusing use of hyperbole is in *Washington State Grange v. Washington State Republican Party* (2008), in which he likens Washington's law to "a law that encourages Oscar the Grouch (Sesame Street's famed bad-taste resident of a garbage can) to state a 'preference' for Campbell's at every point of sale, while barring the soup company from disavowing his endorsement, or indeed using its name at all, in those same crucial locations."[72]

Justice Scalia's use of combative metaphors is in stark contrast to the playful nature of the Oscar the Grouch comparison. In *RAV v. St. Paul*, Justice Scalia writes, "St. Paul has no such authority to license one side of a debate to fight freestyle, while requiring the other to follow Marquis of Queensberry rules."[73] In the same case he argues that the "weapon" of censorship should only be used when there is a compelling state interest.[74] In *Lamb's Chapel*, Justice Scalia writes of the *Lemon* test, "like some ghoul in a late-night horror movie that repeatedly sits up in its grave and shuffles abroad after being repeatedly killed and buried, Lemon stalks our Establishment Clause jurisprudence . . . Its most recent burial, only last Term, was, to be sure, not fully six-feet under. . . . Over the years, however, no fewer than five of the currently sitting Justices have, in their own opinions, personally driven pencils through the creature's heart."[75] He continues, "[t]he secret of the Lemon test's survival, I think, is that it is so easy to kill."[76] He continues his use of deadly metaphors in *Washington State Grange v. Washington State Republican Party* (2008). He states, "association with the party on the general election ballot was fatal."[77] Moreover, allowing candidates running for office to associate themselves with a party without that party's approval distorts the party's message and hijacks its goodwill.[78] He also argues in *New York State Board of Elections v. Lopez Torres* (2008) that a party's associational rights are like a "shield" and a "sword."[79]

Justice Scalia's harsh criticisms, use of hyperbole, and hostile metaphors reveal his emotional attachment to the law and his arguments. He explains that his rhetorical choices are an attempt to get Americans to read the Court's rulings.[80] Mimicking his rhetorical strategy would be folly. Yet there are lessons for the would-be interlocutor embedded in these choices, informed by Cicero's discussion of *ornatus*. One of the resources of *ornatus* is a "quasi-enthymematic model of emotional engagement, in which an orator need not share or display the sought after emotional response."[81] Enthymemes are deductive arguments that rely on probable premises and a kind of subliminal persuasion in which audience members provide missing or suppressed premises. Applying the same principle to *ornatus*, "this mode of theatrical representation gives audience members the pleasure of discovering and applying the appropriate emotion 'on their own.' Just as in the case of the enthymeme, this sense of a discovered attitude or opinion can be key to the rhetorical force of the performance."[82] Thus, the advocate would not directly express a particular emotional state, but instead work to evoke a particular emotional state, a different strategy. Given Justice Scalia's desire to guard against legislating from the bench, one would do well to make him feel that he is fulfilling that duty.

CONCLUSIONS

An analysis of Justice Scalia's decisions on the First Amendment reveals that he primarily relies on history, precedent, and structural modalities to make sense of the law. However, the primary mode of reasoning is historical, which influences his precedential and structural reasoning. Each of these modalities suggest that the ethos of Justice Scalia's decisions is derived from a need for order that can only be found in the consistent application of the law based in the practices and traditions of the framers. His desire to forcefully guard against changes to this order is also reflected in the fashioning of his First Amendment opinions. A classical rhetorical approach would serve potential advocates well, especially the rhetorical possibility embedded in the concept of *ornatus*. Far from a superficial elocutionary device, *ornatus*, which in classical Latin is described as "the weapons and accoutrements of war," would be an indispensable piece of equipment for winning a war of words with Justice Scalia.[83]

NOTES

1. Richard A. Brisbin, *Justice Antonin Scalia and the Conservative Revival* (Baltimore, MD: Johns Hopkins University Press, 1998), 60.

2. Jane Kirtley, "Scalia and His Speeches," *American Journalism Review*, June/July 2004, http://www.ajr.org/Article.asp?id=3686 (accessed August 23, 2009).

3. "Justice Scalia on Life: Part 1," *60 Minutes*, September 15 2008, www.cbsnews.com/video/watch/?id=4448191n&tag=related;photovideo (accessed September 9, 2009).

4. "Justice Scalia on Life: Part 1."

5. Justice Antonin Scalia, "A Theory of Constitutional Interpretation," speech at The Catholic University of America, Washington, DC, October 18, 1996.

6. Scalia, "A Theory of Constitutional Interpretation."

7. Scalia, "A Theory of Constitutional Interpretation."

8. Philip Bobbitt, *Constitutional Interpretation*, 9–10.

9. Bobbitt, *Constitutional Interpretation*, 10.

10. McCreary County v. ACLU, 545 U.S. 844, 896 (2005).

11. 545 U.S. 895.

12. 545 U.S. 886.

13. 545 U.S. 891.

14. Pleasant Grove City v. Summum, 555 U.S. slip op. (2009).

15. Van Orden v. Perry, 545 U.S. 677 (2005).

16. Lamb's Chapel v. Center Moriches Union Free School District, 508 U.S. 384, 400 (1993).

17. 508 U.S. 400.

18. Employment Division v. Smith, 494 U.S. 872 (1990).

19. City of Boerne v. P. F. Flores, Archbishop of San Antonio, and United States, 521 U.S. 507, 539, 540 (1997).

20. Board of Education of Kiryas Joel Village School District v. Grumet, 512 U.S. 687, 732 (1994).

21. 512 U.S. 736.

22. 512 U.S 735.

23. 512 U.S. 735.

24. City of Boerne v. P. F. Flores, Archbishop of San Antonio, and United States, 521 U.S. 507, 537 (1997).

25. 521 U.S. 542.

26. New York State Board of Elections v. Lopez Torres, 552 U.S. 791, 799 (2008).

27. 522 U.S. 799.

28. Citizens United v. Federal Election Commission, 558 U.S. 50 (2010).

29. 558 U.S. ___ 2010.

30. 558 U.S. ___ 2010.

31. 558 U.S. ___ 2010.

32. *Hearings before the Committee on the Judiciary United States Senate Ninety-Ninth Congress Second Session on the Nomination of Judge Antonin Scalia, to Be an Associate Justice of the Supreme Court of the United States*, August 5–6, 1986 (Washington, DC: U.S. Government Printing Office, 1987), 32.

33. Philip Bobbitt, *Constitutional Fate: Theory of the Constitution* (New York: Oxford University Press, 1982), 42.

34. An exception may be Ben Franklin, one of the first American publishers. His biographers have noted books in Franklin's possession that possibly contained "salacious content," and it is unclear if he also published books with containing erotic content. However, "no respected biographer of Franklin's claims that he sold pornography" http://teachinghistory.org/history-content/ask-historian/22470.

35. United States v. Williams, 553 U.S. 285, 288 (2008).

36. 553 U.S. 300.

37. Federal Election Commission v. Wisconsin Right to Life, Inc., 551 U.S. 449, 485 (2007).

38. 551 U.S. 487.

39. 551 U.S. 495.

40. 551 U.S. 495.

41. 551 U.S. 499.

42. McConnell v. Federal Election Commission, 540 U.S. 93, 136 (2003).

43. Federal Election Commission v. Wisconsin Right to Life, Inc., 551 U.S. 449, 501 (2007).

44. Bobbitt, *Constitutional Interpretation*, 74.

45. Antonin Scalia, "Constitutional Interpretation the Old Fashioned Way," speech at Woodrow Wilson International Center for Scholars, Washington, DC, March 14, 2005, http://www.cfif.org/htdocs/freedomline/current/guest_commentary/scalia-constitutional-speech.htm.

46. Joseph A. Russomanno, "A Decade on the Court: The First Amendment Jurisprudence of Justice Antonin Scalia," *Common Law and Policy* (1997): 343.

47. 551 U.S. 503.

48. Kevin A. Ring, *Scalia Dissents: Writing of the Supreme Court's Wittiest, Most Outspoken Justice* (Washington, DC: Regnery 2004), 257.

49. Barnes v. Glen Theatre, Inc., 501 U.S. 560 (1991).

50. 501 U.S. 560, 573.

51. 553 U.S. 285, 288.

52. 553 U.S. 285, 292.

53. RAV v . City of St . Paul , 505 U.S. 377, 395 (1992).

54. 505 U.S. 389.

55. 505 U.S. 391.

56. Washington State Grange v. Washington State Republican Party, 552 U.S. 1184, 1202 (2008).

57. 552 U.S. 1184.

58. Federal Election Commission v. Wisconsin Right to Life, Inc., 551 U.S. 449, 503 (2007).

59. Antonin Scalia and Bryan A. Garner, *Making Your Case: The Art of Persuading Judges* (Thomson West, 2008), 25, 178.

60. Craig R. Smith, *Rhetoric and Human Consciousness*, 2nd ed. (Long Grove, IL: Waveland Press, 2003), 137.

61. Smith, *Rhetoric and Human Consciousness*, 141.

62. Heinrich Lausberg, *Handbook of Literary Rhetoric*, trans. Matthew T. Bliss, Annemiek Jansen, and David E. Orton, ed. David E. Orton and R. Dean Anderson (Boston, MA: Brill, 1998), 243.

63. Raymond Di Lorenzo, "The Critique of Socrates in Cicero's De Oratore: *Ornatus* and the Nature of Wisdom," *Philosophy and Rhetoric*, 11 (1978): 250, 252.

64. Per Fjelstad, "Restraint and Emotion in Cicero's *De Oratore*," *Philosophy and Rhetoric*, 36 (2003): 40.

65. Hanna-Barbara Gerl, "On the Philosophical Dimension of Rhetoric: The Theory of *Ornatus* in Leonardo Bruni," *Philosophy of Rhetoric*, 11 (1978): 182.

66. *Justice Antonin Scalia and the Supreme Court's Conservative Moment* (Westport, CT: Praeger, 1993), 63.

67. Good News Club v. Milford Central School, 533 U.S. 98, 126 (2001).

68. Board of Education of Kiryas Joel Village School District v. Grumet, 512 U.S. 687, 737 (1994).

69. City of Boerne v. Flores, 521 U.S. 507, 536–44 (1997).

70. Federal Election Commission v. Wisconsin Right to Life, Inc., 551 U.S. 449, 490 (2007); emphasis added.

71. Good News Club v. Milford Central School, 533 U.S. 98, 121 (2001).

72. Washington State Grange v. Washington State Republican Party, 552 U.S. 1184, 1201 (2008).

73. RAV v . City of St . Paul , 505 U.S. 377, 392 (1992).

74. 505 U.S. 395.

75. Lamb's Chapel v. Center Moriches Union Free School District, 508 U.S. 384, 398 (1993).

76. 508 U.S. 399.

77. Washington State Grange v. Washington State Republican Party, 552 U.S. 1184, 1199 (2008).

78. 522 U.S. 1200.

79. New York State Board of Elections v. Lopez Torres, 552 U.S. 791, 798 (2008).

80. "Justice Scalia on Life: Part 1."

81. Fjelstad, "Restraint and Emotion in Cicero's *De Oratore*," 40.

82. Fjelstad, "Restraint and Emotion in Cicero's *De Oratore*," 41.

83. Quentin Skinner, *Reason and Rhetoric in the Philosophy of Hobbes* (Cambridge: Cambridge University Press, 1986), 49.

Chapter Six

Associate Justice Kennedy

Kevin A. Johnson

President Ronald Reagan appointed Associate Justice Anthony Kennedy to the Supreme Court in 1988. A careful review of Justice Kennedy's rhetoric reveals that he employs textual, precedential, and prudential arguments to justify his First Amendment decisions. These arguments conceal a deeper ethical perspective that appears to motivate his commitment to First Amendment principles: Justice Kennedy's ethical perspective lies at the heart of his decision making. To demonstrate this claim, I offer a thematic analysis of the arguments that Justice Kennedy has made in his First Amendment opinions, dissents, and concurrences from 1988 to the close of the 2008–2009 session. This close reading of his decision making on First Amendment issues is divided into five sections. The first section examines the importance of Justice Kennedy in First Amendment cases as well as the ethical position that frames his arguments, the second section examines his textual arguments, the third section analyzes his precedential arguments, and the fourth section delves into his prudential arguments. The final section discusses potential implications of Justice Kennedy's rhetorical framing of First Amendment cases. This reading leads to the conclusion that while many legal scholars and practitioners have positioned Justice Kennedy as a conservative justice with a slant against living constitutionalists, his decisions on the First Amendment indicate a conservative brand of ethical commitment disguised by arguments from text, precedence, and prudence. This ethical commitment is of central importance in understanding the rhetorical framework of Justice Kennedy, which has cast him in the role of majority maker. Furthermore, the framework leads Justice Kennedy to interpret the First Amendment to protect the American version of representative democracy as the best purveyor of natural rights endorsed in the Declaration of Independence.

ETHICAL ARGUMENTS

The argument that Justice Kennedy is committed to an ethical interpretation of the First Amendment might at first appear at odds with his actual written decisions. What makes such an argument odd is that Justice Kennedy does not actually write from an ethical perspective. Rather, this chapter contends that he masks his ethical commitment in textual, precedential, and prudential arguments. Understanding Justice Kennedy's ethical commitments is vital to grasping the interpretive scheme of this complicated and pivotal justice.

Because President Reagan appointed Justice Kennedy to the Court, many legal scholars and practitioners might presume that he is inclined to be conservative in his interpretation of the Constitution. However, there is much evidence to suggest that he is a centrist. Kenneth Starr, legal counsel in *Morse v. Frederick* (one the most recent First Amendment cases) described the importance of Justice Kennedy: "As Justice Kennedy went, so went the Court. His centrist position in Bong Hits [i.e., *Morse v. Frederick*], in the face of a narrower, minimalist approach that resolves the case quickly and efficiently, confirms what the early voting in the Roberts Court suggests—that the immediate future of American constitutional law will be in the hands of a single justice. This is, for now, the Kennedy Court."[1] Similarly, Lisa Parshall wrote that "With O'Connor's absence and the increased recognition of Kennedy's centrality and pivotal vote, it has become imperative that the framing of any constitutional argument presented to the Court takes Kennedy's views and preferences into consideration."[2]

If one were to analyze all of Justice Kennedy's arguments about the First Amendment strictly based on the claims made to support his rulings in cases according to Bobbitt's six modalities, one would find that he rarely explicitly bases his decisions on his own ethical commitments. However, a rhetorical analysis reveals the possibility that even though he consistently uses text, precedent, and prudence as the reasons for his decisions, there is an underlying ethical consistency to them. That is, Justice Kennedy might judge cases based on his own ethical commitment, and then retroactively work to construct an argument from text, precedent, and/or prudence that provides an acceptable legal patina.[3] He once alluded to the idea that an ethical commitment might be a consideration in his decision-making process when he stated, "The art of the law, the art of judging, is that you ask yourself, 'Why am I doing this? Why am I thinking this?' . . . You ask, 'Is it logical? Does it make common sense? Is it fair? Does it accord with the law? Does it accord with the Constitution? Does it accord with my own sense of decency and ethics and morality?' And if, at any point along the way, you think you might be wrong, you have to begin all over again."[4] Outside the context of his official decisions, Justice Kennedy has admitted that his own sense of ethics must be congruent with all of the other factors in order to issue a good decision.

There are at least three possible types of decisions that Kennedy might make in the framework that he has laid out in this statement: (a) all of the considerations are congruent with each other, so there is no need to reconsider any of the factors; (b) one or more of the factors do not align with his concept of ethics, so he must change his ethical commitment; and (c) one or more of the factors do not align with his concept of ethics, so he must reconsider the factors to invent arguments that do align with his ethical commitments. If Justice Kennedy were to employ option a, then he would consider his job very easy because he would never have to reconsider any of his decisions. If Justice Kennedy used option b, then one would expect to find a changing ethical commitment based on his belief that his ethical commitment is of little or no importance. This chapter makes the case that Justice Kennedy most likely exercises option c, because his underlying ethical framework has not changed in his decisions about the First Amendment.

Specifically, when interpreting the First Amendment, Justice Kennedy's ethical framework consists of a Hamiltonian skepticism of local authority while he remains ethically committed to protecting his belief in the First Amendment as the protector of freedoms that are essential to a robust and unfettered democratic process that encourages ordinary citizens to engage in creative power at the heart of intellectual life in America. With regard to Justice Kennedy's Hamiltonian skepticism, Kenneth Starr wrote that Justice Kennedy stands "in the grand tradition of Alexander Hamilton in lifting up the primacy of national institutions and embracing a deep skepticism toward local power."[5] Starr concluded that Justice Kennedy seems "willing to have courts exercise their authority to guard against states that would abuse their power."[6] A prime example of his Hamiltonian distrust of local power is found in his concurrence with Justice Alito in *Morse v. Frederick*: "The opinion of the Court does not endorse the broad argument advanced by petitioners and the United States that the First Amendment permits public school officials to censor any speech that interferes with a school's 'educational mission.' . . . This argument can easily be manipulated in dangerous ways, and I would reject it before such abuse occurs."[7] This statement demonstrates that Justice Kennedy is skeptical of the ability for local authorities to respect constitutional freedoms. If Justice Kennedy were not skeptical, and instead trusted local authorities to act reasonably, he would have felt no need to write such a concurrence.

Justice Kennedy's Hamiltonian skepticism is coupled with his ethical commitment to the First Amendment. His version of ethics has several components. First, he views the First Amendment as the protector of freedoms mentioned in its text: religion, speech, press, assembly, and petitioning the government for a redress of grievances. From Justice Kennedy's perspective, central to all of these freedoms is the idea that the First Amendment must protect public space in order for these freedoms to have a place to be exercised. Second, Justice Kennedy is committed to maintaining a robust and unfettered democratic process. In this sense, Justice Kennedy is ethically committed to the idea of an orderly and civil marketplace of ideas. Third, Justice Kennedy is committed to the idea that ordinary citizens should be encouraged to participate in the democratic process if it is to remain healthy. Justice Kennedy seeks to avoid First Amendment restrictions that divorce ordinary citizens from the political process. Fourth, Justice Kennedy is ethically committed to using the First Amendment to encourage creativity. Attempts to regulate speech that stifle creativity are rejected within Justice Kennedy's schematic. Fifth, Justice Kennedy is committed to intellectual life.[8] Justice Kennedy uses the First Amendment as a guardian that encourages critical thinking in order to achieve the best decisions for America. Together, these five parts form the basis for Justice Kennedy's textual, precedential, and prudential arguments, which ultimately ground an ethical thesis based on his belief in natural rights—though not in the precise sense that Philip Bobbitt intended.

Bobbitt wrote, "By ethical argument I mean constitutional argument whose force relies on a characterization of American institutions and the role within them of the American people. It is the character, or ethos, of the American polity that is advanced in ethical argument as the course from which particular decisions derive."[9] In this precise sense, while Justice Kennedy may allude to ethical arguments, he never "relies" on them. Rather, he approaches his interpretation of the First Amendment with an ethical interpretation that relies on text, precedent, and prudence to support his ethical commitment.[10] Examining Justice Kennedy's uses of textual, precedential, and prudential arguments provides a deeper understanding of his interpretive framework for supporting his ethical commitment.

TEXTUAL ARGUMENTS

I begin analyzing Justice Kennedy's perspective on the First Amendment by analyzing his use of textual arguments in his decisions. For Bobbitt, interpreting the Constitution by using textual arguments meant examining a common understanding of the words themselves as they appear in the Constitution without any necessary reference to original intentions of the framers. Bobbitt relied on the work of Justice Joseph Story to describe textual arguments as motivated by the idea that "Constitutions . . . are instruments of a practical nature, founded in the common business of human life, adapted to common wants, designed for common use, and fitted for common under-standing. The people make them; the people adopt them; the people must be supposed to read them . . . ; and cannot be presumed to admit in them any recondite meaning."[11] In other words, the textual argument is rooted in a belief that the Constitution should be interpreted in such a way that it is not difficult for the people to penetrate and that is comprehensible to an ordinary understanding or knowledge.

Justice Kennedy's use of textual arguments is consistent with his ethical commitment to the inclusion of ordinary persons in a healthy democratic process. He alluded to this commitment at a civic education summit: "Some people think government is for experts. That does not accord with basic democratic theory. . . . The law lives in the consciousness of the people. The same can be said of freedom."[12] Justice Kennedy has utilized textual argu-ments to advance his democratic theory on many occasions.

For example, Justice Kennedy's interpretation of the First Amendment using textuality appeared in 1992 in the case of *Lee v. Weisman*. This case involved the issue of whether the inclusion of clergy who offer prayers at official public school ceremonies violates the establishment clause of the First Amendment. Robert E. Lee was a middle school principal who invited a rabbi to speak at Deborah Weisman's graduation ceremony. Daniel Weisman (Deborah's father) filed a claim arguing that the prayer violated the establish-ment clause. In a five to four decision, the Supreme Court ruled for Daniel Weisman.

Writing for the majority, Justice Kennedy interpreted the establishment clause as it appeared in the text of the Constitution. He began by articulating a common person's understanding of graduation ceremonies: "Everyone knows that, in our society and in our culture, high school graduation is one of life's most significant occasions."[13] He then explained the consciousness of the people as more important than rules: "A school rule which excuses atten-dance is beside the point. Attendance may not be required by official decree, yet it is apparent that a student is not free to absent herself from the gradua-tion exercise in any real sense of the term 'voluntary,' for absence would require forfeiture of those intangible benefits which have motivated the stu-dent through youth and all her high school years."[14]

Next, he turned to his argument based on the textual understanding of the establishment clause:

> We recognize that, at graduation time and throughout the course of the educa-tional process, there will be instances when religious values, religious prac-tices, and religious persons will have some interaction with the public schools and their students. See *Board of Ed. of Westside Community Schools (Dist. 66) v. Mergens*, 496 U.S. 226 (1990). But these matters, often questions of accom-modation of religion, are not before us. The sole question presented is whether a religious exercise may be conducted at a graduation ceremony in circum-

stances where, as we have found, young graduates who object are induced to conform. No holding by this Court suggests that a school can persuade or compel a student to participate in a religious exercise. That is being done here, and it is forbidden by the Establishment Clause of the First Amendment. [15]

This statement asserts that the text of the establishment clause allows the state to accommodate religion but does not allow the state to compel someone to participate in religious exercises. For Justice Kennedy, the common understanding of the establishment clause allows for a line to be drawn at the place where government compels people to participate in an actual religious ceremony (i.e., a prayer) as a captive audience, such as at a graduation. Justice Kennedy thereby maintained his commitment to religion as a vital part of the free marketplace of ideas but not a part of a place where the audience is captive.

Another place where Justice Kennedy used textual argument to support his First Amendment interpretation was in the case of *McConnell v. Federal Election Commission* (2003). Senator Mitch McConnell led a group of plaintiffs who sought to overturn the ban on "soft money" put in place by the Campaign Finance Reform Act (CFRA) of 2002. They claimed the ban violated First Amendment freedom of speech. In a five to four decision, the Supreme Court upheld the key provisions of the CFRA. Justice Kennedy concurred in the judgment in part and dissented in part.

His opinion maintained his ethical commitment to robust and unfettered debate as the foundation of democracy by using a textual argument to interpret the First Amendment. Specifically, Justice Kennedy wrote:

> The First Amendment commands that Congress "shall make no law . . . abridging the freedom of speech." The command cannot be read to allow Congress to provide for the imprisonment of those who attempt to establish new political parties and alter the civic discourse. Our pluralistic society is filled with voices expressing new and different viewpoints, speaking through modes and mechanisms that must be allowed to change in response to the demands of an interested public. As communities have grown and technology has evolved, concerted speech not only has become more effective than a single voice but also has become the natural preference and efficacious choice for many Americans. The Court, upholding multiple laws that suppress both spontaneous and concerted speech, leaves us less free than before. Today's decision breaks faith with our tradition of robust and unfettered debate. [16]

This passage refers to both the text of the Constitution as a commandment and to the "preference and efficacious choice for many Americans." While he relied on the text itself as the basis for his claim that the majority decision is a restriction of speech on its face, he simultaneously used such a claim to support his ethical commitment to the participation of "many Americans" in the democratic process.

In 2004, Justice Kennedy would again advance a textual argument for his First Amendment interpretation in the case of *Board of Education of Kiryas Joel Village School District v. Grumet.* This case involved New York's 1989 statute that drew the boundaries of its school districts along lines that allowed the village of Kiryas (a religious enclave of Satmar Hasidim who practice a strict form of Judaism) to have its own district. Taxpayers and the association of state school boards filed a claim that the districting law violated the establishment clause because it limited access only to residents of Kiryas Joel. In a six to three decision, the Supreme Court ruled that the law was an unconstitutional violation of the First Amendment. Justice Kennedy wrote a special concurring opinion, in which he relied upon a textual argument. In fact, Justice Kennedy overturned the precedent established prior to his tenure on the basis of a clear statement grounded in a textual reading. He wrote:

> But for Grand Rapids and Aguilar, the Satmars would have had no need to seek special accommodations or their own school district. Our decisions led them to choose that unfortunate course, with the deficiencies I have described. One misjudgment is no excuse, however, for compounding it with another. We must confront this case as it comes before us, without bending rules to free the Satmars from a predicament into which we put them. The Establishment Clause forbids the government to draw political boundaries on the basis of religious faith. For this reason, I concur in the judgment of the Court. [17]

This statement reflects a textual interpretation of the establishment clause because of its reliance on the interpretation of the clause itself with no other justification. In other words, Justice Kennedy did not make historical, precedential, ethical, or prudential claims in this decision. Rather, he stressed his own definition of the establishment clause. Worth noting here is that Justice Kennedy interpreted the First Amendment in such a way as to prevent religious seclusion from the marketplace of ideas (which, by extension, is necessary for a healthy democracy). In other words, his ruling is consistent with his ethical commitment to preventing the state from creating barriers to public space that foreclose inventive power (the purpose of strict forms of religion is not to invent new meanings).

Justice Kennedy also used textual arguments in the case of *New York State Board of Elections v. Lopez Torres* (2008). This case involved the issue of whether a state judicial appointment system in which appointments are made by political party delegates elected by party members violates the First Amendment freedom of association for voters and candidates. Margarita Lopez Torres sought appointment to the New York Supreme Court but did not have a political party's endorsement. Lopez Torres filed a claim arguing that the system was unconstitutional because it made candidates reliant on associating with political parties. In a unanimous decision, the Supreme

Court held that the system did not violate First Amendment freedom. Justice Kennedy wrote a concurring opinion that appeared to be prudential on its face, but is more grounded in textual claims:

> In light of this longstanding practice and tradition in the States, the appropriate practical response is not to reject judicial elections outright but to find ways to use elections to select judges with the highest qualifications. A judicial election system presents the opportunity, indeed the civic obligation, for voters and the community as a whole to become engaged in the legal process. Judicial elections, if fair and open, could be an essential forum for society to discuss and define the attributes of judicial excellence and to find ways to discern those qualities in the candidates. The organized bar, the legal academy, public advocacy groups, a principled press, and all the other components of functioning democracy must engage in this process. . . . If New York statutes for nominating and electing judges do not produce both the perception and the reality of a system committed to the highest ideals of the law, they ought to be changed and to be changed now. But, as the Court today holds, and for further reasons given in this separate opinion, the present suit does not permit us to invoke the Constitution in order to intervene. [18]

Justice Kennedy based this decision on the inability for the Court to intervene. This argument is based on a textual assertion of the separation of powers in the Constitution—specifically, the power of the Court to intervene in matters of lawmaking. Important to note in this statement is Justice Kennedy's warning about future cases. He argued that future cases may be decided on an ethical commitment to "the highest ideals of the law." If Justice Kennedy were being a "true" strict constructionist, he would have left the claim about the Court's inability to intervene alone. Instead, Justice Kennedy stated that "the present suit does not permit the Court to invoke the Constitution." Thus, he left open the possibility that future suits may invoke the Constitution in order to intervene. Clearly, he may take the opportunity to affirm his ethical commitments if given proper textual, precedential, and/or prudential arguments as support. Having examined his use of textual arguments, we can now turn to the precedential arguments he has used to interpret the First Amendment.

PRECEDENTIAL ARGUMENTS

Precedential arguments, the ones Bobbitt dubbed as "doctrinal," are those that rely on previously established Court rulings in order to formulate a decision consistent with the findings of the Court. According to Bobbitt, precedential arguments are grounded in a view of judicial rules that are "distinguished from the unprincipled *ad hoc* acts of the legislature that need not give any reasons for its decisions, may legislate for one situation only, is not confined to a factual record, and so forth."[19] Justice Kennedy used precedent in numerous decisions about the First Amendment. Each of the uses is consistent with his guiding ethical perspective.

The first case in which Justice Kennedy used precedential argumentation to interpret the First Amendment came in *Ward v. Rock Against Racism* (1989). This case concerned whether a New York ordinance that required the substitution of a city-employed technician and mixing board for a performer's mixer and equipment violated the First Amendment freedom of expression. Members of a rock group claimed that the inability to use their own sound equipment and technicians in a concert in a public forum violated their First Amendment rights. In a six to three vote, the Court upheld the ordinance as constitutional due to the government's compelling interest in maintaining order. Justice Kennedy wrote the majority opinion, in which he used precedent while remaining consistent with his ethical commitment to unfettered democracy: "The city's sound-amplification guideline is narrowly tailored to serve the substantial and content-neutral governmental interests of avoiding excessive sound volume and providing sufficient amplification . . . , and the guideline leaves open ample channels of communication. Accordingly, it is . . . a reasonable regulation of the place and manner of expression."[20] This decision is consistent with his ethical commitment to the democratic process since there were "ample alternative channels of communication." Thus, Justice Kennedy did not see a problem with the restriction and justified his opinion by using cases that establish time, place, and manner exceptions. He also justified his opinion by using cases such as *RAV v. St Paul* that require restrictions on speech to be content neutral. If New York's ordinance had prevented access to alternative channels that ensure a healthy democracy, then it would have breached Justice Kennedy's ethical interpretation and he would thus have ruled very differently.

Justice Kennedy would also affirm his ethical perspective using precedential arguments in *International Society for Krishna Consciousness v. Lee*. This case concerned whether New York City's ban on repetitive solicitation of money within airline terminals while allowing it outside the terminals violated the First Amendment. The International Society for Krishna Consciousness regularly solicits funds in public places and challenged the policy on the basis that it violated its right to speech in a public forum. In a six to three decision, the Supreme Court ruled that an airport terminal is not a public forum and so the regulation did not violate the First Amendment. Justice Kennedy wrote a special concurring opinion.

Justice Kennedy disagreed with the Court's holding on public forum principles while agreeing with the Court that "disallowing in-person solicitation of money for immediate payment" is "a narrow and valid regulation of the time, place, and manner of protected speech in this forum, or else is a valid regulation of the nonspeech element of expressive conduct."[21] Justice Kennedy's disagreement with the Court is rooted in his ethical commitment to ordinary persons' participation in the democratic process. He justified this commitment through the use of a precedential argument:

> The Court's approach is contrary to the underlying purposes of the public forum doctrine. The liberties protected by our doctrine derive from the Assembly, as well as the Speech and Press Clauses of the First Amendment, and are essential to a functioning democracy. See Kalven, The Concept of the Public Forum: *Cox v. Louisiana,* 1965 S.Ct.Rev. 1, 14, 19. Public places are of necessity the locus for discussion of public issues, as well as protest against arbitrary government action. At the heart of our jurisprudence lies the principle that in a free nation citizens must have the right to gather and speak with other persons in public places. The recognition that certain government-owned property is a public forum provides open notice to citizens that their freedoms may be exercised there without fear of a censorial government, adding tangible reinforcement to the idea that we are a free people. . . . One of the primary purposes of the public forum is to provide persons who lack access to more sophisticated media the opportunity to speak. A prohibition on sales forecloses that opportunity for the very persons who need it most.[22]

Justice Kennedy's reliance on *Cox v. Louisiana* and the rhetoric of that which lies at the "heart of our jurisprudence" are ways of appealing to the doctrines of the Court to support his ethical perspective regarding the protection of a healthy democracy, which requires the right of free citizens to gather and speak.

In *Denver Area Consortium v. Federal Communications Commission (FCC),* Justice Kennedy advanced precedential arguments to ground his ethical commitment. This case concerned whether Television Consumer Protection and Competition Act's (TCPCA) provisions violate the First Amendment. The TCPCA provided leased-access-channel cable operators with the ability to censor programming that they believed to be indecent or obscene. The Denver Area Consortium alleged that the TCPCA's provisions granted too much power to regulate speech on cable television. In a six to three decision, the Supreme Court ruled to allow leased-channel cable operators to restrict the transmission of "patently offensive" while at the same time ruling that they do not have the ability to ban offensive or indecent programming on public-access channels.

In his dissenting opinion, Justice Kennedy advanced his ethical perspective by employing interpretive standards of previous decisions. First, Justice Kennedy criticized the majority for failing to "advise us on what standard [the majority] applies to determine whether the state action conforms to the First Amendment."[23] He grounded his dissent by choosing what he perceived to be the applicable precedent:

Sections 10(a) and (c) disadvantage nonobscene, indecent programming, a protected category of expression, *Sable Communications of Cal., Inc. v. FCC*, 492 U.S. 115, 126 (1989), on the basis of its content. The Constitution in general does not tolerate content based restriction of or discrimination against speech. *R. A. V. v. St. Paul*, 505 U.S. 377, 382 (1992) ("Content based regulations are presumptively invalid"); *Carey v. Brown*, 447 U.S. 455, 461-463 (1980); *Police Dept. of Chicago v. Mosley*, 408 U.S. 92, 96 (1972). In the realm of speech and expression, the First Amendment envisions the citizen shaping the government, not the reverse; it removes "governmental restraints from the arena of public discussion, putting the decision as to what views shall be voiced largely into the hands of each of us, in the hope that use of such freedom will ultimately produce a more capable citizenry and more perfect polity." *Cohen v. California*, 403 U.S. 15, 24 (1971). "[E]ach person should decide for him or herself the ideas and beliefs deserving of expression, consideration, and adherence. Our political system and cultural life rest upon this ideal." *Turner Broadcasting System, Inc. v. FCC*, 512 U. S. ___, ___ (1994) (slip op., at 16). We therefore have given "the most exacting scrutiny to regulations that suppress, disadvantage, or impose differential burdens upon speech because of its content." Id., at ___ (slip op., at 17).[24]

Justice Kennedy's dissent is based primarily on precedent. It is important to note here that he opted to not engage in a textual argument despite the majority opinion being primarily based on such argumentation. Instead, Justice Kennedy relied on his democratic vision, rather than being a strict adherent to textualism, precedentialism, or prudentialism. If Justice Kennedy were committed to textualism, he would have attempted to defend a different textual interpretation.

Another important case in which Justice Kennedy invoked a precedential argument about the First Amendment occurred in *Arkansas Educational Television Commission v. Forbes* (1998). This cased concerned whether the First Amendment permits a state-owned public television broadcaster to exclude a ballot-qualified candidate from a debate that the broadcaster sponsors. In 1992, the Arkansas Educational Television Commission (AETC) sponsored a debate between the major-party candidates and excluded independent candidate Ralph Forbes. By a vote of six to three, the Supreme Court ruled that public broadcasters can selectively exclude participants from their sponsored debates if, and only if, the debates were not designed as "public forums."

In his majority opinion, Justice Kennedy opined that the public was not participating in the debate; the party candidates were the participants. Thus, the debate was not a public forum. He wrote that because the debate was a nonpublic forum, "the exclusion of a speaker . . . must not be based on the speaker's viewpoint and must otherwise be reasonable in light of the purpose of the property."[25] He cited *Cornelius v. NAACP Legal Defense and Education Fund* in support of this precedential standard of interpretation:

In this case, the jury found Forbes' exclusion was not based on "objections or
opposition to his views." App. to Pet. for Cert. 23a. The record provides ample
support for this finding, demonstrating as well that AETC's decision to exclude him was reasonable. . . . There is no substance to Forbes' suggestion that
he was excluded because his views were unpopular or out of the mainstream.
His own objective lack of support, not his platform, was the criterion. Indeed,
the very premise of Forbes' contention is mistaken. A candidate with uncon-
ventional views might well enjoy broad support by virtue of a compelling
personality or an exemplary campaign organization. By the same token, a
candidate with a traditional platform might enjoy little support due to an inept
campaign or any number of other reasons. [26]

On the surface, this decision appears to contradict Justice Kennedy's ethical
commitment to the preservation of debate in a healthy democracy, since he
actively excluded a participant from a debate. However, upon closer examination, it is clear he used this opportunity to clarify his definition of the
democratic process. Namely, for Justice Kennedy the democratic process
requires garnering public support through public forums and/or political parties to qualify for inclusion in telecast debates. For Justice Kennedy, therefore, by the time campaigns reach the point of televised debates, the candidates have already had the time and exposure in public forums in order to
meet his standard of legitimate candidacy. So, even though on its face this
case appeared to be in contradiction with Justice Kennedy's ethical commitment, his use of precedential argument refined his position in terms of shedding light on his envisioned ideal democratic process.

In *Ashcroft v. Free Speech Coalition* (April 16, 2002), Justice Kennedy
also employed a precedential argument as a basis for his First Amendment
interpretation. This case concerned the constitutionality of provisions of the
Child Pornography Prevention Act (CPPA) of 1996 that regulated speech not
found to be obscene based on *Miller v. California*, nor obscene as child
pornography as defined in *New York v. Ferber*. The Free Speech Coalition
charged that CPPA was overreaching so as to unconstitutionally violate free
speech rights. In a six to three decision, the Supreme Court agreed with the
Free Speech Coalition. Justice Kennedy wrote the majority opinion.

Consistent with his rejection of laws that are overbroad in their scope,
Justice Kennedy employed the precedents of the Court in his majority opinion:

> The Constitution gives significant protection from overbroad laws that chill
> speech within the First Amendment's vast and privileged sphere. Under this
> principle, the CPPA is unconstitutional on its face if it prohibits a substantial
> amount of protected expression. See *Broadrick v. Oklahoma*, 413 U. S. 601,
> 612 (1973). . . . In sum, §2256(8)(B) covers materials beyond the categories
> recognized in Ferber and Miller, and the reasons the Government offers in
> support of limiting the freedom of speech have no justification in our prece-

dents or in the law of the First Amendment. The provision abridges the freedom to engage in a substantial amount of lawful speech. For this reason, it is
overbroad and unconstitutional.[27]

Not only is this ruling consistent with his ethical perspective of protecting the
marketplace of ideas, it is also consistent with his commitment to the law of
the First Amendment as the executor of democratic freedom. It is important
to note that Justice Kennedy relied on the case precedents in *Broadrick*,
Ferber, and *Miller* to justify his underlying ethical position. Thus, not only
was his reasoning consistent with his ethical perspective, the precedential
argument functioned as support for his ethical commitment.

Another opinion in which Justice Kennedy relied on precedential arguments was *Republican Party of Minnesota v. White* (June 27, 2002). This
case concerned the right of the Minnesota Supreme Court to prohibit candidates for judicial election from announcing their views on disputed legal and
political issues. Minnesota citizens vote for the state's judges by popular
election. In his campaign to become associate justice of the Minnesota Supreme Court, Gregory Wersal claimed that the clause in Minnesota's constitution that prohibited candidates for judicial selection from announcing their
views violated the First Amendment. In a five to four decision, the Supreme
Court agreed that the "announce clause" violated the First Amendment.

In his concurring opinion, Justice Kennedy upheld the precedent of the
Court by refusing the government permission to restrict speech based on its
content. Justice Kennedy's argument was enthymematically rooted in precedent because the precedent against regulating speech based on its content is
firmly established in Supreme Court beliefs. Specifically, he wrote:

> The law in question here contradicts the principle that unabridged speech is the
> foundation of political freedom. . . . By abridging speech based on its content,
> Minnesota impeaches its own system of free and open elections. The State
> may not regulate the content of candidate speech merely because the speakers
> are candidates. . . . Whether the rationale of *Pickering v. Board of Ed. of
> Township High School Dist.* 205, Will Cty., 391 U. S. 563, 568 (1968), and
> *Connick v. Myers*, 461 U. S. 138 (1983), could be extended to allow a general
> speech restriction on sitting judges . . . in order to promote the efficient admin-
> istration of justice, is not an issue raised here. [S]peech may not be controlled
> or abridged in this manner. Even the undoubted interest of the State in the
> excellence of its judiciary does not allow it to restrain candidate speech by
> reason of its content.[28]

Justice Kennedy asserted that content-based restrictions are impermissible.
In the *Denver Area Consortium* case, he explicated case precedent against
content-based restrictions. In this case, however, he took content-based restrictions to be a suppressed premise. The importance of precedent for Justice
Kennedy is demonstrated by his need to refute possible premises that one

might utilize (i.e., *Pickering* and *Connick*). The importance of this use of precedent as a suppressed premise of his First Amendment claim is that he used it in the service of his ethical commitment to a democratic system of "free and open elections." Having examined the many uses of precedential arguments in the service of an ethical commitment, we can now examine Justice Kennedy's deployment of prudential arguments that also serve his ethical vision.

PRUDENTIAL ARGUMENTS

Prudential arguments at their most basic rely on a logic of cost-benefit analysis. According to Bobbitt, "A prudentialist is likely to deride a doctrinal approach as being as naïve as the textual approach is disingenuous."[29] Justice Kennedy is an exception to this brand of prudentialism because his commitment to an ethical perspective on the First Amendment allows him to navigate among being a doctrinalist, a textualist, or a prudentialist depending on which best serves his ethical perspective in the particular case. Justice Kennedy relied on these types of arguments in order to distance himself from an ethics-centered approach to First Amendment interpretation. Bobbitt also described the prudential argument by relying on the writing of Justice Felix Frankfurter. Bobbitt wrote, "prudential approaches are efforts to bring to constitutional decision making 'the impact of actuality,' in Frankfurter's words."[30] Interestingly, Justice Kennedy's brand of prudentialism approaches the measuring of actual costs to the ethical perspective when interpreting the First Amendment. The benefit of interpreting the First Amendment with a prudential calculation is the preservation of Justice Kennedy's ethical commitment. We can see this type of prudentialism in many of his decisions on the First Amendment.

One of his first considerations of prudence occurred in the case of *Texas v. Johnson* (1989). This case concerned whether the desecration of an American flag is a form of protected speech under the First Amendment. Gregory Lee Johnson was sentenced to one year in jail and assessed a two-thousand-dollar fine for burning an American flag as a form of protest against President Reagan's administrative policies; the protest occurred during the Republican convention in Dallas in 1984. In a five to four decision, the Supreme Court ruled that the First Amendment protected burning a flag as a form of expression.

In his concurring opinion, Justice Kennedy wrote of the costs that must be endured for the benefit of the First Amendment. He stated that "Though symbols often are what we ourselves make of them, the flag is a constant in expressing beliefs Americans share, beliefs in law and peace and that freedom which sustains the human spirit. The case here today forces recognition of the costs to which those beliefs commit us. It is poignant but fundamental that the flag protects those who hold it in contempt."[31] The prudential cost-benefit argument was made in a way that reflected Justice Kennedy's belief in the ultimate benefit of protecting the freedom of expression. This case demonstrated the thin line between Justice Kennedy's brand of prudentialism and ethics-based argumentation, since the benefit of the First Amendment protection for burning the American flag is the maintenance of Justice Kennedy's ethical commitment to expression as the foundation of a vibrant democracy.

In *Rosenberger v. University of Virginia*, Justice Kennedy also advanced his use of prudential argumentation in the service of his ethical vision. This case concerned whether or not the University of Virginia violated First Amendment rights by denying a student-run Christian magazine the same resources as secular student-run magazines. Ronald Rosenberger was a University of Virginia student who asked the university for $5,800 from a student activities fund to subsidize the cost of the student-run Christian magazine. Rosenberger filed a complaint when the university refused funding on the basis that the magazine "primarily promotes or manifests a particular belief in or about a deity or an ultimate reality." In a five to four decision, the Supreme Court ruled in favor of Rosenberger and held that the university restriction amounted to viewpoint discrimination.

In his majority opinion, Justice Kennedy found an opportunity to advance a prudential argument about the benefits of the ruling in securing his ethical perspective about the First Amendment:

> For the University, by regulation, to cast disapproval on particular viewpoints of its students risks the suppression of free speech and creative inquiry in one of the vital centers for the nation's intellectual life, its college and university campuses. . . . The prohibition on funding on behalf of publications that "primarily promot[e] or manifes[t] a particular belie[f] in or about a deity or an ultimate reality," in its ordinary and commonsense meaning, has a vast potential reach. . . . Were the prohibition applied with much vigor at all, it would bar funding of essays by hypothetical student contributors named Plato, Spinoza, and Descartes. And if the regulation covers . . . those student journalistic efforts which primarily manifest or promote a belief that there is no deity and no ultimate reality, then undergraduates named Karl Marx, Bertrand Russell, and Jean-Paul Sartre would likewise have some of their major essays excluded from student publications. If any manifestation of beliefs in first principles disqualifies the writing, as seems to be the case, it is indeed difficult to name renowned thinkers whose writings would be accepted, save perhaps for articles disclaiming all connection to their ultimate philosophy. Plato could contrive perhaps to submit an acceptable essay on making pasta or peanut butter cookies, provided he did not point out their (necessary) imperfections.[32]

Here, Justice Kennedy's prudential arguments took two forms. First, he claimed that the cost of restrictions would be the destruction of the "nation's intellectual life." Second, he advanced the pragmatic argument that the university's policy would rule basically everything out of funding. These prudential arguments are consistent with his ethical commitment to protecting the national intellectual life. And it is important to note that Justice Kennedy's need to protect against perceived threats to creative inquiry may influence his thoughts in arguments about the rights to creative property.

Another case in which Justice Kennedy used prudential argumentation was *Ashcroft v. ACLU* (May 13, 2002). This case concerned whether the COPA used "community standards" to identify "material that is harmful to minors" in accordance with First Amendment freedoms. The ACLU charged that COPA was overbroad. In an eight to one decision, the Court offered a limited opinion by ruling only that COPA's reliance on community standards alone did not render the statute substantially overbroad. However, they remanded the case for further review. [33]

In his concurrence with the majority decision, Justice Kennedy used a prudential argument that sheds more light on his ethical perspective on the First Amendment. In this case, he simply had too many questions unanswered in order to reach a decision as to how the case fit within his ethical commitments, so he deferred it for further analysis. He stated that "There may be grave doubts that COPA is consistent with the First Amendment; but we should not make that determination with so many questions unanswered. The Court of Appeals should undertake a comprehensive analysis in the first instance." [34] This statement may appear rather benign, but it reveals two things about his First Amendment interpretation. First, this decision demonstrated Justice Kennedy's own commitment to intellectual inquiry as essential to a healthy democracy. He demonstrates that intellectual pursuits, in order to reach reasoned judgment in a democracy, require systematic and comprehensive analysis. Second, there is an ordered process for the analysis of important issues that face a nation. In this case, the process involves reaching more firm analyses at the court of appeals before cases are decided by the Supreme Court. Each of these revelations may be taken as a consistent approach toward his ethical perspective.

One of Justice Kennedy's most important uses of prudential argument in his First Amendment jurisprudence occurred in *Randall v. Sorrell* (2006). This case concerned the issue of whether expenditure limits for political candidates violate the First Amendment freedom of speech. Vermont passed a campaign finance law that restricted the amount candidates could spend on their campaigns. Neil Randall, a state legislator, sued Vermont attorney general William Sorrell claiming that *Buckley v. Valeo* ruled that all expenditure limits were unconstitutional. In a six to three decision, the Supreme Court ruled in favor of Randall's interpretation of *Buckley*.

In his opinion, Justice Kennedy argued that there were prudential considerations for his ruling, namely, that the majority opinion arbitrarily placed monetary limits that are not based in pragmatic considerations for how manipulation circumvents any judicial limitations. Specifically, he wrote:

> That new order may cause more problems than it solves. On a routine, operational level the present system requires us to explain why $200 is too restrictive a limit while $1,500 is not. Our own experience gives us little basis to make these judgments, and certainly no traditional or well-established body of law exists to offer guidance. . . . [P]olitical action committees . . . can manipulate the system and attract their own elite power brokers, who operate in ways obscure to the ordinary citizen. Viewed within the legal universe we have ratified and helped create, the result the plurality reaches is correct; given my own skepticism regarding that system and its operation, however, it seems to me appropriate to concur only in the judgment.[35]

There are two forms of the prudential argument in this statement. First, prudentialism is manifest in a pragmatic claim about the impossibility of operationally defining exactly what limit is too restrictive. Second, Justice Kennedy referred to the brand of prudentialism that assessed the "impact of actuality."[36] He showed his concern with the way the Court's decision might impact the ordinary citizen. And, of course, such concern may stem from Justice Kennedy's concern for the ordinary person's participation (and by extension, natural rights) as vital to a healthy democracy.

CONCLUSIONS

In sum, Justice Kennedy is perhaps the most important vote when arguing in front of the Supreme Court because he is often the crucial swing vote. From a rhetorical perspective, earning his vote requires a sophisticated case based on the matrix of textual, precedential, and prudential arguments that are consistent with his ethical perspective on the First Amendment. The legal practitioner may even choose to dedicate a substantial part of his or her argument to Justice Kennedy's ethical perspective in order to allow Justice Kennedy to utilize whatever type of argument is necessary to affirm such a perspective.

This chapter has demonstrated that Justice Kennedy's ethical framework consists of a Hamiltonian skepticism of local authority while he remains committed to protecting his belief in the First Amendment as the protector of freedoms that are essential to a robust and unfettered democratic process that encourages ordinary citizens to engage in the creative power at the heart of intellectual life in America. Through an analysis of his First Amendment decisions, this chapter has specified some of the finer points involved in Justice Kennedy's ethical framework for First Amendment interpretation.

This chapter has suggested that ignoring ethical arguments in the hopes of earning Justice Kennedy's vote on textual, precedential, and/or prudential grounds would be a mistake because his ethical perspective is what grounds his reasoning in First Amendment cases. Specifically, his written opinions on the First Amendment demonstrate that textual arguments are used to overrule precedent. Prudential arguments and textual arguments are employed when precedent is murky and/or challenges Justice Kennedy's ethical perspective. The one thing that remains constant and that can be counted on is his ethical perspective. While textual, precedential, and prudential arguments change from case to case, Justice Kennedy's ethical perspective does not.

The major implication of Justice Kennedy's use of textual, precedential, and prudential arguments is that they all function to reinforce his underlying ethical perspective on the First Amendment. One might even claim that Justice Kennedy is a closet advocate of a higher, natural law that evolves over time. He may never officially say that he interprets the Constitution from a living document perspective; instead, he will likely choose the textual, precedential, and/or prudential arguments that suit him best in the particular case to warrant his ethical position. Perhaps the reason for his cover lies in his own desire to not be associated with judicial activism.

Regardless of the reason, Justice Kennedy's rhetoric in his First Amendment decisions speaks to his commitment to natural rights. The well-known view of natural rights in the Declaration asserts that "all men are created equal, that they are endowed by their Creator with certain unalienable Rights, that among these are Life, Liberty, and the pursuit of Happiness." The next and lesser-known part of the Declaration is perhaps most important for understanding the interpretive framework of Justice Kennedy. That is, "to secure these rights, Governments are instituted among Men, deriving their just powers from the consent of the governed,—That whenever any Form of Government becomes destructive of these ends, it is the Right of the People to alter or to abolish it, and to institute new Government, laying its foundation on such principles and organizing its power in such form, as to them shall seem most likely to effect their Safety and Happiness." This passage best represents Justice Kennedy's view.

He interprets the First Amendment in accordance with a special kind of evolving ethical perspective that is often quite compatible with those who see the Constitution as a living document. For Justice Kennedy, democracy is the means to securing the natural rights alluded to in the Declaration of Independence. More specifically, Justice Kennedy believes that the purpose of the First Amendment is to facilitate democratic participation as the best protector against any other "Form of Government becom[ing] destructive of [natural rights]." As such, the First Amendment preserves democracy as the best vehicle for sustaining life, liberty, safety, and happiness. At the same time, Justice Kennedy maintains an unwavering belief that "the people" are morally conservative and have become more sophisticated in their approach to various issues. Changes in the American ethos from a conservative position may be translated to mean a maturing of natural rights by way of confronting new and innovative circumstances. In this way, Justice Kennedy is an evolving conservative who complicates Bobbitt's interpretive schema by affording a type of ethical interpretation that is not reserved for liberal judicial decision making.

NOTES

1. Kenneth Starr, "Symposium: Speech and the Public Schools after *Morse v. Frederick*: Paper Symposium: Our Libertarian Court: Bong Hits and the Enduring Hamiltonian-Jeffersonian Colloquy," *Lewis and Clark Law Review* (Spring 2008): 7.

2. Lisa K. Parshall, "Embracing the Living Constitution: Justice Anthony M. Kennedy's Move away from a Conservative Methodology of Constitutional Interpretation," *North Carolina Central Law Review* (2007).

3. For example, in the recent case of *Citizen's United v. Federal Elections Commission*, Justice Kennedy wrote the majority opinion of the Court that ruled against limitations placed on corporate and union financing of campaign advertising. According to Justice Kennedy, there were three primary reasons for ruling campaign finance restrictions unconstitutional: "First is the uncertainty caused by the litigating position of the government. . . . Second, substantial time would be required to bring clarity to the application of the statutory provision on these points in order to avoid any chilling effect caused by improper interpretation. . . . Third, is the primary importance of speech itself to the integrity of the election process." Justice Kennedy thus showed that his primary consideration is for the preservation of the election process—a view that we will discuss later in this chapter as consistent with his ethical commitment to an "unfettered democratic process." 558 U.S. ___ (2010), slip op., 15–16.

4. Justice Anthony Kennedy, speech to the general assembly of the Florida Bar's Annual Meeting, June 24, 2005.

5. Starr, "Symposium," 9.

6. Starr, "Symposium," 15.

7. 551 U.S. 393, 423 (2007).

8. His commitment to creativity and intellectual life was recently reinforced in his concurring opinion in *Christian Legal Society Chapter v. Martinez*. He wrote, "Law students come from many different backgrounds and have but three years to meet each other and develop their skills. They do so by participating in a community that teaches them how to create arguments in a convincing, rational, and respectful manner and to express doubt and disagreement in a professional way. . . . A vibrant dialogue is not possible if students wall themselves off from opposing points of view." 561 U.S. ___ (2010), slip op., 4.

9. Bobbitt, *Constitutional Fate*, 94.

10. I am reminded of Aristotle's enthymeme, a deductive argument based on probable premises that requires the audience to fill in the most obvious premise. Perhaps the ethical claims are the suppressed premises of Justice Kennedy's constitutional arguments.

11. Bobbitt, *Constitutional Fate*, 25–26.

12. Justice Anthony Kennedy, "Federal Judges Convene Civic Education Summit," *The Third Branch*, available at www.uscourts.gov/ttb/july02ttb/convene.html (accessed August, 1, 2009), paragraph 3.

13. 505 U.S. 577, 595 (1992).

14. 505 U.S. 577, 595 (1992).

15. 505 U.S. 577, 598–99 (1992).

16. 540 U.S. 93, 341 (2003).

17. 512 U.S. 687, 731 (1994).

18. 552 U.S. 196, 212–13 (2008).

19. Bobbitt, *Constitutional Fate*, 43.

20. 491 U.S. 781, 803 (1989).

21. 505 U.S. 672, 703 (1992).

22. 505 U.S. 672, 696–709 (1992).

23. 518 U.S. 727 (1996).

24. 518 U.S. 727, 782 (1996).

25. 523 U.S. 666, 682 (1998).

26. 523 U.S. 666, 682–83 (1998).

27. 535 U.S. 234, 244–56 (2002).

28. 536 U.S. 765, 794–96 (2002).

29. Bobbitt, *Constitutional Fate*, 67.

30. Bobbitt, *Constitutional Fate*, 66.

31. 491 U.S. 397, 421 (1989).

32. 515 U.S. 819, 836–37 (1995).

33. This is the remand version of *Ashcroft v. ACLU.*

34. 535 U.S. 564, 602 (2002).

35. 548 U.S. 230, 264–65 (2006).

36. This references Justice Frankfurter's description of the prudential argument at the beginning of this section.

Chapter Seven

Associate Justice Souter

Megan Loden

> The first lesson, simple as it is, is that whatever court we're in, whatever we are doing, at the end of our task some human is going to be affected. Some human life is going to be changed by what we do. And so we better use every power of our hearts and minds to get those rulings right.—Associate Justice David Souter[1]

When President George H. W. Bush nominated David Hackett Souter to the Supreme Court on July 25, 1990, it came as a surprise to many. Bush had originally planned on nominating Clarence Thomas to Justice Brennan's open seat, but ultimately decided to nominate Souter instead due to Thomas's "lack of experience"[2] at that juncture. Ironically, Souter was only two months into his post on the First Circuit Court of Appeals; nonetheless, he was confirmed in the Senate by a vote of ninety to nine on October 9, 1990. Soon after his confirmation, Souter was called "an enigma, maybe with a capital E,"[3] due in part to the criticism and praise he received from both politicians and media commentators during the nomination process. During his first few years on the Court, Souter quickly disappointed conservatives by aligning himself with the liberal side of the Court on some cases, a practice that became more pronounced the longer he remained on the Court. What Souter did not do, however, was engage in Washington's social scene, making him not just an enigma on the bench, but a peculiarly quiet member of the establishment. "David H. Souter had no agenda 19 years ago when he took his seat on the Supreme Court, but he did have a goal: not to become a creature of Washington, a captive of the privileges and power that came with the job he was entitled to hold for the rest of his life."[4]

However, this chapter is not about Souter's personal life—which he kept from the media—or even his rumored daily lunch of yogurt and an entire apple (core and all). This chapter is about the Harvard Law School graduate and Rhodes Scholar's key opinions in many First Amendment areas. A close examination of Souter's opinions reveals their importance, and how rhetoric functions within them, realizing that "The hallmark of rhetoric as an art is that it is audience based."[5] The object of this chapter is to profile Justice Souter's rhetoric during his nomination hearings, and in significant First Amendment cases, to present a conceptual (and critical) understanding of his rhetorical frame regarding First Amendment case law. This chapter will use the theory of Philip Bobbitt from his 1991 book *Constitutional Interpretation* and other works.[6] More specifically, this chapter will discuss how Souter's rhetoric in three significant First Amendment cases fits with three of Bobbitt's modalities of argument: historical, doctrinal, and prudential. The chapter will conclude with additional patterns and implications of Souter's rhetoric on the Court as a whole and, finally, discuss Associate Justice Sonia Sotomayor, who replaced Souter on the bench while this book was being written.

SOUTER'S NOMINATION HEARINGS

When Souter was nominated by the president to the Supreme Court on July 25, 1990, many were surprised. Analysis of his nomination hearings reveals this surprise mirrored not only in the rhetoric of those questioning Souter, but in his responses. Souter's surprise about his nomination is initially expressed in his opening statements:

> I came to the notice of probably most of you on this committee when I stood next to the President and tried-again, with great difficulty, that afternoon in late July to express some sense of the honor that I felt, despite the surprise and even shock of the event to me. . . . I mentioned to you the great surprise that I had on July 23[7] in finding myself where I was. I certainly found very quickly that I had no reason to be surprised at the interest which the United States and, actually, a good deal of the world suddenly took in me as an individual.[8]

Souter would maintain his humble confidence throughout his nomination hearings. He explained that his experiences in public legal service were what taught him how the government "really works" and that his tenure as a trial judge exposed him to the "condition of people."[9] His comments persuaded many that he was suited for the Court.

It was not until the concluding lines of his opening statement that Souter provided the first glimpse into the modalities that he would later utilize: "I am conscious [of those two lessons] as I sit here today, suddenly finding myself the nominee of the President of the United States to undertake the greatest responsibility that any judge in our Republic can undertake: The responsibility to join with eight other people, to make the promises of the Constitution a reality for our time, and to preserve that Constitution for the generations that will follow us after we are gone from here."[10]

In this passage, Souter hinted that he would embrace the historical and doctrinal modalities of argument, ones on which he would heavily rely during his tenure on the Court.

Throughout the remainder of the nomination hearings, the toughest questions Souter faced came from the nine senators who would vote against Souter, including Ted Kennedy and John Kerry, Democrats of Massachusetts. These senators, along with others, attempted to portray Souter as a right-wing Republican whose professional record provoked little controversy and no paper trail. President Bush had publicly mentioned that Souter's lack of paper trail was a positive trait, but the senators disagreed. Souter was asked difficult questions regarding his position on *Roe v. Wade*,[11] *Griswold v. Connecticut*,[12] and *Oregon v. Mitchell*[13] (among others); Souter was consistent with his responses, making multiple references to the framers' intent and using the structural modality as a moderating tactic to shift discussions from one amendment to another. In a response to a question from Chairman (now vice president) Joseph Biden (D-Delaware) regarding his "school" of thought for reading the Constitution, Justice Souter responded by saying that "in any interpretive enterprise, I have to start with the text and I do not have a basis for doubting that somewhat obvious and straightforward meaning of the text."[14] The following day, in response to a question from Senator Kennedy regarding the same topic, Souter explained, "I think the reasons then for the remarkable and blessed endurance of the American Constitution are extraordinarily pragmatic reasons. It rests upon a recognition of where its power forms and it is structured with recognition that power will be abused unless it is limited and divided and restrained."[15] As many of his critics predicted, Souter did not say much in his nomination hearings that surprised the Senate, but instead gave confident, diplomatic responses that relied heavily on the document which he had been nominated to interpret. Thus, Souter's rhetoric in his nomination hearings foreshadowed his vision for the Supreme Court.

ROSENBERGER AND THE HISTORIC MODALITY

Closely related to the doctrine of original intent, Bobbitt's historical modality implies a strategy that relies on the intentions of the framers of the Constitution. *Rosenberger v. Rector and Visitors of the University of Virginia* of 1995 concerned the University of Virginia's practice of providing student organizations with money for the printing costs of their publications.[16] This money came from the university's student activity fee (SAF), a mandatory fee imposed on students. One of the university's student organizations was denied funding for its magazine, *Wide Awake: A Christian Perspective at the University of Virginia*. The organization claimed that its free speech rights were being violated, and in a five to four decision, the Supreme Court ruled that the University of Virginia, a public institution, inappropriately denied funding to this student organization. The majority based its ruling on a denial of free press as opposed to addressing the establishment clause issue. Dodging this issue may have inspired Justice Souter, in one of his earliest First Amendment opinions, to write a dissenting opinion. He stated, "The Court today, for the first time, approves direct funding of core religions activities by an arm of the State. It does so, however, only after erroneous treatment of some familiar principles of law implementing the First Amendment's Establishment and Speech Clauses, and by viewing the very funds in question as beyond the reach of the Establishment Clause's funding restrictions as such."[17]

From the very beginning of this opinion, Souter makes it clear that the majority opinion violates the intent of the framers. Referencing such past cases as *Wolman v. Walter*,[18] *Meek v. Pittenger*,[19] and *Tilton v. Richardson*,[20] Souter explains that "in the absence of a forthright disavowal, one can only assume that the Court does not mean to eliminate one half of the Establishment Clause's purpose."[21] With reference to the purpose of the establishment clause, Justice Souter resurrects the intent of the framers' rhetoric. Souter concludes his dissent by stating, "Since I cannot see the future I cannot tell whether today's decision portends much more than making a shambles out of student activity fees in college."[22] Souter mocks the majority's decision by descending from his legal rhetoric and arguing that if the majority's interpretation is not from original intent, it is "making a shambles" out of the case.

In *Constitutional Fate*, Bobbitt wrote, "When one argues a court's experience with parsing documents, or its time for reflection, or its relative institution from political pressure, and so forth . . . one is already committed to the view that enforcing rules derived from the constitutional text is the legitimate task at hand."[23] In *Rosenberger v. Virginia*, Souter is doing just that by claiming that the majority is incorrectly interpreting the original intent of the Constitution, and therefore not "enforcing rules derived from the constitutional text." Also noteworthy, in the rhetoric of his decision in *Rosenberger*, Souter showed his conservative side, which was later sometimes superseded by his liberal tendencies.

GARCETTI AND THE DOCTRINAL MODALITY

Garcetti v. Ceballos (2006) contains one of Souter's lesser-known First Amendment Supreme Court opinions.[24] However, it is important to understanding his doctrinal argumentation. The case concerns whether the First Amendment protects a public employee's on-duty expression, in this case a deputy district attorney who wrote and circulated a memorandum suggesting that a deputy sheriff lied in a search warrant affidavit. The Court ruled, in a five to four decision, that because the district attorney's statements were made from his position as a public employee, rather than as a private citizen, he had no First Amendment protection from his employers. Justice Souter led the dissenters. He begins his argument by referencing what is the first of almost thirty cases quoted in the dissent:

> The significant, albeit qualified, protection of public employees who irritate the government is understood to flow from the First Amendment, in part, because a government paycheck does nothing to eliminate the value to an individual speaking on public matters, and there is no good reason for categorically discounting a speaker's interest in commenting on a matter of public concern just because the government employs him. Still, the First Amendment safeguard rests on something more.[25] . . . "Government employees are often in the best position to know what ails the agencies for which they work."[26]

Using Bobbitt's doctrinal modality, that is, a heavy reliance on precedent, Souter's dissenting opinion took critical aim at the majority's interpretation of existing doctrines. "Souter's forceful dissent in *Garcetti v. Ceballos* . . . offered up a strong case against the majority's 'categorical exclusion of First Amendment protection' for whistle-blowers."[27] Moreover, Souter consistently uses phrases such as "the key to understanding the difference between this case and . . . ," "the fallacy of the majority's misunderstanding," and, finally, "defined in the classic sense"[28] to reaffirm his reliance on past cases, and to protest the majority discouraging speech from public employees that might unearth bad practices.

Even in the footnotes of his dissenting opinion, Souter writes, "According to the majority's logic, the litigation it encourages would have the unfortunate result of demanding permanent judicial intervention in the conduct of governmental operations."[29] Immediately following this statement, Souter lists cases where these practices were struck down, extending his doctrinal argument. In this way, Souter played a significant role in ensuring that the Court maintained its precedence in its interpretation of the First Amendment.[30] As Bobbitt explained, precedential rhetoric, like Souter's in *Garcetti v. Ceballos*, is the essence of doctrinal argumentation by members of the Court.

Precedents are established to support not only the Constitution, but its constituents. Interestingly, in the aftermath of *Garcetti v. Ceballos*, a slew of public employees who reported wrongdoing lost their cases. "It would not be surprising if at some point the Court revisited this matter, and turned to Souter's dissent for guidance."[31]

COHEN AND THE PRUDENTIAL MODALITY

Souter also finds the prudential modality appealing.[32] Bobbitt explained that the prudential modality "is derived from a calculus of costs and benefits, when the facts are taken into account."[33] Essentially, this modality takes a balanced approach, trying to determine the best outcome for a complex situation. *Cohen v. Cowles Media Company* (1991) reveals Justice Souter doing just that.

In one of his first *free-press* cases (not many came along during his tenure), Souter dissented in another five to four opinion. *Cohen v. Cowles Media Company* was a case in which the Supreme Court held that freedom of the press does not exempt journalists from generally applicable laws. During the 1982 Minnesota gubernatorial race, petitioner Cohen, who was associated with one party's campaign, gave court records concerning another party's candidate for lieutenant governor to a reporter after receiving a promise of confidentiality.

Justice Souter's dissent argued for a textbook cost-benefit analysis. Souter wrote, "Nor can I accept the majority's position that we may dispense with balancing because the burden on publication is in a sense 'self-imposed' by the newspaper's voluntary promise of confidentiality."[34] The emphasis on balance indicates a controversy that has "weight" on both sides (in which the public interest is given more weight in the decision-making calculus); thus the public interest is addressed as the heart of the decision-making calculus:

> The importance of this public interest is integral to the balance that should be struck in this case. There can be no doubt that the fact of Cohen's identity expanded the universe of information relevant to the choice faced by Minnesota voters in that State's 1982 gubernatorial election, the publication of which was thus of the sort quintessentially subject to strict First Amendment protection. . . . Because I believe the State's interest in enforcing a newspaper's promise of confidentiality insufficient to outweigh the interest in unfettered publication of the information revealed in this case, I respectfully dissent.[35]

In this short dissent, Souter effectively argued that the public interest out-weighed the interest in protecting the contract. This utilization of the pruden-tial modality parallels Bobbitt's conceptualization of the term and further frames Souter's overarching view of the First Amendment during his time on the Court.

CONCLUSIONS

After analyzing the historical, doctrinal, and prudential modalities employed by Justice Souter, it is easier to frame his First Amendment dissents and general perception of the Court. David Souter wrote his college senior thesis on the jurist Oliver Wendell Holmes, Jr., and throughout his tenure on the Supreme Court many compared Souter to Holmes, for a variety of reasons.[36] Notably, like Holmes, Souter was "at his First Amendment best in his dis-senting opinions."[37] There are many possible reasons as to why this was the case, but an easy answer is that it was Souter's historical, doctrinal, and prudential modalities, which blurred the lines between constitutionalist and judicial activist and conservative and liberal readings of the Constitution.

In one instance, *National Endowment for the Arts v. Finley*,[38] Souter's solitary dissent is noted to be one of the best on artistic expression and the problems created when such expression is squelched by discrimination. The case dealt with the National Endowment for the Arts's (NEA's) discretion to award financial grants. In his lone dissent, Souter sympathized with defen-dant Karen Finley, one of a group of artists that sought equal treatment from the NEA. Souter argued that that freedom of *artistic* expression can be dis-criminatory if the guidelines for grants are too vague and thus can be used in arbitrary ways.

These opinions are the ones for which Souter will go down in history, dissecting the law and often working "outside the lines." In his 2007 book *The Nine*, legal expert Jeffrey Toobin wrote that "[Souter] believed that law existed to preserve the stability of society and that adherence to precedent best guaranteed a limited and predictable role for the judiciary."[39] Souter just happened to do much of his preserving while disagreeing with the Court majority. Statistically, in First Amendment cases, Souter dissented 59 per-cent of the time, higher than any of the current justices, a testament to just how much of an enigma he was.[40] This is not to say that Souter did not have an impact on majority and concurring opinions. He is often referenced for leading the court's majority in the infamous 2005 *McCreary County v. ACLU*,[41] where the Court ordered the removal of a Ten Commandments display from a Kentucky courthouse, or for his upholding of *Roe v. Wade*[42] in 1992. But, as a whole, Souter "did his thing" for the First Amendment and did it a little differently than everyone else.

On April 30, 2009, National Public Radio (NPR) was the first media source to announce that Justice Souter would be retiring at the conclusion of Court's term. Per his "no camera" policies, Souter did not immediately comment on this news, but on the final day of the Court's 2008–2009 term, June 29, 2009, Souter wrapped up what was a nineteen-year tenure on the bench. There are many differing opinions of Souter, his personal life, and his First Amendment dissents, but Souter's general perception of the Court and the Constitution was clear. First Amendment Legal Center correspondent Tony Mauro summarizes it this way: "Souter has left a significant mark on the Court's First Amendment jurisprudence. It is not the legacy of a First Amendment absolutist like Hugo Black, or a tireless First Amendment champion like William Brennan Jr. It is the record of a practical common-law judge who balanced the competing interests and precedents before him and came out with the most sensible answer he could devise."[43]

INTRODUCING ASSOCIATE JUSTICE SOTOMAYOR

Factors in Justice Souter's decision to retire no doubt included the election of President Obama, who was more than likely going to appoint a successor attuned to the moderate-to-liberal principles Souter followed during his late tenure. On May 26, 2009, President Obama nominated Judge Sonia Sotomayor to the Supreme Court, which would make her the Court's second sitting female, the third female ever appointed, and the first-ever Hispanic justice.[44] Prior to her nomination, Sotomayor was a judge for the Second Circuit Court of Appeals, and before that, a judge of the District Court for the Southern District of New York. Sotomayor assumed her role on the Court on August 6, 2009, after a Senate confirmation vote of sixty-eight to thirty-one.

Although the sixty-eight to thirty-one vote was considered a defeat by some conservatives, "Republicans contend that they had [succeeded] in framing the confirmation debate in a way that could influence Obama's future nominations through the federal judiciary, including the Supreme Court if vacancies arise."[45] The vote was a culmination of many elements of the career path of Sotomayor, whose personal narrative quickly gained attention from the American public. Sotomayor was raised by her widowed mother in the South Bronx housing projects, attended Princeton University and Yale Law School, and then began her ascent through the federal judiciary after spending time as a judge of the United States District Court in Southern New York and the Second Circuit Court of Appeals. President Obama referred to her narrative after her confirmation hearings by stating, "Core American ideals—justice, equality, and opportunity—are the very ideals that have made Judge Sotomayor's own uniquely American journey possible."[46]

However, the exploration of her quintessential American story did not shed much light on Sotomayor's past, present, and future regarding First Amendment law. During her nomination hearings, Sotomayor was heavily questioned on her positions on First Amendment issues and then criticized for her "roundabout" answers. For example, in the opening statement of her nomination hearings, Sotomayor stated:

> In the past month, many Senators have asked me about my judicial philosophy. It is simple: fidelity to the law. The task of a judge is not to make the law—it is to apply the law. And it is clear, I believe, that my record in two courts reflects my rigorous commitment to interpreting the Constitution according to its terms; interpreting statutes according to their terms and Congress' intent; and hewing faithfully to precedents established by the Supreme Court and my Circuit Court. . . . That is why I generally structure my opinions by setting out what the law requires and then by explaining why a contrary position, sympathetic or not, is accepted or rejected.[47]

While Sotomayor referred to the doctrinal and historical modalities that Souter employed, in this statement Sotomayor also uses phrases such as "I believe" and "generally," which led the Judiciary Committee's members to request more specific responses. She satisfied the leading Democrats on the committee. On the final day of questioning, for example, Senator John Kerry of Massachusetts asked, "Will this nominee protect the civil rights and liberties enshrined in the Constitution and protected by law that we have fought so long and hard for? Will this nominee support Congress's power to enact critical legislation? I have concluded that she is someone with whom our rights and freedoms are safe."[48] The nomination hearings were followed with a few days of debate on the Senate floor. Some senators claimed there were still unanswered questions regarding Sotomayor's stance on affirmative action, abortion, and other issues. However, Sotomayor's stance on the First Amendment might be characterized as mainstream:

> Judge Sotomayor was part of a unanimous panel in 94.1% of the First Amendment cases in which she participated,[49] more frequently than the Circuit's rate of 90.9%. She dissented in only 3 of her 68 First Amendment cases, or in less than 5% of these decisions. Additionally, in cases involving a First Amendment claim, Judge Sotomayor voted to overturn the challenged action 25 percent of the time. However, she voted to overturn the lower court or agency's decision less frequently than the circuit average—in 36.8% of her decisions as opposed to a circuit rate of 43.8 percent.[50]

On August 17, 2009, Justice Sotomayor cast her first vote from the Supreme Court bench by joining three "liberal" justices in an unsuccessful attempt to stop a pending execution for Jason Getsy of Ohio on an appeal from the Court of Appeals.[51] On September 9, 2009, oral arguments for Sotomayor's first major Supreme Court decision began. This key campaign finance case, *Citizens United v. Federal Election Commission*,[52] dealt with the First Amendment rights of corporations and unions. The lower courts had denied Citizens United's motion for a "preliminary injunction to stop the Federal Election Commission (FEC) from enforcing provisions of the Bipartisan Campaign Reform Act, or McCain-Feingold Act, which prevented the film *Hillary: The Movie* from being shown on cable stations during the 2008 Democratic Primaries."[53] Essentially, the Supreme Court's majority struck down a provision of the McCain–Feingold Act that prevented for-profit and not-for-profit corporations and unions from broadcasting "electioneering communications" within a thirty-day window before a presidential primary and a sixty-day window before the general elections. The decision overruled *Austin v. Michigan Chamber of Commerce*[54] and partially overruled *McConnell v. Federal Election Commission*.[55]

The dissent, written by Justice Stevens (see chapter 4), was joined by Justice Ginsburg, Justice Breyer, and Justice Sotomayor. The opinion concurred with the Court's decision to sustain disclosure provisions in the law; that is, contributors and funders must be disclosed by campaigns. But it "dissented with the principal holding the majority opinion"[56] with regard to allowing unions and corporations to participate in campaign advertising. The ninety-page dissent held that the Court's ruling "threatens to undermine the integrity of elected institutions across the nation. The path it has taken to reach its outcome will, I fear, do damage to this institution."[57]

Similar to many of Justice Souter's dissents, Justice Stevens relied predominantly on the historical and doctrinal modalities in his opinion. For example, in the second paragraph of the opinion, he states, "The basic premise underlying the Court's ruling is its iteration, and constant reiteration, of the proposition that the First Amendment bars regulatory distinctions based on a speaker's identity, including its 'identity' as a corporation. While that glittering generality has rhetorical appeal, it is not a correct statement of the law."[58] A similar sentiment is expressed at the conclusion of the opinion.

> Today's decision is backwards in many senses. It elevates the majority's agenda over the litigants' submissions, facial attacks over as-applied claims, broad constitutional theories over narrow statutory grounds, individual dissenting opinions over precedential holdings, assertion over tradition, absolutism over empiricism, rhetoric over reality. Our colleagues have arrived at the conclusion that *Austin* must be overruled and that [it] is facially unconstitutional only

after mischaracterizing both the reach and rationale of those authorities, and after bypassing or ignoring rules of judicial restraint used to cabin the Court's lawmaking power.[59]

In both of these excerpts, Stevens emphasized the importance of precedent and a solid interpretation of not only the First Amendment but the Constitution in general. While Sotomayor did not write an opinion (nor, as of this writing, has she on any First Amendment cases since her tenure on the Court began), her decision to side with Stevens places her toward the left of the bench.

On June 21, 2010, Sotomayor revealed more of her biases in another First Amendment decision by joining with Justice Breyer's dissenting opinion. The case, *Holder v. Humanitarian Law Project*,[60] revisited a 1996 law that makes aiding terrorists a criminal act. Specifically, the case (on a six to three decision) rejected the plaintiffs' claims that U.S. law prohibiting the knowing provision of "material support or resources"[61] to foreign organizations that engage in terrorist activity constitutes an infringement on free speech and association rights under the First Amendment. The dissent reads, "I cannot agree with the Court's conclusion that the Constitution permits the Government to prosecute the plaintiffs criminally for engaging in coordinated teaching and advocacy furthering the designated organizations' lawful political objectives."[62] While Sotomayor did not author an opinion, her decision to side with Breyer supports previous analysis in this chapter that she mirrors Souter in his reliance on the historical, doctrinal, and prudential modes of argument.

The bottom line is that Sotomayor will likely continue to vote as if she were a liberal Souter. At the time of this writing, after participating in twenty-two Supreme Court decisions in which there was at least one dissenting vote, Justice Sotomayor has revealed her liberal tendencies. She voted with Justice Ginsburg 82 percent of the time, while voting with justices Alito, Scalia, and Thomas 41 percent of the time. Her dissent in campaign reform legislation places her on the opposite side of the fence from the "conservative five" on this important First Amendment issue. If her short record is any indication, Sotomayor will continue to embrace historical, doctrinal, and prudential modes of argument.[63] In a handful of notable cases she presided over in the past, including *Pappas v. Guiliani*,[64] *United States v. Quattrone*,[65] and *Dominger v. Niehoff*,[66] Sotomayor relies heavily on precedent and does not seem concerned with whether she is being called a liberal or criticized for relying on a strict reading of the Constitution: "Critics from the right continue to spout slogans about neutrality and objectivity in reasoning, as if anyone could set aside all they know and have lived through in their assessments of case. . . . Judge Sotomayor has simply stated up front what most of us know full well: identify affects experience, and experience makes a difference in our judgment."[67]

NOTES

1. *Hearings before the Senate Committee on the Judiciary United States Senate One Hundred First Congress First Session on the Nomination of David H. Souter to Be an Associate Justice of the Supreme Court of the United States*, September 13–19, 1990 (Washington, DC: U.S. Government Printing Office, 1991), 49.
   2. See "Anchoring the Court's New Center," *New York Times*, June 3, 1991: 18–21.
   3. Transcripts of interview with First Amendment lawyer Bruce Sandford, October 1990, available at www.firstamendmentcenter.org (accessed September 1, 2009).
   4. See "Justice Souter: Justice Unbound," *New York Times*, May 3, 2009.
   5. Craig R. Smith, chapter 1 of this book.
   6. Bobbitt, *Constitutional Interpretation*.
   7. Souter actually found out about his nomination from President Bush two days before it was formally announced.
   8. *Hearings on the Nomination of David H. Souter*, 49.
   9. *Hearings on the Nomination of David H. Souter*, 49–50.
   10. *Hearings on the Nomination of David H. Souter*, 51.
   11. 410 U.S. 113 (1973).
   12. 381 U.S. 479 (1965).
   13. 400 U.S. 112 (1970).
   14. *Hearings on the Nomination of David H. Souter*, 73.
   15. *Hearings on the Nomination of David H. Souter*, 76.
   16. 515 U.S. 819 (1995).
   17. See transcripts of 515 U.S. 819 (1995), available from www.law.cornell.edu/author.php.souter.
   18. 433 U.S. 229 (1977).
   19. 421 U.S. 349 (1975).
   20. 403 U.S. 672 (1971).
   21. See transcripts of 515 U.S. 819 (1995), available at http://www.law.cornell.edu/author.php.souter.
   22. See transcripts of 515 U.S. 819 (1995), available at http://www.law.cornell.edu/author.php.souter.
   23. Bobbitt, *Constitutional Interpretation*, 17.
   24. 547 U.S. 410 (2006).
   25. See transcripts of 547 U.S. 410 (2006), available at http://www.law.cornell.edu/author.php.souter.
   26. Souter used this quotation from Waters v. Churchill, 511 U.S. 661 (1994).
   27. From "Justice Souter and the First Amendment," First Amendment Center Online Symposium, available at http://www.firstamendmentcenter.org (accessed September 7, 2009).
   28. See transcripts of 547 U.S. 410 (2006), available at http://www.law.cornell.edu/author.php.souter.
   29. See transcripts of 547 U.S. 410 (2006), available at http://www.law.cornell.edu/author.php.souter.
   30. See transcripts of 547 U.S. 410 (2006), available at http://www.law.cornell.edu/author.php.souter.
   31. From "Justice Souter and the First Amendment," First Amendment Center Online Symposium, available at http://www.firstamendmentcenter.org (accessed September 7, 2009).
   32. See transcripts of 501 U.S. 663 (1991), available at http://www.law.cornell.edu/author.php.souter.

33. Bobbitt, *Constitutional Interpretation*, 17.

34. See transcripts of 501 U.S. 663 (1991), available at http://www.law.cornell.edu/author.php.souter.

35. See transcripts of 501 U.S. 663 (1991), available at http://www.law.cornell.edu/author.php.souter.

36. From "Justice Souter, Justice Holmes, the First Amendment, and Yankee Independence," First Amendment Center Online Symposium, available at http://www.firstamendmentcenter.org (accessed September 7, 2009).

37. From "Justice Souter, Justice Holmes, the First Amendment, and Yankee Independence," First Amendment Center Online Symposium, available at http://www.firstamendmentcenter.org (accessed September 7, 2009).

38. 524 U.S. 569 (1998).

39. Jeffrey Toobin, *The Nine: Inside the Secret World of the Supreme Court* (New York: Doubleday, 2007), 276.

40. Lee Epstein, Jeffrey A. Segal, Harold J. Spaeth, and Thomas G. Walker, *The Supreme Court Compendium: Data, Decisions, and Development* (Washington, DC: CQ Press, 2007), 625.

41. 545 U.S. 844 (2005).

42. 410 U.S. 113 (1973).

43. From "Justice Souter's First Amendment Legacy: Not Absolutionist," First Amendment Center Online Symposium, available at http://www.firstamendmentcenter.org (accessed September 7, 2009).

44. There is a debate about whether Associate Justice Cardozo, who sat on the Court from 1932 to 1937, was the first Hispanic. Cardozo's ancestors were of Portuguese descent.

45. See "Sotomayor Wins Confirmation," *Washington Post*, August 7, 2009: A1.

46. "A Breakthrough Judge: What She Always Wanted," *New York Times*, August 25, 2009: A1.

47. *Hearings before the Senate Committee on the Judiciary United States Senate One Hundred Second Congress First Session on the Nomination of Sonia M. Sotomayor to Be an Associate Justice of the Supreme Court of the United States*, July 13–16, 2009, available at http://cspan.org/Supreme-Court-Sotomayor-Senate-Confirmation-Hearings.aspx.

48. *Hearings on the Nomination of Sonia M. Sotomayor*, 131.

49. Referencing decision by the Second Circuit Court of Appeals.

50. "Judging Sonia Sotomayor," *Time*, July 13, 2009: 33.

51. "Sotomayor on Losing End in Ohio Man's Death Appeal," Associated Press, August 17, 2009.

52. 558 U.S. ___ (2010).

53. "Justices to Revisit 'Hillary' Documentary," *New York Times*, August 29, 2009.

54. 494 U.S. 652(1990).

55. 540 U.S. 93 (2003).

56. "Justices to Revisit 'Hillary' Documentary."

57. See transcripts of 558 U.S. ___ (2010), available at http://www.law.cornell.edu/supct/html/08-205.ZS.html.

58. See transcripts of 558 U.S. ___ (2010), available at http://www.law.cornell.edu/supct/html/08-205.ZS.html.

59. See transcripts of 558 U.S. ___ (2010), available at http://www.law.cornell.edu/supct/html/08-205.ZS.html.

60. 561 U.S. ___ (2010).

61. See transcripts of 561 U.S. ___ (2010), available at http://www.law.cornell.edu/supct/html/08-205.ZS.html.

62. See transcripts of 561 U.S. ___ (2010), available at http://www.law.cornell.edu/supct/html/08-205.ZS.html.

63. See, for example, her opinions for the unanimous Supreme Court in the following cases: *Matrixx Initiatives, Inc., et al., Petitioners v. James Siracusano et al.* (563 U.S. ____ (2011) Sip. Op.), *Chase Bank USA, n.a., Petitioner v. James A. McCoy, individually and on behalf of all others similarly situated* (562 U.S. ___ (2011) Slip. Op.

64. 290 F. 3d 143 (2002).
65. 402 F. 3d 304 (2005).
66. 554 F. 3d 56 (2009).
67. "Sotomayor's Reasoning," *Huffington Post*, August 9, 2009: 11.

Chapter Eight

Associate Justice Breyer

Amy L. Heyse

Associate Justice Stephen Breyer was appointed to the Supreme Court in 1994 by President Bill Clinton. A careful review of Justice Breyer's rhetoric reveals that, like Justice John Paul Stevens and Justice David Souter, he consistently frames his decisions with precedential, ethical, and prudential arguments. To demonstrate this method of decision making, this chapter offers a thematic analysis of the claims Breyer made during his 1994 nomination hearings as well as his First Amendment opinions, dissents, and concurrences from 1994 to the close of the 2008–2009 session. In order to closely examine each type of argument, the chapter is divided into four sections. The first section analyzes Justice Breyer's precedential rhetoric, the second section examines his ethical arguments, and the third studies Justice Breyer's prudential reasoning. Each section also considers the metaphors Justice Breyer employs to support his positions. The chapter concludes in the final section with a discussion of the potential implications of Justice Breyer's rhetorical framing of First Amendment cases.

PRECEDENTIAL RHETORIC

Breyer has employed a precedential or doctrinal modality with his rhetoric ever since his nomination. The precedential modality, as Smith explains, relies on "'doctrinal' rulings [that] have been established to guide the Court, normally by substantial majorities."[1] In other words, the precedential rhetor appeals to past "doctrines" and decisions in order to justify and support his or her position in present cases. Bobbitt pointed out, however, that "doctrinal arguments are not confined to arguments originating in case law; there are also precedents of other institutions, e.g., the practices of earlier Presidents as well as the various corollaries incident to fashioning rules on the basis of precedent."[2] Furthermore, the Court is obliged to overrule itself when it determines that a precedent "was wrongly decided and should not be applied."[3] The precedential modality is clearly evident in Justice Breyer's judicial rhetoric.

In his 1994 nomination statement, Breyer appealed to precedent when he referred to the "grand tradition" of the Court and promised to honor "the guarantees of fairness and of freedom that the Constitution provides."[4] The U.S. Constitution is, of course, the penultimate judicial doctrine to cite when arguing from precedent, but one may also rely on previous laws, rulings, and regulations, as Breyer explained:

> The opportunity to study law as a whole helped me understand that everything in the law is related to every other thing, and always, as Holmes pointed out, that whole law reflects not so much logic, as history and experience. Academic lawyers, practicing lawyers, government lawyers, and judges, in my opinion, have a special responsibility to try to understand how different parts of that seamless web of the law interact with each other, and how legal decisions will actually work in practice to affect people and to help them.[5]

The "history and experience" of law as well as previous "legal decisions" would guide Breyer's judgments, not just "logic." Put differently, precedent would help Breyer make decisions that would "affect and help" people in the present and future—a statement that hints at his ethical perspective as well.

Justice Breyer continued to express a precedential stance once seated on the bench. In his opinion in *Tory v. Cochran* (2005), Justice Breyer cited multiple California court cases and previous U.S. court decisions as warrants for his decision. This libel case concerned an injunction against Ulysses Tory to stop picketing Johnnie L. Cochran, Jr.'s office with defaming signs. Cochran—famed defense attorney for high-profile clients such as O. J. Simpson—had sued and was awarded an injunction against Tory—a former client of his—for marching in front of Cochran's office holding signs accusing his one-time attorney of thieving and accepting bribes. Justice Breyer cited California cases such as *People v. Gonzalez* and U.S. court cases such as *Firefighters v. Stotts* to argue that Cochran's death during the hearing made the injunction a violation of Tory's free speech and the case should therefore be returned to the California courts.[6]

Justice Breyer also made arguments from precedent in the complex ruling of *McConnell v. Federal Election Commission* (2003) by referring to a "65-year-old FCC regulation" and arguing that the Court must "follow the Government's regulation-related references to the relevant regulatory records, related FCC regulatory conclusions, and the FCC's enforcement experience."[7] Brought by Senator Mitch McConnell, then head of the Republican Senatorial Campaign Committee, the *McConnell* case questioned the constitutionality of the BCRA of 2002. The Court, including Justice Breyer, disagreed with the plaintiff's claim that the BCRA infringed on First Amendment rights by limiting the amount of soft money that may be used to register voters.

Even as recently as January 21, 2009, it was evident that Justice Breyer had maintained his precedential stance. Writing the opinion for a unanimous Court ruling in *Locke v. Karass*, Justice Breyer plainly appealed to precedent: "Prior decisions of this Court frame the question before us."[8] In fact, Justice Breyer organized the entire opinion around legal precedents, noting previous Supreme Court cases and even citing specific judges, such as Justice John Marshall.[9] The First Amendment issue at hand in *Locke v. Karass* was whether or not the costs of national litigation by a national union may be chargeable to local nonmembers without violating their free speech. Justice Breyer concluded that "The record then leads us to find that the national litigation expenses before us are both appropriately related to collective bargaining and reciprocal. Consequently, consistent with our precedent, those expenses are chargeable."[10] The concern with consistency of "the record" from past to present is deeply embedded in the precedential perspective.

Justice Breyer's most explicit and elaborate defense of legal precedent, though, may be found in the 2006 ruling in *Randall v. Sorrell*. In this case, the plaintiffs argued that a Vermont law, which placed an unusually strict cap on financial donations made to politicians, violated free speech. The Court agreed, but in such a way as to preserve precedents that had allowed caps on fundraising that were "reasonable." Early in the opinion, Justice Breyer explained that his decision was based on the "well-established precedent" of *Buckley* v. *Valeo*, which the plaintiffs charged was "a controlling—and unfavorable—precedent."[11] Much of Justice Breyer's opinion was devoted to explaining and defending *Buckley* as a valuable precedent and as a valid basis of his ruling: "Over the last 30 years, in considering the constitutionality of a host of different campaign finance statutes, this Court has repeatedly adhered to *Buckley*'s constraints."[12] To support his assertion, Justice Breyer listed seven cases that the Court decided based on *Buckley*, adding yet another layer of precedent to his argument.

The *Randall* opinion is also significant because of Justice Breyer's explanation of stare decisis, or "the basic legal principle that commands judicial respect for a court's earlier decisions and the rules of law they embody."[13] In other words, Justice Breyer defined and defended a strict form of the precedential modality:

> The Court has pointed out that *stare decisis* "promotes the evenhanded, predictable, and consistent development of legal principles, fosters reliance on judicial decisions, and contributes to the actual and perceived integrity of the

judicial process." . . . *Stare decisis* thereby avoids the instability and unfairness that accompany disruption of settled legal expectations. For this reason, the rule of law demands that adhering to our prior case law be the norm. Departure from precedent is exceptional, and requires "special justification."[14]

Arguing that the respondents did not justify why *Buckley* should be overruled and abandoned as a valuable precedent, Justice Breyer concluded that "Overruling *Buckley* now would dramatically undermine this reliance on our settled precedent," thereby invalidating past decisions and being uninformative to the present case.[15]

Embedded in Justice Breyer's precedential rhetoric are metaphors that depict the law as a complicated "web" through which he must "guide" the American people, if not his colleagues. After all, the Supreme Court alone, not to mention state and local laws, has decided thousands of cases over two hundred years. In his 1994 statement to the judiciary committee, Breyer explained that as a Supreme Court judge, he would "guide" the American people through the "labyrinth of rules and regulations" and the "vast web" and "vast array" of legal complexities that so often "restrain" our "very human goals" and "freedom."[16] In fact, Breyer twice mentioned the "vast web" of laws he would navigate in his position as justice. These metaphors create accessible images that clarify Justice Breyer's positions and bolster his precedential perspective.

ETHICAL ARGUMENTS

In addition to the precedential modality, Justice Breyer has crafted an ethical stance with his Court rhetoric. As Smith explains, "ethicists take into account changes in the American ethos," which allows them to argue that "if the framers were alive today they would apply their principles to new constituencies or developments in the current context."[17] In fact, ethicists believe in a "living constitution" that may be adapted to the "ever-changing" context of the United States.[18] The ethical judge is thus concerned with the present needs and concerns of the American people—based on fundamental constitutional beliefs—and rules accordingly.

Breyer has consistently fashioned himself as an ethical judge and explained such commitments in his nomination statement: "I believe that the law must work for people. . . . to help the many different individuals who make up America—from so many different backgrounds and circumstances, with so many different needs and hopes—its purpose is to help them live together productively, harmoniously, and in freedom."[19] Spoken like a true ethicist. Breyer revealed his belief that the Supreme Court's duty is to put the law and the U.S. Constitution to work for the American people in order to make their lives more productive, harmonious, and free. Breyer's ethical position, after all, reflects the original principles of the framers, "to form a more perfect union, establish justice, insure domestic tranquility, provide for the common defense, promote the general welfare, and secure the blessings of liberty to ourselves and our posterity."[20] Breyer positions himself as a guarantor of that tradition.

While the ethical perspective has assisted the justices in their arguments for myriad types of cases, new technologies especially have challenged the Court to make their decisions with little direct help from the Founders; that is, the Founders did not and could not account for the impact of new technologies such as the Internet and mass media on the First Amendment. That is why the ethical modality, wherein the justices evoke the fundamental commitments of the evolving American ethos, has been invaluable in First Amendment cases that involve new technologies. Three instances are instructive in Justice Breyer's case.

First, in his concurrence in *Bartnicki v. Vopper* (2001), Justice Breyer stated that "the Constitution demands legislative efforts to tailor the laws in order reasonably to reconcile media freedom with personal, speech-related privacy."[21] The American values of free speech and privacy surfaced when Justice Breyer argued that journalists could not be held liable for broadcasting illegally obtained information—the case at bar concerned the radio broadcasting of an illegally taped conversation between a union official and union members about a teacher's strike. Explaining further the American principle of privacy in the age of evolving technology, Justice Breyer asserted, "Clandestine and pervasive invasions of privacy, unlike the simple theft of documents from a bedroom, are genuine possibilities as a result of continuously advancing technologies. Eavesdropping on ordinary cellular phone conversations in the street (which many callers seem to tolerate) is a very different matter from eavesdropping on encrypted cellular phone conversations or those carried on in the bedroom."[22] The Founders could not have accounted for "encrypted cellular phone conversations" and all "advancing technologies," but they were able to set forth a code of privacy that would assist the Supreme Court justices like Justice Breyer in ruling on such cases for centuries.

Second, in *Ashcroft v. ACLU, II* (2004), Justice Breyer dissented from the majority opinion that the Child Online Protection Act (COPA)—an act meant to keep children from viewing obscene material on the Internet—was unconstitutional. A major argument of the opinion was that free speech would be limited if the government enforced the use of online filtering software. In his dissent, Justice Breyer appealed to the long-revered American moral commitments to free speech as well as to protecting children, or in his words, the "compelling congressional goal [of] protecting children from exposure to commercial pornography."[23] Justice Breyer's dissent was ethical because in the "real world" of today, "the obscene and the nonobscene do not come tied neatly into separate, easily distinguishable, packages"[24] and "more than 28 million school age children have both parents or their sole parent in the work force, at least 5 million children are left alone at home without supervision each week, and many of those children will spend afternoons and evenings with friends who may well have access to computers and more lenient parents."[25] Justice Breyer's ethical argument is that realities and technologies of the present era may have changed—as detailed in the facts and figures here—but America's commitments to its children and to free speech have not.

Third, this same ethical rationale surfaces in the 2003 ruling *Eldred v. Ashcroft*. Again dissenting from the majority opinion, Justice Breyer employed the ethical modality to argue that it is unconstitutional for Congress to pass legislation to extend copyright terms. Eldred and other users of public domain works argued that the Sonny Bono Copyright Term Extension Act, which added twenty years to existing and future copyrights, distorted the balance between private incentive and enrichment of the public domain.[26] Justice Breyer concluded, "This statute will cause serious expression-related harm" because it will "likely restrict traditional dissemination of copyrighted works. It will likely inhibit new forms of dissemination through the use of new technology. It threatens to interfere with efforts to preserve our Nation's historical and cultural heritage and efforts to use that heritage, say, to educate our Nation's children."[27] Justice Breyer appealed here to long-held values in the American ethos: children, technology, tradition, history, and culture. And again, even though the technology has changed, the American commitment to the First Amendment and values embedded in our sacred documents has not.

While Justice Breyer's ethical metaphors are not as rich and vivid as his precedential and prudential metaphors, we do find some evidence of his metaphoric expression. For instance, Justice Breyer often said that "the law must work for people," thereby personifying "the law" as something (or someone) that must "work" for us. In order for laws to work best for the people, Justice Breyer explains how we must "tailor the laws" to best suit us. Both of these metaphors reflect an ethical position—that is, "tailoring" or adjusting laws so that they "work" for the American people.

PRUDENTIAL REASONING

Along with the precedential and ethical modalities, Justice Breyer has often evoked the prudential modality in his First Amendment opinions, dissents, and concurrences (although not explicitly in his nomination statement). Bobbitt explains that the prudential modality "is derived from a calculus of costs and benefits, when the facts are taken into account," thereby weighing the potential advantages of a particular decision against potential detriments.[28] The prudent judge will appeal to the "practical wisdom of using the courts in a particular way."[29] Justice Breyer's prudential perspective is observable in many of his arguments.

In his opinion in *McConnell v. Federal Election Commission* (2003)—the case involving the constitutionality of the BCRA—Justice Breyer weighed the relative time and cost of filing FCC-mandated "candidate requests" with the plaintiff's claim that such actions were "intolerabl[y] burdensome and invasive."[30] Justice Breyer concluded, "The FCC has consistently estimated that its 'candidate request' regulation imposes upon each licensee an additional administrative burden of six to seven hours of work per year. . . . That burden means annual costs of a few hundred dollars at most, a microscopic amount compared to the many millions of dollars of revenue broadcasters receive from candidates who wish to advertise."[31] Taking his position further, Justice Breyer explained that "Compared to these longstanding record-keeping requirements, an additional six to seven hours is a small drop in a very large bucket."[32] Thus, Justice Breyer's prudential approach considers the time and energy involved in filing candidate requests with the claims of the plaintiffs. Coming to a practical conclusion, Justice Breyer illustrated how the benefits of the case far outweighed the burdens of such action.

In his opinion in *Randall v. Sorrell* (2006)—the case regarding Vermont's strict campaign contribution limits—Justice Breyer argued that it was prudent to rule in Randall's favor because the relative cost of doing otherwise would threaten freedom of speech. Writing that "At some point the constitutional risks to the democratic electoral process become too great," Justice Breyer asserted that "lower" limits did not mean "better" and "contribution limits that are too low can also harm the electoral process."[33] Justice Breyer made similar prudential arguments based on relative comparisons in his concurrence to *Bartnicki v. Vopper* (2001)—the case involving the legal broadcasting of illegally obtained material—when he mused, "I would ask whether the statutes strike a reasonable balance between their speech-restricting and speech-enhancing consequences. Or do they instead impose restrictions on speech that are disproportionate when measured against their corresponding privacy and speech-related benefits, taking into account the kind, the importance, and the extent of these benefits, as well as the need for the restrictions in order to secure those benefits?"[34] Justice Breyer assessed the costs and benefits of contribution limits with the advantages and disadvantages to free speech. This rhetorical strategy is a hallmark of the prudential perspective.

Similarly, in his dissent of *Ashcroft v. ACLU, II* (2004), Justice Breyer argued that the protection of children from obscene material outweighs the small burden placed on adults by implementing restrictions on Internet pornography websites: "In sum, the Act at most imposes a modest additional burden on adult access to legally obscene material, perhaps imposing a similar burden on access to some protected borderline obscene material as well."[35] Furthermore, Justice Breyer concluded that the "minor burdens" placed on adults who wish to view the constitutionally protected material "may [be] overcome at modest cost."[36] The prudent judge decides the degree of "burdens"—whether they are "minor," "modest," or greater—and rules accordingly.

Justice Breyer evoked the metaphoric image of scales in his prudential rhetoric as he "weighs" evidence. As Bobbitt explained, the prudential modality "often gives rise to a 'balancing test' (the balance being a scales, not a tightrope)," which manifests itself as metaphors in Justice Breyer's prudential reasoning.[37] When deciding whether the requirements imposed by the FCC "impose disproportionate administrative burdens" on broadcasters in *McConnell v. Federal Election Commission*, Justice Breyer began, "On the one hand, the burdens are likely less heavy than many that other FCC regulations have imposed."[38] But, he continued, "On the other hand, the burdens are likely heavier than those imposed by BCRA §504's other provisions, previously discussed."[39] The image emerges of Justice Breyer holding each observation in his hands as he carefully balances and weighs them.

Once he judiciously considered each argument on the scales of justice, Justice Breyer employed diminutive and superlative language to justify his decisions. Again in *McConnell v. Federal Election Commission*, Justice Breyer discussed the "microscopic amount" of money spent on filing candidate requests "compared to the many millions of dollars" of candidate revenue, the "slight" imposition on the First Amendment by the FCC statutes "compared to the strong enforcement-related interests that it serves," and the relative insignificance of "an additional six to seven hours" of administrative work that amounted to "a small drop in a very large bucket."[40] When put on the scales—or dropped in the "very large bucket"—the "slight" and "strong" can be compared to each other and a decision better warranted and justified.

CONCLUSIONS

Based on this analysis, I conclude that Justice Breyer's rhetoric positions him as a pragmatic judge. The historical, structural, and textual modalities are typically employed by judges who wish to uphold the exact letter of the law and honor the original intent of the Founders, perhaps reflecting an idealistic perspective. Conversely, judges who exploit the precedential, ethical, and prudential modalities present themselves as concerned with the pragmatics of law and how it impacts the day-to-day lives of contemporary Americans. Of course, the modalities are not mutually exclusive, since they often overlap and may even appear in the same sentence. Furthermore, judges are not exclusively bound to their modalities; in other words, an ethical judge may invoke the historical modality to make a case. Generally speaking, however, Justice Breyer remains true to a pragmatic approach and attendant rhetorical modalities.[41]

In First Amendment cases, Justice Breyer's arguments and metaphors illustrate his desire for free speech laws to benefit the people and demands of today. With this knowledge, an advocate arguing before the Court and hoping to sway Justice Breyer may consider making appeals to precedent and asserting that his or her case is consistent with a "web" of good laws. An advocate may also consider making appeals to ethics in order to persuade Justice Breyer, finding ways to make constitutional values such as privacy and protecting children "work" today. Making appeals to the prudential modality may also serve the advocate well when addressing Justice Breyer, making sure to "weigh" the advantages and disadvantages of free speech on realities of the day.

These particular arguments and metaphors will continue to be important in framing First Amendment cases, especially as technology and mass media continue to evolve. That is, it may prove difficult for the justices to argue using the textual or originalist modalities in cases involving Internet technology, while the precedential, prudential, and especially the ethical judges may have an easier time with it. These arguments and metaphors will be particularly instructive for advocates who argue First Amendment cases before this Court in the age of technology, and for the rhetorical critics who study them.

NOTES

1. Craig R. Smith, chapter 1 in this book.
2. Bobbitt, *Constitutional Interpretation*, 18.
3. Bobbitt, *Constitutional Interpretation*, 18.
4. *Hearings before the Committee on the Judiciary United States Senate One Hundred Third Congress Second Session on the Nomination of Stephen G. Breyer to Be an Associate Justice of the Supreme Court of the United States*, July 12–15, 1994 (Washington, DC: U.S. Government Printing Office, 1995), 21.
5. *Hearings on the Nomination of Stephen G. Breyer*, 20.
6. 544 U.S. 734, 737 (2005).
7. 540 U.S. 93, 238, 245 (2003).
8. 555 U.S. ___ (2009), slip op., 4.
9. 555 U.S. ___ (2009), slip op., 8.
10. 555 U.S. ___ (2009), slip op., 13.
11. 548 U.S. 230, 236, 242 (2006).
12. 548 U.S. 230, 242 (2006).
13. 548 U.S. 230, 243 (2006).
14. 548 U.S. 230, 244 (2006).
15. 548 U.S. 230, 244 (2006).

16. *Hearings on the Nomination of Stephen G. Breyer*, 20–21.

17. Smith, chapter 1 of this book.

18. Smith, chapter 1 of this book.

19. *Hearings on the Nomination of Stephen G. Breyer*, 20–21.

20. Preamble to the U.S. Constitution, retrieved from http://www.law.cornell.edu/constitution/index.html

21. 532 U.S. 514, 538 (2001).

22. 532 U.S. 514, 541 (2001).

23. 542 U.S. 656, 677 (2004).

24. 542 U.S. 656, 691 (2004).

25. 542 U.S. 656, 685 (2004).

26. Openlaw on *Eldred v. Ashcroft*, http://cyber.law.harvard.edu/eldredvreno/.

27. 537 U.S.186, 266 (2003).

28. Bobbitt, *Constitutional Interpretation*, 17.

29. Bobbitt, *Constitutional Fate*, 7.

30. 540 U.S. 93, 235 (2003).

31. 540 U.S. 93, 235 (2003).

32. 540 U.S. 93, 236 (2003).

33. 548 U.S. 230, 248, 249 (2006).

34. 532 U.S. 514, 536 (2001).

35. 542 U.S. 656, 683 (2004).

36. 542 U.S. 656, 689 (2004).

37. Bobbitt, *Constitutional Interpretation*, 17.

38. 540 U.S. 93, 241–42 (2003).

39. 540 U.S. 93, 242 (2003).

40. 540 U.S. 93, 235, 246, 236 (2003).

41. At press time for this book, Justice Breyer maintained his pragmatic stance regarding First Amendment cases. In the final paragraph of his dissent in *Holder, et al. v. Law Project, et al.*, slip op. 08-1498 (2010)—a case that "make[s] it a crime to provide support, including humanitarian aid, literature distribution and political advocacy, to any foreign entity that the government has designated as a 'terrorist' group" (Center for Constitutional Rights, available at http://ccrjustice.org/holder-v-humanitarian-law-project)—Breyer appealed to the precedent of the U.S. Constitution, stating that the majority ruling is not ethical because it "deprives the individuals before us of the protection that the First Amendment demands," and argues that the decision is not prudential because it "has failed to require tailoring of means to fit compelling ends" (23).

Chapter Nine

Associate Justice Ginsburg

Katie L. Gibson

Ruth Bader Ginsburg was nominated to the Supreme Court by President Bill Clinton in 1993. Judge Ginsburg was overwhelmingly confirmed as the second woman to serve on the Supreme Court of the United States; only three senators opposed her nomination. Justice Ginsburg's reasoning from the nation's highest bench demonstrates a judicial philosophy that embraces a "living Constitution."[1] This chapter analyzes Justice Ginsburg's rhetoric from her confirmation hearings and in her written opinions on the First Amendment to argue that her constitutional interpretation is justified primarily through precedential and ethical reasoning. Unlike the historical modality, the precedential and ethical modalities ground Justice Ginsburg's endorsement of an evolving Constitution. Testifying in her Senate confirmation hearings, Ginsburg asserted, "I think the Framers were intending to create a more perfect union that would become ever more perfect over time."[2] The interpretation of the Constitution as a dynamic document is supported by a judicial "conscience" that legitimates case law and the contemporary American ethos as warrants for constitutional argument. Although Justice Ginsburg has penned comparably few opinions on the First Amendment, a close look at these writings reveals a mixed modal style that suggests a strong preference for precedential and ethical reasoning.

PRECEDENTIAL REASONING

Precedential reasoning looks to past decisions and relies on established traditions and practices as the primary warrants for solving constitutional disputes. Justice Ginsburg's dissent in *Agostini v. Felton* (1997) illustrates her

129

precedential stance. The Court majority in *Agostini* reviewed and overturned its own decision in *Aguilar v. Felton* (1985). In the earlier case of *Aguilar*, the Court held that a New York City program that sent public school teachers into parochial schools to provide remedial instruction to disadvantaged children resulted in an "excessive entanglement" of church and state and, therefore, violated the establishment clause of the First Amendment.[3] Twelve years later, however, the Court overturned this precedent. In *Agostini v. Felton*, the majority insisted that developments in establishment clause law rendered the earlier judgment in *Aguilar* erroneous and unjust.[4] Justice Ginsburg dissented. A review of Justice Ginsburg's dissent demonstrates that her arguments are grounded in a precedential judicial ethic that assigns ultimate value to stare decisis and to the consistency of legal practice and procedure.

Ginsburg's precedential stance is clearly revealed in her characterization of the majority opinion as arbitrary and haphazard. She begins her opinion, "The Court today *finds a way* to rehear a legal question decided in respondents' favor in this very case some 12 years ago."[5] Ginsburg's opening shot at the majority's reasoning is telling because she implies her strict preference for order and precedent, while characterizing the majority's "[find] a way" jurisprudence as suffering from a lack of principle and respect for appropriate procedure. She asserts, "This Court's Rules do not countenance the rehearing here granted."[6] Ginsburg's repeated references to rules and procedures throughout the opinion bolster her precedential stance. She continues, "I am aware of no case in which we have extended the time for rehearing. . . . [N]othing in our procedures allows us to grant rehearing, timely or not."[7] And again, beginning the third paragraph, she asserts, "Lacking any rule or practice allowing us to reconsider the *Aguilar* judgment directly, the majority accepts as a substitute a rule governing relief from judgments or orders of the federal trial courts."[8] Ginsburg's precedential stance demands a certain reverence for rules, traditions, and precedent. Thus, her rhetoric of dissent emphasizes the failure of the Court to abide by the appropriate rules and procedures and casts these failures as the cause of the decision's ultimate illegitimacy.

At the heart of Justice Ginsburg's dissent in *Agostini* is an insistence on precedential respect. She criticizes the majority for attempting "to make today's use of Rule 60(b) palatable" and accuses her colleagues of "bend[ing] Rule 60(b) to a purpose."[9] Justice Ginsburg points squarely to precedent to rebut the majority's application of Rule 60(b), and she plainly asserts that previous case law offers "firm instruction" on its proper use.[10] Justice Ginsburg's "firm instruction" thus stands in contrast to the majority's "problematic" application of a law—a law bent to a purpose without principle and made palatable after the fact. In closing, Justice Ginsburg states:

> Unlike the majority, I find just cause to await the arrival of *Helms, Pearl II*, or perhaps another case in which our review appropriately may be sought, before deciding whether *Aguilar* should remain the law of the land. That cause lies in the maintenance of integrity in the interpretation of procedural rules, preservation of the responsive, non-agenda-setting character of this Court, and avoidance of invitations to reconsider cases based on "speculat[ions] on chances from changes in [the Court's membership]."[11]

Justice Ginsburg's closing remarks question the character of her colleagues. For Ginsburg, the measure of judicial character is precedential respect—the "maintenance of integrity" in following case law and abiding by proper procedure. Within Ginsburg's precedential framework, the majority's decision to overturn its precedent in *Aguilar* is cast as arbitrary, disingenuous, and political.

Justice Ginsburg's precedential stance also anchors her recent majority opinion in *Hastings Christian Fellowship Society v. Martinez* (2010). In *Hastings Christian Fellowship Society*, the Court rejected a First Amendment challenge brought by a Christian student organization and ruled in favor of a public law school that refused official recognition of the Christian group because it failed to comply with the school's nondiscrimination policy by barring gay students from membership. Again, Ginsburg's precedential ethic is featured as she opens her argument with criticism of the petitioners and of the Court's dissent for failing to respect the joint stipulation of facts in the case. She criticizes the Christian Legal Society for their "unseemly attempt to escape from the stipulation and shift its target"[12] and takes aim at Justice Alito's dissent claiming "time and time again the dissent races away from the facts to which CLS stipulated."[13] Here again, Justice Ginsburg's reasoning turns on the proper application of legal rules and the following of correct procedure. Ginsburg explains "We are not writing on a blank slate,"[14] reminding her reader of the case history and tradition that drive her precedential interpretive stance.

Justice Ginsburg's precedential rhetoric in *Agostini v. Felton* and *Hastings Christian Fellowship Society v. Martinez* projects a rigid stylistic tone. In the doctrinal style, the repeated references to rules, procedures, and precedent may encourage a more formal judicial tone than other modalities. In any case, the rigidity of the tone that the modality of precedential interpretation may encourage should not suggest a corresponding rigidity in the justice's view of the Constitution. The precedential modality, in fact, is seen by many as a method of reasoning that contradicts originalism and strict constructionism and, instead, bolsters the concept of a living Constitution. Commenting on the relationship between precedential reasoning and originalism, Paulson writes, "Stare decisis contradicts the premise of originalism—that it is the original meaning of the words of the text, and not anything else, that controls constitutional interpretation. To whatever extent precedents inconsistent with original meaning are accepted as controlling (whether sometimes and to some extent, or always and absolutely), such acceptance undermines—even refutes—the premises that are supposed to justify originalism."[15] Despite the strict formal tone that emerges from Ginsburg's precedential references to stare decisis, established rules, and proper procedures, it is important to note that the interpretive consciousness often driving precedential reasoning recognizes an understanding of the Constitution that is much more flexible and boundless than a formal tone may suggest.

ETHICAL REASONING

Like precedential reasoning, ethical reasoning also recognizes the legitimacy of a living Constitution. Unlike historical reasoning, which demands adherence to original meanings, ethicists maintain that reasoning *between the lines* of the Constitution is necessary in order to properly account for a changing context and evolving American ethos. In *Hastings Christian Fellowship Society v. Martinez* (2010), Justice Ginsburg clearly articulates her ethical interpretive stance, stating, "Our inquiry is shaped by the educational context in which it arises."[16] The ethical interpreter understands proper constitutional interpretation to be responsive to particular contexts. Justice Ginsburg's testimony at her confirmation hearings affirmed her ethical constitutional stance. She testified: "One of the world's greatest jurists, Judge Learned Hand, said that the spirit of liberty that imbues our Constitution must lie, first and foremost, in the hearts of the men and women who compose this great nation."[17] Instead of looking backward—to the intentions and motives of the Founders—the ethicist looks first and foremost to the contemporary American ethos, to "the hearts of the men and women who compose this great nation." Ginsburg's reference to Learned Hand communicates a commitment to the present and to the citizens who compose this nation *today*.

Ginsburg's praise of Judge Learned Hand's reference to the "spirit of liberty that imbues our Constitution" also points to a measure of plasticity that is constitutive of the ethical modality. Justice Ginsburg's majority opinion in *Cutter v. Wilkinson*[18] highlights her ethical stance and her understanding of the Constitution as a living and flexible document. In *Cutter*, the Supreme Court denied an establishment clause claim and affirmed the constitutionality of the Religious Land Use and Institutionalized Persons Act (RLUIPA). While the Act prohibited the government from imposing a substantial burden on a prisoner's free exercise of religion, prison officials claimed that RLUIPA violated the establishment clause of the First Amendment.[19] Writing for a unanimous Court, Justice Ginsburg opens with a metaphor that underpins the logic of her reasoning: "Just last Term, in *Locke v.*

Davey, 540 U.S. 712 (2004), the Court reaffirmed that 'there is room for play in the joints between' the Free Exercise and Establishment Clauses, allowing the government to accommodate religion beyond free exercise requirements, without offense to the Establishment Clause."[20] While language choice and metaphor selection might appear happenstance to the untrained eye, a rhetorical approach to the study of judicial opinion exposes the guiding logic and hidden assumptions operative in such choices. Here, Justice Ginsburg's metaphor for constitutional interpretation as "room for play in the joints" reveals her ethicist stance as well as her broader philosophy of constitutional interpretation. In the following passage, Justice Ginsburg identifies the key issues at stake in *Cutter* and invokes the "room for play" metaphor once more—reiterating its controlling logic:

> The Religion Clauses of the First Amendment provide: "Congress shall make no law respecting an establishment of religion, or prohibiting the free exercise thereof." The first of the two Clauses, commonly called the Establishment Clause, commands a separation of church and state. The second, the Free Exercise Clause, requires government respect for, and noninterference with, the religious beliefs and practices of our Nation's people. While the two Clauses express complementary values, they often exert conflicting pressures. . . . Our decisions recognize that "there is room for play in the joints" between the Clauses.[21]

Justice Ginsburg points to rhetorical precedent, citing a metaphor first used by Chief Justice Warren Burger in *Walz v. Tax Commission* (1970).[22] At the time *Walz* was decided, the Court was persuaded that Thomas Jefferson's metaphor of the "wall"—dividing church and state—was too restrictive.[23] Chief Justice Burger introduced a new rhetorical construct that replaced the absolute separation demanded by the "wall" with the possibility of a benevolent shared space. Combining her precedential and ethical stances, Justice Ginsburg relies on the rhetorical precedent in *Walz* to legitimate the flexibility of her ethical stance in *Cutter*. The metaphor "room for play in the joints" eschews the dogmatism of the strict constructionists and originalists. Instead, the metaphor validates the ethicist's interpretive practice of reading between the lines, responding to changing contexts, and listening to an evolving American ethos. Sharon Keller explains, "Play, as the portal to innovation and creativity, can be the enemy of settled expectations and predictability."[24] Certainly, the metaphor of "play in the joints" stands in contrast to the historicist's precept of original intent and the textualist's demand for "plain reading."

While *Cutter* provides insight as to how Justice Ginsburg interprets the religion clauses of the First Amendment and to the measure of flexibility her judicial conscience allows, her dissent in *Federal Communications Commission v. Fox Television Stations, Inc., et al.* (2009) reveals her ethicist approach to freedom of expression. While the Court's majority ducked the First Amendment issue in this case, Ginsburg features freedom of expression at the center of her dissent. For this reason, it is a valuable text for our study.

The central question at issue in *FCC v. Fox* was whether the FCC acted arbitrarily and capriciously in changing its policy under federal law to prohibit the televised broadcast of "fleeting expletives."[25] In a five to four decision, the majority upheld the government's power to restrict the broadcast of a single four-letter word. While the majority bypassed the bigger question of whether the ban violated the First Amendment, Justice Ginsburg's dissent acknowledged the elephant in the room, asserting "there is no way to hide the long shadow the First Amendment casts over what the Commission has done. Today's decision does nothing to diminish that shadow." Ginsburg's dissent sees the ethical modality as the appropriate lens through which the First Amendment issues in this case should be judged. Citing Justice Brennan's dissent in *FCC v. Pacifica* (1978), Ginsburg writes, "Justice Brennan observed that the Government should take care before enjoining the broadcast of words or expressions spoken by many 'in our land of cultural pluralism.' That comment, fitting in the 1970s, is even more potent today. If the reserved constitutional question reaches this Court, we should be mindful that words unpalatable to some may be 'commonplace' for others, 'the stuff of everyday conversations.'"[26] Reasoning from an ethical stance, Ginsburg's assertion that Justice Brennan's argument was "fitting in the 1970s, [and] is even more potent today" validates an approach to constitutional interpretation that is necessarily responsive to changing contexts. While the historicist looks to the intent of the framers and the textualist looks to the written text of the Constitution, Justice Ginsburg looks to the American ethos and points to contemporary cultural pluralism and the practices of "everyday conversations" as warrants for her First Amendment argument.

The central position of the American ethos in Justice Ginsburg's judicial conscience was clearly evident in her confirmation hearing. Ginsburg spoke specifically about the evolving nature of this ethos, testifying, "'We the People' has grown ever larger. So now it includes people who were once held in bondage. It includes women who were left out of the political community at the start."[27] For the ethicist, constitutional interpretation requires judicial responsiveness to the ethos of the "people." Note the sharp difference from Attorney General Edwin Meese's assertion that "The text of the document and the original intention of those who framed it would be the judicial standard in giving effect to the Constitution."[28] In stark contrast to an originalist approach that genuflects to the past, the ethical modality observed in Justice Ginsburg's rhetoric in her confirmation hearings and in her written opinions on the First Amendment relies on a framework of interpretation that is adapted to the present.

CONCLUSIONS

Justice Ginsburg's mixed modal style of precedential and ethical reasoning requires respect for stare decisis and legal tradition while demanding flexibility and responsiveness to an evolving American ethos. Ginsburg's Senate testimony provides insight into the interpretive balance she strikes between the precedential and ethical modalities. She demonstrates her doctrinal ethic as she urges caution on the part of judges who wish to deconstruct established law: "It is very easy to tear down, to deconstruct. It is not so easy to construct. I as a general matter would never tear down unless I am sure that I have a better building to replace what is being torn down."[29] While a precedential ethic places high value on stability and tradition, Ginsburg reminds us that precedential reasoning does allow for changes and shifts in legal doctrine—provided that such shifts are rigorously argued and exceptionally warranted. On the other hand, in Justice Ginsburg's Senate testimony, she was also careful to protect against the charge that the ethical modality is arbitrary and activist. She asserts, "The courts don't react to public opinion polls. They do react to what Professor Freund described as, not the weather of the day, but the climate of the age."[30] Despite the constitutional flexibility that the ethical modality permits, Ginsburg lends a measure of stability to this interpretive lens, anchoring it in the "climate of the age" and separating her interpretive ethic from the politics of opinion polls.

This study has demonstrated how Justice Ginsburg balances the commitments of stability and change that animate the precedential and ethical modalities. Advocates before the Supreme Court would be wise to frame their arguments with a similar concern for balance and demonstrate respect for the competing interests of stability and change that often divide their robed interlocutors.

While Justice Ginsburg's First Amendment opinions and her Senate testimony provide evidence of a judicial stance that is predominantly precedential and ethical, she has a practice of mixing modalities and demonstrates a willingness to employ even the historical modality—a method of reasoning seemingly out of step with her very understanding of the Constitution—in order to build consensus. Read, for example, Ginsburg's reasoning in her unanimous *Eldred v. Ashcroft* (2003) opinion:

> The Copyright Clause and First Amendment were adopted close in time. This proximity indicates that, in the Framers' view, copyright's limited monopolies are compatible with free speech principles. Indeed, copyright's purpose is to *promote* the creation and publication of free expression. As *Harper & Row* observed: "[T]he Framers intended copyright itself to be the engine of free expression. By establishing a marketable right to the use of one's expression, copyright supplies the economic incentive to create and disseminate ideas."[31]

Ginsburg embraces the precept of original intent as she looks back to the context of the framers and attempts to discern their motives. Again, her Senate testimony provides insight into the rhetorical strategy observed in *Eldred*. The following passage suggests that Justice Ginsburg—although clearly committed to living constitutionalism—is not beholden to reasoning from any specific modality in her effort to build consensus. She testifies, "Willingness to entertain the position of the other person, readiness to rethink one's own views, are important attitudes on a collegial court. If your colleagues, who are intelligent people and deserve respect, have a different view, perhaps you should then pause and rethink, Am I right? Is there a way that we can come together? Is this a case where it really doesn't matter so much which way the law goes as long as it is clear?"[32] While this study demonstrates Justice Ginsburg's preference for doctrinal and ethical reasoning, it is clear that she is willing to embrace the preferred modalities of her colleagues in order to build consensus.

In closing, I suggest that advocates before the highest court may benefit from crafting arguments that speak to multiple modalities. Although Justice Ginsburg is certainly persuaded by First Amendment arguments that are grounded by doctrinal and ethical warrants, advocates would be wise to present a mixed-modal argument that provides Ginsburg with the available means of persuasion to build consensus among her colleagues.

NOTES

1. Adam Winkler, "A Revolution Too Soon: Woman Suffragists and The 'Living Constitution,'" *New York University Law Review*, 76 (2001): 1463. Winkler explains, "Based on the idea that society changes and evolves, living constitutionalism requires that constitutional controversies, in the words of Justice Oliver Wendell Holmes Jr., 'must be considered in the light of our whole experience and not merely in that of what was said a hundred years ago.'"

2. *Hearings before the Committee on the Judiciary United States Senate One Hundred Third Congress First Session on the Nomination of Ruth Bader Ginsburg to be an Associate Justice of the Supreme Court of the United States*, July 20–23, 1993 (Washington, DC: U.S. Government Printing Office, 1994), 127.

3. The three-part *Lemon* test was established in Lemon v. Kurtzman, 403 U.S. 602 (1971). The *Lemon* test laid out a three-pronged requirement for legislation dealing with religion: (1) The government's action must have a secular legislative purpose; (2) The government's action must not have the primary effect of either advancing or inhibiting religion; (3) The government's action must not result in an "excessive government entanglement" with religion.

4. Agostini v. Felton, 521 U.S. 203 (1997). *Agostini* resulted in a loosening of the *Lemon* test. Justice O'Connor argued: "We therefore hold that a federally funded program providing supplemental remedial instruction to disadvantaged children on a neutral basis is not invalid under the Establishment Clause when such instruction is given on the premises of sectarian schools by government employees pursuant to a program containing safeguards such as those present here," 236.

5. Agostini v. Felton, 521 U.S., 223, 255; emphasis added.

6. Agostini v. Felton, 521 U.S., 223, 255.

7. Agostini v. Felton, 521 U.S., 223, 255.

8. Agostini v. Felton, 521 U.S., 223, 255.

9. Explaining Rule 60(b), Justice Ginsburg states, "Under that rule, a district court may, in its discretion, grant relief from a final judgment with prospective effect if the party seeking modification can show 'a significant change in factual conditions or law' that renders continued operation of the judgment inequitable," 256.

10. Justice Ginsburg cites Rodriguez de Quijas v. Shearson/American Express, Inc., 490 U.S. 477, 484 (1989) as guiding precedent, Agostini v. Felton, 521 U.S., 223, 259.

11. Agostini v. Felton, 521 U.S., 223, 260.

12. Hastings Christian Fellowship Society v. Martinez et al., 561 U.S. ___ (2010).

13. Hastings Christian Fellowship Society v. Martinez et al., 561 U.S. ___ (2010).

14. Hastings Christian Fellowship Society v. Martinez et al., 561 U.S. ___ (2010).

15. Michael S. Paulsen, "Reconciled With Precedent? A Symposium on Stare Decisis: The Intrinsically Corrupting Influence of Precedent," *Constitutional Commentary*, 22 (2005): 289.

16. Hastings Christian Fellowship Society v. Martinez et al., 561 U.S. ___ (2010).

17. *Hearings on the Nomination of Ruth Bader Ginsburg*, 54.

18. 544 U.S. 709 (2005).

19. A group of Ohio inmates brought suit under the Religious Land Use and Institutionalized Persons Act claiming that prison officials violated the law by failing to make accommodations for their practice of "nonmainstream" religions—Satanism, Wicca, and Asatru. Ohio responded by claiming the law improperly advanced religion in violation of the establishment clause, and the Sixth U.S. Circuit Court of Appeals struck down the law. The Supreme Court reversed the Sixth Circuit ruling.

20. Cutter v. Wilkinson, 544 U.S. 709, 713.

21. 544 U.S. 709, 719.

22. The Court stated: "The course of constitutional neutrality in this area cannot be an absolutely straight line; rigidity could well defeat the basic purpose of these provisions, which is to insure that no religion be sponsored or favored, none commanded, and none inhibited. The general principle deducible from the First Amendment and all that has been said by the Court is this: that we will not tolerate either governmentally established religion or governmental interference with religion. Short of those expressly proscribed governmental acts there is room for play in the joints productive of a benevolent neutrality which will permit religious exercise to exist without sponsorship and without interference," 397 U.S. 664, 669 (1970).

23. See Gillette v. United States, 401 U.S. 437 (1971): "The metaphor of a 'wall' or impassable barrier between Church and State, taken too literally, may mislead constitutional analysis . . . , but the Establishment Clause stands at least for the proposition that when government activities touch on the religious sphere, they must be secular in purpose, evenhanded in operation, and neutral in primary impact," 450.

24. Sharon Keller, "The Rules of the Game: 'Play in the Joints' Between the Religion Clauses," *Rutgers Journal of Law and Religion*, 7 (2006).

25. In 1978, the high court ruled in FCC v. Pacifica Foundation that the government had the right to prohibit the broadcast of indecent words and notably declared that broadcasting had "the most limited First Amendment protection." From the time of this ruling until 2004, the FCC only punished broadcasters for sustained and repeated use of indecent language. In 2004, however, in response to rock singer Bono's use of the *f* word during the Golden Globe Awards, the FCC changed its policy to prohibit the broadcast of a single vulgar word. In July of 2010, the Second Court of Appeals reopened this issue by unanimously ruling in a follow-up *FOX v. FCC* case that the FCC's rules about contextual and implied indecency were overbroad and arbitrary, thereby striking them down.

26. Citing FCC v. Pacifica, 438 U.S.775, 776 (1978).

27. *Hearings on the Nomination of Ruth Bader Ginsburg*, 119.

28. Attorney General Edwin Meese III, speech before the American Bar Association, July 9, 1985, as reprinted in *The Great Debate: Interpreting Our Written Constitution* (Washington, DC: The Federalist Society, 1986), 1.

29. *Hearings on the Nomination of Ruth Bader Ginsburg*, 155.

30. *Hearings on the Nomination of Ruth Bader Ginsburg*, 221.

31. Citing Harper and Row v. Nation Enterprises, 471 U.S. 539, 558 (1985).

32. *Hearings on the Nomination of Ruth Bader Ginsburg,* 201.

Chapter Ten

Associate Justice Thomas

Kevin A. Johnson

President George H. W. Bush nominated Judge Clarence Thomas to the Supreme Court in 1991. After very controversial hearings, he took his oath of office following the closest Senate vote to confirm a Supreme Court nominee in more than a century (fifty-two for, forty-eight opposed). A review of Justice Thomas's rhetoric reveals that he consistently frames his arguments about the First Amendment with historical, precedential, and prudential arguments. To demonstrate his method of decision making, this chapter offers a thematic analysis of the claims Justice Thomas made during his 1991 nomination hearings as well as First Amendment opinions from 1991 to the close of the 2008–2009 session. In order to closely examine each type of argument that he employs, this chapter is divided into four sections. The first section analyzes Justice Thomas's historical arguments, the second section examines his precedential arguments, and the third section delves into his prudential arguments. Each section also considers the rhetorical functions of the arguments he has advanced. This chapter concludes with a discussion of the potential implications of Justice Thomas's rhetorical framing of First Amendment cases. The thesis that this chapter advances is that whereas Justice Thomas's historical arguments are important in his framing of the First Amendment, scholars and legal practitioners would be foolish to neglect the arguably more central place that precedent and prudence occupy in Justice Thomas's decisions.

HISTORICAL RHETORIC

Legal scholars and practitioners have long thought of Justice Thomas as an originalist. For example, Bradley Jacob wrote that while Antonin Scalia is the "contemporary Godfather of the originalist movement," there is "another Justice on the Supreme Court, a quiet Justice who rarely speaks during oral argument and is not famous for his lectures or books on this topic, who may be as much or more committed to the principles of originalism as Justice Scalia. That Justice, of course, is Clarence Thomas."[1] Originalism has its basis in historical rhetoric, since justices that are originalist in their orientation "stand for an original textual meaning that has been lost or discarded by other modern judges and scholars."[2] The purpose of this section is to document the historical rhetoric of Justice Thomas in his nomination process and First Amendment decisions. Doing so will highlight some of the reasons for scholars characterizing Justice Thomas as an originalist. However, as we shall see later in this chapter, Justice Thomas is a much more complicated thinker on the First Amendment than a strictly originalist label implies.[3]

With Justice Thomas having been labeled an originalist, the fact that he has employed historical rhetoric in both his confirmation hearings and subsequent decisions comes as no surprise. Indeed, as Bobbitt (1982) noted, "Historical arguments depend on a determination of the original understanding of the constitutional provision to be construed."[4] Justice Thomas presumes to be exemplary in determining the "original" understanding of the Constitution, and by extension the First Amendment. He indicated the importance of such determination in his confirmation hearings prior to becoming a Supreme Court justice.

Senator Herb Kohl (D-Wisconsin) questioned Justice Thomas about the way his personal beliefs might impact his ability to judge cases that came before the Supreme Court. Specifically, he asked Justice Thomas about this statement in 1985: "As for prayer, my mother says that when they took that out of schools, the schools went to hell. She may be right. Religion certainly is a source of positive values and we need to get as many positive values in schools as possible."[5] Senator Kohl asked Justice Thomas, "You're being considered for the Supreme Court and you will be in a position to set precedents, so your personal views are of great consequence. So, we'd like to ask you this. The Supreme Court has repeatedly ruled that prayer in the schools violates the First Amendment. Given your statement in 1985, could you explain your views on prayer in school today?"[6] Justice Thomas replied with a blend of historical and precedential rhetoric: "From my standpoint, as a citizen of this country and as a judge, the metaphor of the Jeffersonian 'wall of separation' is an important metaphor. The Court has established the *Lemon* test to analyze the Establishment Clause cases and I have no quarrel with that test. The Court of course has had difficulty in applying the *Lemon* test and is grappling with that as we sit here, I would assume, and over the few years—past few years. But the concept itself, the Jeffersonian 'Wall of Separation,' the *Lemon* test, neither of those do I quarrel with."[7] In this particular statement, Justice Thomas acknowledged the importance he placed on a historical interpretation of the First Amendment. The historical argument is particularly important in this instance because of Justice Thomas's willingness to default to the Jeffersonian "wall of separation" (a historical argument) when he faced the nearly impossible task of advancing a precedential (i.e., the "difficulty" of applying the *Lemon* test).

However, in actual practice in his First Amendment rulings, Justice Thomas rarely, if ever, has made mention of historical arguments with as much commonality as one would assume one would find based on his statements from the confirmation hearings. There are at least three cases in which the historical argument surfaced as justification for Justice Thomas's decision. In chronological order, the cases were *McIntyre v. Ohio Elections Commission* (April 19, 1995), *Rosenberger v. University of Virginia* (June 29, 1995), and *Morse v. Frederick* (2007). Note that Justice Thomas served on the Court for four years before making a First Amendment decision involving the historical argument.

McIntyre v. Ohio Elections Commission concerned the issue of whether the government may constitutionally prohibit the distribution of campaign literature that does not contain the name and address of the person issuing it. Margaret McIntyre was a resident of Westerville, Ohio, and opposed her local school district's request for a tax levy. McIntyre expressed her disagreement by preparing and distributing handbills to persons attending a meeting concerning the handbill. Some of the handbills identified herself as the author, while others were signed "CONCERNED PARENTS AND TAX PAYERS." The Ohio Elections Commission found that Mrs. McIntyre had violated election law and fined her one hundred dollars because of the anonymity of some of the handbills (the ones that did not identify herself as the author). In a seven to two decision, the Supreme Court ruled in favor of McIntyre, finding that anonymous speech about important public issues was core political speech and that any attempt to regulate this speech must be "narrowly tailored." While Justice Stevens wrote the majority opinion, Justice Thomas wrote a concurring decision that highlights his rhetorical use of the historical argument.

In his concurring opinion, Justice Thomas wrote extensively about the importance of interpreting the First Amendment in a way consistent with the framers of the Constitution. I quote Justice Thomas at length to provide a feel for the extent of his conviction regarding the historical argument:

The First Amendment states that the government "shall make no law . . . abridging the freedom of speech, or of the press." . . . When interpreting the Free Speech and Press Clauses, we must be guided by their original meaning, for "[t]he Constitution is a written instrument. As such its meaning does not alter. That which it meant when adopted, it means now." . . . We have long recognized that the meaning of the Constitution "must necessarily depend on the words of the constitution [and] the meaning and intention of the convention which framed and proposed it for adoption and ratification to the conventions . . . in the several states." . . . We should seek the original understanding when we interpret the Speech and Press Clauses, just as we do when we read the Religion Clauses of the First Amendment. When the Framers did not discuss the precise question at issue, we have turned to "what history reveals was the contemporaneous understanding of [the Establishment Clause's] guarantees." . . . "[T]he line we must draw between the permissible and the impermissible is one which accords with history and faithfully reflects the understanding of the Founding Fathers."[8]

Justice Thomas then argued that prohibiting anonymous political speech was unconstitutional based on the Founders' intentions. Specifically, he wrote that "the historical evidence indicates that Founding-era Americans opposed attempts to require that anonymous authors reveal their identities on the ground that forced disclosure violated the 'freedom of the press.'"[9]

Justice Thomas also relied upon the historical argument in *Rosenberger v. University of Virginia.* The case concerned whether a public university that pays printing costs for a number of student publications can deny that benefit to a student-run religious publication. On a five to four vote, the Supreme Court ruled that the distribution of moneys in the fund was a neutral supply of benefits, despite the dissent's protestations that the distribution of fund proceeds to a religious organization should be considered an unconstitutional tax for the benefit of a religious activity. While he voted in the majority, Justice Thomas wrote a concurring opinion to refute the claims of the dissenting opinion.

He answered the historical claims of the dissenting opinion by advancing his own historical argument. Specifically, he wrote that "history provides an answer for the constitutional question posed by this case, but it is not the one given by the dissent. The dissent identifies no evidence that the framers intended to disable religious entities from participating on neutral terms in evenhanded government programs. The evidence that does exist points in the opposite direction and provides ample support for today's decision."[10] From a rhetorical perspective, Justice Thomas's need to respond to the claims of the dissenting opinion demonstrated the importance of the historical argument as part of the justice's repertoire.

Most recently, Justice Thomas provided a historical argument for his interpretation of the Constitution in *Morse v. Frederick* (a.k.a. the "Bong Hits 4 Jesus" case). This case concerned whether the First Amendment allows public schools to prohibit students from displaying messages that alleg-edly promote the use of illegal substances at so-called school-sponsored events. Deborah Morse, high school principal, suspended student Joseph Frederick after he displayed a banner reading "BONG HiTS 4 JESUS" across the street from the school during the 2002 Olympic Torch relay run. The Court ruled in an unusual four to one to four decision that the suspension of Frederick did not violate his First Amendment rights. In his concurring deci-sion, Justice Thomas took the most radical position by denying First Amend-ment rights to students in schools altogether.

Justice Thomas based his decision on a historical argument about schools at the time of the writing of the First Amendment. According to Kenneth Starr, "Consistent with his iconoclastic approach to constitutional issues, Justice Thomas called for a housekeeping in the Court's student free speech cases. . . . Justice Thomas based his concurrence on his view of the original purpose and protection of the Constitution."[11] Specifically, Justice Thomas wrote:

> [T]he history of public education suggests that the First Amendment, as origi-nally understood, does not protect student speech in public schools. Although colonial schools were exclusively private, public education proliferated in the early 1800s. By the time the State ratified the Fourteenth Amendment, public schools had become relatively common. . . . If students in public schools were originally understood as having free-speech rights, one would have expected nineteenth-century schools to have respected those rights and courts to have enforced them. They did not.[12]

Worth noting is that Justice Thomas employed this historical argument in order to discount the *Tinker* case of 1969, in which the Court had ruled that students do not lose their First Amendment rights at the schoolhouse door. Thus, as we turn to the precedential arguments, we have a specific point at which Justice Thomas defaults to the historical argument only when he finds that there is a blatant disregard for historical interpretation in the Constitu-tion.

PRECEDENTIAL ARGUMENTS

Precedential arguments are those that rely on claims established in previous case law (i.e., stare decisis) in order to generate a ruling about the nature and scope of constitutional rights. As noted in the previous section, scholars and legal practitioners are quick to point out that Justice Thomas is primarily an originalist. However, I hope to show in this and the following sections that Justice Thomas has based many of his decisions on precedent and prudence.

From a rhetorical perspective, he has employed precedent and prudence on the condition that he does not find there to be a conflict between the historical argument and precedential and prudential arguments. Thus, understanding the kinds of precedential and prudential arguments he has defended is centrally important to navigating his interpretation of First Amendment freedoms.

Before his confirmation to the Court, Justice Thomas provided symptoms of the vital role that he gave to Court precedent. For example, in his confirmation hearings, there were two specific examples in which he discussed the importance of Court precedent. First, there was his interaction with Senator Strom Thurmond (R-South Carolina), who was concerned with how Justice Thomas would interpret the First Amendment when it came to religious freedoms. Thurmond cited the opinion of Justice Scalia for *Employment Division v. Smith* and asked Justice Thomas, "Would you please briefly discuss the impact this decision has on the compelling interest test established in *Sherbert v. Verner* in 1963?"[13] Justice Thomas replied by stating:

> Of course, Justice Scalia's decision was, in essence, that since the general criminal statutes outlawed the use of peyote, I think in that case, that one could not claim that it was a violation of their First Amendment to exercise their religious beliefs, that this preclusion by statute had occurred or that you could not use it in a religious exercise of any sort or religious celebration. What Justice Scalia did was actually use a different test than had been used in the past. He avoided using the *Sherbert* test. Justice O'Connor used the compelling interest test, she used *Sherbert* test and reached the same result, if I remember the case right. I think it is an important departure from prior approaches and it's one that anyone who approaches these cases should be concerned about or at least be watchful for.[14]

This reply indicates his skepticism toward establishing new precedent by way of a new test for evaluating cases in front of the Court. It also demonstrates his general commitment to the test that Scalia used that came before the *Sherbert* test. From a rhetorical perspective this is symptomatic of Justice Thomas's larger commitment to the history of the Court, not just the history of the framers, as documented in his use of historical argument.

A second instance of precedential rhetoric in Justice Thomas's confirmation hearings occurred in his interaction with Senator Patrick Leahy (D-Vermont), who was concerned about how Justice Thomas might interpret cases pertaining to scientific expression. He asked Justice Thomas the general question, "I'm not trying to give you a specific case, you understand, Judge. I just want to make sure we differentiate between the types of speech. But a scientific debate—First Amendment protections?"[15] Justice Thomas replied, "We value all of our speech. What I'm trying to say is I don't limit the—and see no reason and haven't seen the Court limit our freedom of speech to whether or not we're talking about science or whether we're talking about politics. Certainly the Court has attempted to accord protection of speech such as on, for example, the most recent case, being the *Texas v. Johnson*, the flag burning case."[16] Of course, Justice Thomas was referring to the specific case of *Texas v. Johnson* as precedential justification for his interpretation of the First Amendment. While this answer may be supported by a historical argument, it is worth noting that Justice Thomas did not make such a justification, as he did elsewhere in his confirmation hearings, when he referred to both the *Lemon* test (as precedential) *and* the Jeffersonian "wall of separation" (as historical). To the contrary, in this instance, he failed to even mention the historical argument.

After his confirmation hearings, Justice Thomas has consistently employed the precedential argument in his decisions regarding the First Amendment. For example, in *Dawson v. Delaware* (1992), Justice Thomas relied on the use of precedent in his written decision. *Dawson v. Delaware* concerned whether a criminal defendant's First Amendment right to freedom of association prevents the prosecution from introducing evidence of the defendant's gang membership. David Dawson was a member of the Aryan Brotherhood (a prison gang) and was accused of first-degree murder and various other crimes. The defense sought to exclude evidence of Dawson's gang membership in the murder trial on the basis of such evidence violating his First Amendment freedom of association. In an eight to one decision, the Court ruled that evidence of his gang membership was admissible evidence for the prosecution and did not violate Dawson's First Amendment rights, particularly the right to confidential assembly.

In his majority opinion, Justice Thomas used primarily precedential reasoning to justify his argument:

> We have long held that the Constitution permits courts and juries to consider character evidence in sentencing proceedings. See *Williams v. New York*, 337 U.S. 241, 247 (1949). Until today, we have never hinted that the First Amendment limits the aspects of a defendant's character that they may consider. To the contrary, we have emphasized that the sentencing authority "may appropriately conduct an inquiry broad in scope, largely unlimited either as to the kind of information he may consider, or the source from which it may come." *United States v. Tucker*, 404 U.S. 443, 446 (1972). In *Williams*, for example, we upheld a New York law that encouraged the sentencing judge to consider evidence about the defendant's "past life, health, habits, conduct, and mental and moral propensities," 337 U.S., at 245, a phrase easily broad enough to encompass a substantial amount of First Amendment activity. Writing for the Court, Justice Black specifically identified religion and interests as sentencing considerations that may "give the sentencing judge a composite picture of the defendant."[17]

He reasoned that the Court has always held affiliations as admissible evidence. Worth noting is that while the precedents may be consistent with the Constitution's framers' intentions, Justice Thomas does not rely on the parts of previous decisions that discuss such intentions. Rather, he has consistently shown a rhetorical preference for citing those aspects of previous law that establish a precedential argument for his opinions.

Justice Thomas also relied heavily on precedential arguments in *Mitchell v. Helms* (2000). This case determined whether Chapter 2 of the Education Consolidation and Improvement Act of 1981, which provides federal funds to state and local education agencies to purchase and lend neutral, secular, and nonreligious materials, and which allocates funds to public and private—secular and sectarian—schools on an equal per-student basis, violates the establishment clause of the First Amendment. In a six to three decision, the Court ruled that Chapter 2 did not violate the establishment clause of the First Amendment. Justice Thomas wrote the majority opinion for the Court and relied heavily on precedential arguments in order to justify the position of the Court:

> Our recent precedents, particularly *Zobrest*, require us to reject respondents' argument. For *Zobrest* gave no consideration to divertibility or even to actual diversion. Had such things mattered to the Court in *Zobrest*, we would have found the case to be quite easy—for striking down rather than, as we did, upholding the program—which is just how the dissent saw the case. See, e.g., 509 U. S., at 18 (Blackmun, J., dissenting) ("Until now, the Court never has authorized a public employee to participate directly in religious indoctrination"); id., at 22 ("[G]overnment crosses the boundary when it furnishes the medium for communication of a religious message. . . . [A] state-employed sign-language interpreter would serve as the conduit for James' religious education, thereby assisting Salpointe [High School] in its mission of religious indoctrination"); id., at 23 (interpreter "is likely to place the imprimatur of governmental approval upon the favored religion"); see generally id., at 18–23. Quite clearly, then, we did not, as respondents do, think that the use of governmental aid to further religious indoctrination was synonymous with religious indoctrination by the government or that such use of aid created any improper incentives.[18]

There are two important assessments to be made with respect to this use of the precedential argument. First, Justice Thomas appealed to the history of the Court, rather than the history of the framers of the Constitution, in supporting his argument. Second, he relied on the recent decisions of the Court rather than choosing to rely on older precedents.[19] These two observations suggest that Justice Thomas may begin his decisions with the precedents of the Court and then, only if necessary, turn to the framers when interpreting the First Amendment.

More evidence of Justice Thomas's reliance on precedential arguments is found in *Shaw v. Murphy* (April 18, 2001). This case determined whether prison inmates have a First Amendment right to assist inmates in legal matters that enhance their constitutional protections. Pat Tracy asked fellow prison inmate Kevin Murphy, a trained inmate law clerk, for legal assistance. Murphy wrote a letter to Tracy urging him not to plead guilty to a charge of assaulting a guard. Prison guard Robert Shaw intercepted Murphy's letter and charged him with violating prison rules. In a nine to zero decision, the Supreme Court ruled that prison officials do not violate inmates' First Amendment rights if the prison regulation is reasonably related to a legitimate penological interest. Justice Thomas wrote the majority opinion, in which he invoked the *Turner* test[20] as a basis for his argument to deny the prisoner's claim to First Amendment rights:

> Because *Turner* provides the test for evaluating prisoners' First Amendment challenges, the issue before us is whether *Turner* permits an increase in constitutional protection whenever a prisoner's communication includes legal advice. We conclude that it does not. To increase the constitutional protection based upon the content of a communication first requires an assessment of the value of that content. But the *Turner* test, by its terms, simply does not accommodate valuations of content. On the contrary, the *Turner* factors concern only the relationship between the asserted penological interests and the prison regulation.[21]

Contrary to the belief that Justice Thomas consistently relies upon an originalist interpretation of the Constitution as his measuring stick, his opinion here relied on the *Turner* test. Because the *Turner* test is not explicitly in the Constitution or in the debates of the framers, it is clear that Justice Thomas relied on a precedential argument rather than a historical one in this case.

Two months after the Court ruled on *Shaw v. Murphy*, the Court ruled on *Good News Club v. Milford Central School*. The case pertained to two First Amendment issues: (1) whether a public school policy creating a limited public forum that expressly bans religious groups from school facilities constitutes viewpoint discrimination in violation of freedom of speech and (2) whether allowing the Good News Club to use school facilities for meetings would have constituted a violation of the establishment clause. Milford Central School had refused access to its facilities by the Good News Club on the basis that the club's meetings would be "the equivalent of religious worship . . . rather than the expression of religious views or values on a secular subject." In a six to three decision, the Court held that the school did engage in expressible viewpoint discrimination by denying the club permission to use its facilities, and that permitting the club to hold meetings in school facilities would not have violated the establishment clause. Justice Thomas wrote the majority opinion for the Court while upholding several of the

Court's precedents. For example, he used the *Rosenberger*, *Lamb's Chapel*, and *Cornelius* case precedents to rule on the issue of viewpoint discrimination:

> When the State establishes a limited public forum, the State is not required to and does not allow persons to engage in every type of speech. The State may be justified "in reserving [its forum] for certain groups or for the discussion of certain topics." *Rosenberger v. Rector and Visitors of Univ. of Va.*, 515 U. S. 819, 829 (1995); see also *Lamb's Chapel*, supra, at 392–393. The State's power to restrict speech, however, is not without limits. The restriction must not discriminate against speech on the basis of viewpoint, *Rosenberger*, supra, at 829, and the restriction must be "reasonable in light of the purpose served by the forum," *Cornelius v. NAACP Legal Defense & Ed. Fund, Inc.*, 473 U. S. 788, 806 (1985). Applying this test, we first address whether the exclusion constituted viewpoint discrimination. We are guided in our analysis by two of our prior opinions, *Lamb's Chapel* and *Rosenberger*. In *Lamb's Chapel*, we held that a school district violated the Free Speech Clause of the First Amendment when it excluded a private group from presenting films at the school based solely on the films' discussions of family values from a religious perspective. Likewise, in *Rosenberger*, we held that a university's refusal to fund a student publication because the publication addressed issues from a religious perspective violated the Free Speech Clause. Concluding that Milford's exclusion of the Good News Club based on its religious nature is indistinguishable from the exclusions in these cases, we hold that the exclusion constitutes viewpoint discrimination. Because the restriction is viewpoint discriminatory, we need not decide whether it is unreasonable in light of the purposes served by the forum.[22]

This passage is telling because the test that Justice Thomas employed was not a test that was discussed by the framers of the Constitution. And, perhaps more importantly, this decision informs us about what Justice Thomas did not discuss in his confirmation hearings—namely, that the Jeffersonian "wall of separation" that he was so adamant about in his hearing does not apply to the walls of a public school.

The final case of significance in which Justice Thomas relied upon precedential arguments was *Washington State Grange v. Washington State Republican Party* (2008). This case concerned whether a "blanket primary" restrains political parties' supporters from their First Amendment freedom of association. The blanket primary was a system that advanced the two candidates with the most votes, regardless of political affiliation, to the general election. In a seven to two decision, the Court upheld the system by ruling that political parties' supporters did not have their constitutional freedom of association infringed upon by the new political process. Justice Thomas delivered the majority opinion of the Court, in which he relied solely on precedential arguments to make his case. He rejected each of the contentions of the Washington State Republican Party because "They all depend, not on any facial requirement of I-872, but on the possibility that voters will be confused as to the meaning of the party-preference designation."[23] Justice Thomas noted that such contentions were rooted in "sheer speculation" and that there was no basis to "presume that a well-informed electorate will interpret a candidate's party-preference designation to mean that the candidate is the party's chosen nominee or representative."[24] Furthermore, Justice Thomas acknowledged that "it is possible that voters will misinterpret that candidates' party-preference designation as reflecting endorsement by the parties. But these cases involve a facial challenge, and we cannot strike down I-872 on its face based on the mere possibility of voter confusion."[25] Justice Thomas provided numerous case precedents to justify his decision:

> See *Yazoo*, 226 U.S., at 219 ("[T]his court must deal with the case in hand and not with imaginary ones"); *Pullman Co. v. Knott*, 235 U. S. 23, 26 (1914) (A statute "is not to be upset upon hypothetical and unreal possibilities, if it would be good upon the facts as they are"). Because respondents brought their suit as a facial challenge, we have no evidentiary record against which to assess their assertions that voters will be confused. See *Timmons*, 520 U. S., at 375–376 (Stevens, J., dissenting) (rejecting judgments based on "imaginative theoretical sources of voter confusion" and "entirely hypothetical" outcomes). Indeed, because I-872 has never been implemented, we do not even have ballots indicating how party preference will be displayed. It stands to reason that whether voters will be confused by the party-preference designations will depend in significant part on the form of the ballot.[26]

Justice Thomas, therefore, relied on *Yazoo*, *Pullman*, and *Timmons* to justify his decision in this case. An important note to consider is that while Justice Scalia is often referred to as the champion of the originalist movement, Justice Thomas differed with his opinion on this case, and the justification that Justice Thomas used was based solely in Court precedent. In addition to Justice Thomas's heavy use of the precedential arguments in his First Amendment rulings, he tends to employ prudential arguments on a fairly consistent basis.

PRUDENTIAL ARGUMENTS

According to Bobbitt, when using the prudential form of argument, a Supreme Court justice "need not treat the merits of the particular controversy" but rather make an argument about "the practical wisdom of using the courts in a particular way."[27] Such practical wisdom often takes the form of pragmatic argumentation and may subvert certain constitutional protections due to the logistical difficulties of providing given protections. Interestingly, Justice Thomas did not advance prudential arguments about the First Amendment in his confirmation hearings, even though they have occupied significant space in his First Amendment decisions.

Justice Thomas first employed the prudential argument relating to the First Amendment in 2000 in his majority opinion in *Mitchell v. Helms*. While he also relied on precedential arguments in this case, as noted in the previous section, the prudential argument was important to his mode of constitutional interpretation. Specifically, he wrote:

> The dissent serves up a smorgasbord of 11 factors that, depending on the facts of each case "in all its particularity," post, at 11, could be relevant to the constitutionality of a school-aid program. And those 11 are a bare minimum. We are reassured that there are likely more. See post, at 19, 22. Presumably they will be revealed in future cases, as needed, but at least one additional factor is evident from the dissent itself: The dissent resurrects the concern for political divisiveness that once occupied the Court but that post-*Aguilar* cases have rightly disregarded. Compare post, at 1, 6, 36, 37, 45, n. 27, with *Agostini*, supra, at 233–234; *Bowen*, 487 U. S., at 617, n. 14; *Amos*, 483 U. S., at 339–40, n. 17. As Justice O'Connor explained in dissent in *Aguilar*: "It is curious indeed to base our interpretation of the Constitution on speculation as to the likelihood of a phenomenon which the parties may create merely by prosecuting a lawsuit." 473 U. S., at 429. While the dissent delights in the perverse chaos that all these factors produce, post, at 34; see also post, at 2, 19–20, the Constitution becomes unnecessarily clouded, and legislators, litigants, and lower courts groan, as the history of this case amply demonstrates.[28]

Justice Thomas's decision in this case was, therefore, partly based on the pragmatic argument of being "uncloudy" so that legislators, litigants, and lower courts do not "groan" when speculating about legal factors. He did not make the case that the eleven minimum factors would not help to secure First Amendment rights. Rather, he used the eleven minimum factors as the premise of an argument for potential confusion about First Amendment rights and the difficulties with which government administration is confronted.

Justice Thomas also employed both the precedential and prudential arguments in *Shaw v. Murphy*. In his majority opinion, Justice Thomas expressed a concern for the impact of this ruling on creating additional governmental oversight: "If courts were permitted to enhance constitutional protection based on their assessments of the content of the particular communications, courts would be in a position to assume a greater role in decisions affecting prison administration."[29] He continued by citing precedent: "Seeking to avoid 'unnecessarily perpetuat[ing] the involvement of the federal courts in affairs of prison administration,' *Turner*, 482 U.S., at 89 (quoting *Martinez*, supra, at 407) [alteration in original], we reject an alteration of the *Turner* analysis that would entail additional federal-court oversight."[30] Thus, Justice

Thomas not only carefully crafted his decision to reflect that which would be prudent, he also rhetorically crafted his decision in such a way as to rely on the authority of the Court in the *Turner* case. In other words, for Justice Thomas, prudence has precedence.

Moreover, there are a few cases in which Justice Thomas relied primarily on the prudential argument in order to interpret the First Amendment. For instance, in *Ashcroft v. Free Speech Coalition* (2002), Justice Thomas wrote about the enforcement issues of online child pornography. This case concerned whether the provisions of the Child Pornography Prevention Act (CPPA) of 1996, which concerned the shipment, distribution, receipt, reproduction, sale, or possession of any visual depiction that "appears to be of a minor engaging in sexually explicit conduct," violates the First Amendment The Free Speech Coalition charged that the "appears to be a minor" and "conveys the impression" clauses suffer from overbreadth and are thus a violation of the First Amendment.[31] The Supreme Court voted six to three on the "appears to be a minor" clause and seven to two on the "conveys the impression" clause to the effect that both clauses were violations of First Amendment freedoms.[32] Justice Thomas wrote the majority opinion, in which he conveyed genuine concern for the pragmatic ability of law enforcement officials to sufficiently enforce child pornography laws. Specifically, he wrote that "the Government points to no case in which a defendant has been acquitted based on a 'computer-generated images' defense."[33] He continued, "Technology may evolve to the point where it becomes impossible to enforce actual child pornography laws because the Government cannot prove that certain images are of real children. In the event this occurs, the Government should not be foreclosed from enacting a regulation of virtual child pornography that contains an appropriate affirmative defense or some other narrowly drawn restriction."[34] So, while Justice Thomas decided in this case against the federal government because of the overbroad clauses of the CPPA, he provided the rationale for future restrictions of First Amendment freedom based on the pragmatic concern for the government's ability to regulate child pornography on the Internet.

Two years later, Justice Thomas used prudential arguments in another case involving Attorney General John Ashcroft. Like the previous case, *Ashcroft v. ACLU* (2004) concerned the government's ability to regulate Internet pornography through the Child Online Protection Act (COPA). The government claimed that Congress had fixed the problems of the CPPA and that there was no constitutional violation. However, the Court held that the government was to be held enjoined from enforcing COPA absent further action by the court of appeals or the district court. Justice Thomas delivered the opinion of the Court for certain sections of the statement.

In section four of the Court's decision, Justice Thomas made clear his belief in the relevance of the prudential argument concerning the First Amendment. Justice Thomas began this section by highlighting the issue of overbreadth: "We do not express any view as to whether COPA suffers from substantial overbreadth for other reasons, whether the statute is unconstitutionally vague, or whether the District Court correctly concluded that the statute likely will not survive strict scrutiny analysis once adjudication of the case is completed below."[35] He invoked the prudential considerations in resolving such issues: "While respondents urge us to resolve these questions at this time, prudence dictates allowing the Court of Appeals to first examine these difficult issues. . . . [W]e could not do so without addressing matters yet to be considered by the Court of Appeals."[36] Justice Thomas used the prudential argument to specifically avoid and/or delay interpreting the First Amendment. If his decisions regarding the First Amendment's application to the Internet are any indication, we might speculate that Justice Thomas is not ready to render a judgment on First Amendment cases regarding the Internet—perhaps due to their complexity (the eleven or more standards) or due to this being a relatively new technological application of the First Amendment. Regardless, in cases involving the Internet, arguments about prudence are vital to Justice Thomas's approach to the First Amendment.[37] Prudence is a concern, but it does not trump overbroad legislation unless there is a demonstration that enforcement against obscenity is an impossibility. If Justice Thomas perceives that enforcement is impossible without causing an overly broad law, he will most likely rule in favor of prudence and against the First Amendment's requirement that legislation be narrowly tailored.

However, cases concerning the Internet are not the only cases in which we find Justice Thomas's use of the prudential argument. This argument also appeared in *Tory v. Cochran* (2005), which concerned the issue of whether the death of a person who may have been libeled makes a case moot. Ulysses Tory was a former client of Johnnie Cochran, Jr., and picketed his offices for years claiming that Cochran was a liar and a thief. Cochran obtained an injunction barring Tory from speaking about Cochran or his firm in any public forum. Tory appealed the injunction on First Amendment grounds. Cochran died a week after the oral arguments, but Tory's lawyer argued that the case was not moot because the injunction barred Tory from speaking about Cochran's firm, which survived Cochran's death. In a seven to two decision, the Supreme Court ruled that the case was now moot.

Justice Thomas dissented and argued that the case should not have been dismissed as moot based on a prudential argument. Before providing the grounds for his dissent, Justice Thomas characterized the Court's majority opinion: "The Court purports to save petitioners the uncertainty of possible enforcement of the injunction, and thereby to prevent any chill on their First Amendment rights, by vacating the decision below. But . . . the Court . . .

only invites further litigation by pronouncing that 'injunctive relief may still be warranted,' conceding that 'any appropriate party remains free to ask such relief, and 'express[ing] no view on the constitutional validity of any such new relief.'"[38] Then Justice Thomas provided reasons for why "further litigation" is imprudent; he noted that "What the Court means by 'any appropriate party' is unclear. Perhaps the Court means . . . Cochran's widow, who has taken his place in this suit. Or perhaps it means the Cochran firm, which has never been a party to this case, but may now (if 'appropriate') intervene and attempt to enjoin the defamation of a now-deceased third party. The Court's decision invites the doubts it seeks to avoid. . . . The more prudent course is to dismiss the writ as improvidently granted."[39] What we learn from this particular case from a rhetorical perspective is that arguments rooted in the opposition's vagueness may be compelling for Justice Thomas if they are coupled with arguments about increases in litigation based on a Supreme Court decision. More simply, Justice Thomas views his interpretations of the First Amendment as necessitating a decrease in litigation and a more efficient criminal justice system. If interpreting the First Amendment at the Supreme Court level risks vagueness, he will most likely rule against it.

With regard to the prudential form, the final case worth examining is *Randall v. Sorrell* (2006). As we have seen in previous chapters, this case involved the issue of whether Vermont's mandatory limits on candidate expenditures violated the precedent set in *Buckley v. Valeo*. Vermont passed its campaign finance law and placed a three-hundred-thousand-dollar spending cap on gubernatorial candidates, while applying lesser limits for other state political contests. Contributions to state campaigns were limited to as little as two hundred dollars per election cycle for state House races. The Court ruled six to three to reject Vermont's campaign finance limits on the basis that such limits constrained speech by telling candidates and voters how much campaigning was sufficient. Justice Thomas, who has wanted to overturn *Buckley v. Valeo* for many years because he is opposed to campaign limits, dissented and based his dissent on prudential concerns. He described the Court's majority opinion as advancing a two-step test. "The plurality sets forth what appears to be a two-step process for evaluating the validity of contribution limits: First, determine whether there are 'danger signs' in a particular case that the limits are too low; and, second, use 'independent judicial judgment' to 'review the record independently and carefully with an eye toward assessing the statute's "tailoring," that is, towards assessing the proportionality of the restrictions.'"[40] He claimed that "Neither step of this test can be reduced to a workable inquiry to be performed by States attempting to comply with this Court's jurisprudence."[41] He took particular issue with the first step on prudential grounds. "As to the first step, it is entirely unclear how to determine whether limits are so low as to constitute 'danger signs' that require a court to 'examine the record independently and carefully.'"[42] It is worth noting that Justice Thomas relied on a prudential argument as it pertained to pragmatic concerns. Whereas Bobbitt identified a type of prudential argument that weighs the costs and benefits, Justice Thomas is less concerned with the costs and benefits than he is with the pragmatic burdens of the criminal justice system. This suggests a need to expand Bobbitt's initial considerations of the constitutive dimensions of prudentialism.

CONCLUSIONS

Over the course of his tenure on the Supreme Court, Justice Thomas has primarily interpreted the First Amendment through historical, precedential, and prudential arguments. There are at least two observations worth noting. First, his reliance on historical arguments tends to bookend his career—they were relevant for him at the confirmation hearings and in his early decisions, they disappeared for a significant amount of time, and they resurfaced in his more recent decisions. Second, Justice Thomas relied on historical arguments more when writing concurring decisions and almost never in his majority or dissenting opinion. When writing majority and dissenting opinions for the Court, Justice Thomas tended to rely on precedential and prudential arguments in his decision.

The first rhetorical implication of this observation is that Justice Thomas's interpretive schema views the historical argument as only one criterion that advocates must address in order to persuade him. Advocates must at the same time take into account precedent and prudence. For Justice Thomas, the historical argument appears to be debatable in terms of what the framers meant by the First Amendment. Perhaps more important, if advocates do not make a compelling precedential *and* prudential argument, they are probably less likely to win Justice Thomas's vote. If historical arguments were centrally important to Justice Thomas's interpretation of the First Amendment, one would expect to see such arguments reflected in his decisions on a more consistent basis. The only time Justice Thomas wrote against precedent and in favor of the historical argument was in *Morse v. Frederick*, in which he sought to overturn the *Tinker* precedent. In this case, Justice Thomas viewed *Tinker* as a blatant disregard of the framers' intent when crafting the Constitution. This predilection implies that in order to persuade Justice Thomas, one needs to use a historical argument as an opening gambit rather than as an end goal. It is not inconceivable that an advocate may win both the precedential and/or prudential arguments, which may, in turn, influence Justice Thomas's view of historical interpretation. If the debate about history becomes difficult to resolve, Justice Thomas is likely to defer to precedent and prudence in making his decision. Thus, it is wise for the advocate trying to earn Justice Thomas's vote to learn from his interpretive framework of history, precedent, and prudence.

A second implication of Justice Thomas's interpretations of the First Amendment is that tradition is the guiding rhetorical trope. The historical and precedential arguments are symptomatic of his belief in the tradition of the Court as it is rooted in the authority given to it by the framers of the Constitution. The prudential arguments function to maintain the order of the Court in its management of the justice system and enable the tradition to continue. Thus, scholars and legal practitioners are certainly correct in their claim that Justice Thomas is an originalist. However, my analysis has suggested that Justice Thomas is a special kind of originalist. He is what I would call a traditionalist originalist because while believing that the original interpretations of the Constitution are relevant, Justice Thomas is more concerned with the traditions of the Court, which happen to include the framers' intent. This is evident in many cases in which he relied on prudential arguments when the framers' intentions were uncertain after and/or because of rigorous debate.[43]

From a rhetorical perspective, Justice Thomas's reliance on tradition (i.e., his historical and precedential claims) commits fallacies of *ad antiquitam* (claiming that since something has survived the tests of time or is simply old it must be good or valid). However, the fallacy is of little consequence because the fallacy is true for Justice Thomas in the sense that tradition becomes a way for him to rationalize a position on the First Amendment. According to Edward Shils, "Tradita can become objects of fervent attachment to the quality of pastness which is seen in them; they may be accepted in a manner which takes them for granted as the only reasonable thing to do or believe."[44] Thus, exemplars or custodians of tradition such as Justice Thomas and previous interpreters of First Amendment law provide interpretive significance to a cultural history that creates meaning in individuals. And it is in this lineage that Justice Thomas views himself, as a justice who passes on such meaning.

Tradition is, therefore, an authoritative voice that speaks to Justice Thomas. To put it another way, from Justice Thomas's perspective, the framers are the basis of the constitutional gospel. The justices that spread the word of the constitutional gospel are disciples of the framers. Justice Thomas is a traditionalist originalist when interpreting the First Amendment because he seeks to be the type of disciple that passes on the words of the constitutional gospel (via the framers) and its disciples (Supreme Court precedent) while at the same time protecting the Court's legitimacy through pragmatic considerations (prudential arguments). Thus, scholars and legal practitioners would be wise to frame arguments in terms of not only historical claims about original intent, but also the precedential and prudential arguments that have come to occupy Justice Thomas's beliefs about the First Amendment.

NOTES

1. Bradley P. Jacob, "Will the Real Constitutional Originalist Please Stand Up?" *Creighton Law Review*, 40 (2007): 595–650, 595–96.

2. Jacob, "Will the Real," 599.

3. While some scholars characterize Justice Thomas as holding firm to a belief in natural rights, there are few, if any, such appeals found in his First Amendment decisions.

4. Bobbitt, *Constitutional Fate*, 9.

5. *Nomination of Judge Clarence Thomas to Be Associate Justice of the Supreme Court of the United States: Hearings before the Committee on the Judiciary* (Washington, DC: Government Printing Office, October, 1991), available in part at http://www.firstamendmentjournal.com/about.aspx?id=18942 (accessed July 15, 2010).

6. *Nomination of Judge Clarence Thomas.*

7. *Nomination of Judge Clarence Thomas.*

8. 514 U.S. 334, 359 (1995).

9. 514 U.S. 334, 361 (1995).

10. 515 U.S. 819, 863 (1995).

11. Kenneth W. Starr, "Our Libertarian Court: Bong Hits 4 and the Enduring Hamiltonian-Jeffersonian Colloquy," *Lewis and Clark Law Review*, 12 (2008): 4.

12. 551 U.S. 393, 410–11 (2007).

13. *Nomination of Judge Clarence Thomas.*

14. *Nomination of Judge Clarence Thomas.*

15. *Nomination of Judge Clarence Thomas.*

16. *Nomination of Judge Clarence Thomas.*

17. 503 U.S. 159, 177 (1992).

18. 530 U.S. 793, 820–21 (2000).

19. This may seem obvious at first since recent precedents overturn previous ones. However, Justice Thomas does not necessarily fall in line in terms of relying on recent precedents. Rather, he has on occasion cited previous precedents as being more valid than recent ones (as in his citing of previous cases to justify his desire to overturn *Tinker*).

20. See Turner v. Safley, 482 U.S. 78 (1987). The *Turner* test is composed of four factors to determine the constitutionality of a prison regulation: (1) there must be a valid, rational connection between the prison regulation and the legitimate governmental interest put forward to justify it, (2) there must be alternative means of exercising the right that remain open to prison inmates, (3) a court must asses the impact accommodation of the asserted constitutional right will have on guards and other inmates, and on the allocation of prison resources generally, and (4) a court must determine if the prison had alternatives for achieving the same end—the absence of ready alternatives is evidence of the reasonableness of a prison regulation.

21. 532 U.S. 223, 230 (2001).

22. 533 U.S. 98, 106–7 (2001).

23. Case 06-713, 454.

24. Case 06-713, 454.

25. Case 06-713, 455.

26. Case 06-713, 455.

27. Bobbitt, *Constitutional Fate*, 7.

28. 530 U.S. 793, 825–26 (2000).

29. 532 U.S. 223, 230 (2001).

30. 532 U.S. 223, 230–31 (2001).

31. "*Ashcroft v. Free Speech Coalition,*" *Oyez: U.S. Supreme Court Media*, available at www.oyez.org/cases/2000-2009/2001/2001_00_795.

32. "*Ashcroft v. Free Speech Coalition,*" *Oyez.*

33. 535 U.S. 234, 259 (2002).

34. 535 U.S. 234, 259 (2002).

35. 535 U.S. 234, 585-86 (2002).

36. 535 U.S. 234, 586 (2002).

37. In the most recent case of *Citizen's United v. Federal Election Commission*, the Internet provided the only concern for Justice Thomas that compelled him to join in all but part four of the Court's decision. He wrote that "'the advent of the Internet' enables 'prompt disclosure of expenditures,' which 'provide[s]' political opponents 'with the information needed' to intimidate and retaliate against their foes. . . . I cannot endorse a view of the First Amendment that subjects citizens of this Nation to death threats, ruined careers, damaged or defaced property, or preemptive and threatening warning letters as the price for engaging in 'core political speech, the 'primary object of First Amendment protection.'" Thus, the pragmatic approach to preventing violence is pivotal in Justice Thomas's jurisprudence, which is skeptical of, if not resistant to, the Internet. 558 U.S. ___ (2010), slip. op. 6.

38. 544 U.S. 734, 740 (2005).

39. 544 U.S. 734, 740 (2005).

40. 548 U.S. 230, 267–68 (2006).

41. 548 U.S. 230, 268 (2006).

42. 548 U.S. 230, 268 (2006).

43. See, for instance, the example of Mitchell v. Helms, whereby he does not negate that the complicated standards may protect First Amendment rights (even if within the framers' intent), but rather relies on prudence as a basis for his decision.

44. Edward Shils, *Tradition* (Chicago: University of Illinois Press, 1981), 13.

Chapter Eleven

Associate Justice Alito

Tim West

> I think that freedom of speech and freedom of the press and all the freedoms set out in the First Amendment are matters of the utmost importance . . . If anybody reviews the opinions that I have written in the area of freedom of expression and other First Amendment . . . they will see that I strongly support those rights.—Samuel Alito, hearing before the Senate Judiciary Committee [1]

Associate Justice Samuel A. Alito, Jr., began his tenure on the United States Supreme Court on January 31, 2006. He was nominated by George W. Bush on October 31, 2005, and eventually replaced Sandra Day O'Connor after a contentious Senate confirmation vote. [2] After a failed filibuster attempt by Senator John Kerry (D-Massachusetts), the Senate confirmed Justice Alito on a partisan fifty-eight to forty-two vote, which made him the 110th justice of the Supreme Court. [3] Despite being the focus of a heated debate on Capitol Hill, Justice Alito brought a substantial amount of judicial experience to the high court. After graduating from Princeton and earning his JD at Yale Law School in 1975, Alito went on to serve as deputy assistant attorney general for the Department of Justice in 1985, U.S. attorney for the District of New Jersey in 1987, and appellant judge for the United States Third Circuit Court of Appeals from 1990 to 2005.

After a few decisions on the bench, Justice Alito received the nickname "Scalito" due to his affinity for (and ideological similarities to) the conservative justice Antonin Scalia. [4] However, as we shall see, Justice Alito tends to differ from Scalia when it comes to the application of the First Amendment. Regarding the issues of freedom of speech, press, and especially religion, Alito is more of a libertarian than Scalia and several other conservative members of the Court. [5]

This chapter will analyze the rhetorical strategies employed by Alito in First Amendment challenges that reached the Supreme Court. These strategies, or modalities, as described by Phillip Bobbitt, provide rationales for Supreme Court rulings that evolve into a judicial conscience.[6] In order to access Alito's use of modalities, I will analyze modalities as they appear within Justice Alito's rhetoric. By observing the modalities that he favors, this chapter will highlight rhetorical frames that appeal to him so that advocates can gain an understanding of Justice Alito's decision-making calculus. Initially, I will look at the modalities that surfaced in Judge Alito's nomination hearings, then dissect the modalities that were utilized during two of his most significant First Amendment opinions, *Hein v. Freedom from Religion Foundation* (2007)[7] and *Davis v. Federal Election Commission* (2008),[8] and conclude by examining the rhetorical implications of the modalities Justice Alito preferred.

CONFIRMATION HEARINGS

Unlike Chief Justice Roberts, who admitted that he had little experience in adjudicating First Amendment court cases, Justice Alito had a number of prior rulings he could discuss during his confirmation hearings. Thanks to Alito's lengthy tenure as an appellant judge and his 361 authored opinions, the Senate Judiciary Committee and the Senate at large were able to inquire about a wide array of First Amendment topics during Alito's nomination process.

After the successful appointment of John G. Roberts as the chief justice of the Supreme Court, the Senate faced the fact that the conservative majority of the Court was being increased. Due to this shift, most Democratic politicians on Capitol Hill were ready to challenge President Bush's next appointee. During Alito's hearing before the Senate's Judiciary Committee, Senator Patrick Leahy (D-Vermont) foreshadowed the imminent fight regarding Alito's appointment by emphasizing Bush's failed appointment of Harriet Miers and backhandedly criticizing Alito by saying:

> Supreme Court nominations should not be conducted through a series of winks and nods designed to reassure a small faction of our population, while leaving the American people in the dark. And no President, I think we would all agree, should be allowed to pack the courts, and especially the Supreme Court, with nominees selected to enshrine Presidential claims of Government power. The checks and balances that should be provided by the courts, Congress and the Constitution are too important to be sacrificed to a narrow partisan agenda. This hearing is the opportunity for the American people to learn what Samuel

Alito thinks about their fundamental constitutional rights and whether he—
you, Judge—will protect their liberty, their privacy and their autonomy from
Government intrusion.[9]

However, not all politicians were as critical as Leahy. Senator Mike DeWine
(R-Ohio), who displayed a more cordial tone, asked the first questions regarding Alito's opinions on the First Amendment. DeWine began by seeking
Alito's opinion on the application of the First Amendment in cases involving
the protection of pornography through freedom of expression. Alito answered by saying:

> Pornography on the Internet illustrates the fact that although the task of the
> judiciary is to apply principles that are in the Constitution and not make up its
> own principles, to apply those to different factual situations when the world
> changes, and in particular, in the First Amendment context, when means of
> communication changes. The job of applying the principles that have been
> worked out—and I think in this area worked out with a great deal of effort over
> a period of time—in the pre-Internet world, applying those to the world of the
> Internet is a really difficult problem, and I understand it. Congress has been
> struggling with it, and I know the judiciary has been struggling with it. The
> law, of course, as you know, constitutional law draws a distinction between
> obscenity, which has no First Amendment protection but is subject to a very
> strict definition, and pornography, which is not obscenity but is sexually relat-
> ed materials, with respect to minors, the Supreme Court has said that it's
> permissible for a State to regulate the sale of pornography to minors, has
> greater authority there. I think that's [*Ginsberg v. New York* (1968)]. It has
> greater authority there than it does with respect to the distribution of pornogra-
> phy to adults.[10]

Alito's response revealed one of the modalities that Alito favors. By admit-
ting that the judiciary is struggling with the issue of Internet pornography due
to the lack of specific constitutional guidance, Alito was overtly acknowledging that the "ethical" modality was used to frame his decisions.

Bobbitt defined the ethical modality as "moral commitments of the
American ethos that are reflected in the Constitution."[11] In answering Senator DeWine, Alito endorsed the utility of this modality when *clear* precedent
or constitutional guidance is not available; however, he also acknowledged
the importance of the doctrinal modality by concluding with a reference to
precedent regarding the state's ability to regulate the sale and distribution of
pornography to minors as established in *Ginsberg v. New York* (1968).[12]

The doctrinal modality is essentially the reliance on precedent to guide
future rulings, and Alito employed this modality several times during his
confirmation hearings. During Alito's questioning by the Senate subcommit-
tee, he relied on the doctrine of stare decisis in more than twenty questions.
Stare decisis, which is a synonym for the doctrinal modality, relies on prece-

dential rulings.[13] In Alito's case, the doctrinal and ethical modalities work in coordination. That is, Alito established a foundation for his rulings with his doctrinal approach and then built on that foundation with the ethical modality.

It should come as no surprise then that as questioning continued, Senator Schumer (D–New York) pressed Alito regarding instances where the Supreme Court deviated from stare decisis, including *United Artists v. Warrington* (2003), *Beauty Time v. VU Skin Systems* (1997), and *Rappa v. New Castle* (1994). Alito explained that he had no choice but to follow the Supreme Court's lead because of his respect for "vertical *stare decisis*"; that is, the Supreme Court decides the law of the land and hands it down to lower courts, which are bound to follow the precedents. Alito continued, in response to *United Artists*: "you have a Supreme Court decision intervening, and in that situation I thought it was our obligation—and I wrote the majority opinion there—to follow what the Supreme Court had said."[14] Alito's precedential rhetoric illustrated his tendency to favor this modality as a starting point for decisions.

Earlier, in response to Senator DeWine's question about the government's ability to restrict public speech, Justice Alito demonstrated his willingness to use the structural modality while on the bench: "I think that freedom of speech and freedom of the press and all the freedoms set out in the First Amendment are matters of the utmost importance. Freedom of speech is not only important for its own sake, but it is vital to the preservation of our form of government, and I think that if anybody reviews [the] opinions that I've written in the area of freedom of expression and other First Amendment areas they will see that I strongly support those rights." Bobbitt explained that structural modalities are "largely factless and [depend] on deceptively simple logical moves from the entire Constitutional text, rather than its parts."[15] Alito's response to DeWine conformed to the structural modality because he alleged that democracy would not exist without freedom of speech (which may be true; however, in terms of a being a legal response, this is a nonwarranted, nonfactual claim) and because he argued that the potential implications justify his reasoning. Moreover, Alito's statement employed the doctrinal modality because he used past rulings to forecast the future. By combining the structural modality with the doctrinal modality, Alito was "help[ing] the Court balance one right against the other"[16] so that they require "a heavy burden of proof."[17]

Samuel Alito was approved by the Senate's judiciary committee on a partisan ten to eight vote on January 24, 2006.[18] On the following day, the full Senate began its discussion of his nomination. The debate over Alito's qualifications and judicial ideology raged until January 31, 2006, when he was confirmed on a fifty-eight to forty-two vote.[19]

Over the past three years, Justice Alito has been faithful to the rationale that appeared in his confirmation hearings by primarily relying on structural and doctrinal modalities. Interestingly, during his short time on the Court, Alito has yet to apply the ethical modality to his most important decisions. In order to evaluate Alito's use of modalities, the remainder of this chapter will examine three of his most significant First Amendment opinions.

HEIN RULING

Hein v. Freedom from Religion Foundation (2007)[20] was "a lawsuit by a Wisconsin-based group of atheists and agnostics against the White House Office of Faith-Based and Community Initiatives."[21] The petitioners claimed that President Bush's faith-based initiatives, which set up conferences for religious groups to help them secure financial assistance, violated the "establishment clause" of the First Amendment because the initiatives blurred the lines between church and state. The Freedom from Religion Foundation filed suit because they believed that all citizens should have access to the funds that were being allocated to religious groups, which some argued was allowed due to precedent set by *Flast v. Cohen* (1968),[22] even though that decision was narrowly confined to its unique circumstances.

On June 25, 2007, Justice Alito announced in a five to four decision that Bush's faith-based programs *were* constitutional. Chief Justice Roberts, Jr., and Justice Anthony M. Kennedy joined in Justice Alito's opinion, while justices Scalia and Thomas wrote concurring opinions. The dissenters argued that the ruling violated the establishment clause.

Near the beginning of Alito's opinion, one of his modalities of decision making was revealed:

> It has long been established . . . that the payment of taxes is generally not enough to establish standing to challenge an action taken by the Federal Government. In light of the size of the federal budget, it is a complete fiction to argue that an unconstitutional federal expenditure causes an individual federal taxpayer any measurable economic harm. And if every federal taxpayer could sue to challenge any Government expenditure, the federal courts would cease to function as courts of law and would be cast in the role of general complaint bureaus.[23]

Alito's comment was interesting because it introduced the use of the prudential modality. Prudential reasoning is the cost-benefit assessment of a given ruling that Bobbitt summarized as "the particular wisdom of using the courts in a particular way."[24] Alito introduced this modality (which was not present during his hearing to the Senate or the Senate Judiciary Committee) in the face of the precedent set by *Flast v. Cohen* (1968).[25] He addressed the problem with *Flast* by arguing that the decision was not meant to apply to other situations: "we leave *Flast* as we found it . . . It is significant that, in the four decades since its creation, that *Flast* exception has largely been confined to its facts."[26] Alito used his statement on *Flast* to explain why he was not relying on the doctrinal paradigm in this case. Justices Scalia and Thomas, who favored retaining *Flast* as a precedent, noticed this passage and remarked "there is no intellectual justification for this limitation."[27]

Alito also used a prudential-doctrinal hybrid modality to explain his logic for ruling against the petitioner's claim for monetary reimbursement by arguing that "a plaintiff raising only a generally available grievance about government—claiming only harm to his and every citizen's interest in proper application of the Constitution and laws, and seeking relief that no more directly and tangibly benefits him than it does the public at large—does not state an Article III case or controversy. *Lujan v. Defenders of Wildlife* (1992)."[28] In this case, Alito used the hybrid modality to bolster the logic behind his application of prudential and doctrinal modalities. The combination of modalities was rhetorically effective because it enabled Alito to adhere to his structuralist philosophy while simultaneously addressing the implications of his ruling. He used this framing strategy to increase the appeal of his ruling because he believed that the prudential implications of such an action would create a better domestic situation for charities.

Two trends were evident in Alito's opinion on *Hein v. Freedom from Religion Foundation* (2007). First, he showed an affinity for prudential rhetoric. Despite framing his decision-making process as strictly doctrinal and structural during his confirmation hearings, the rhetoric of his opinion in *Hein v. Freedom from Religion Foundation* (2007) revealed that he is not averse to using cost-benefit arguments. Second, despite the introduction of prudential principles, *Hein v. Freedom from Religion Foundation* (2007) also reinforced Alito's reliance on doctrinal logic in order to determine the outcome of legal questions.

DAVIS RULING

Davis v. FEC (2008)[29] involved a challenge to the so-called Millionaire's Amendment of the Bipartisan Campaign Reform Act (BCRA) of 2002. The Millionaire's Amendment was intended to ensure that candidates who were not wealthy could compete against opponents who were wealthy, since prior to the amendment wealthy candidates were not restricted from using their own funds in an unlimited manner. Specifically, this amendment raised campaign finance limits for candidates whose opponent's personal funds amount

(OPFA) exceeded $350,000 dollars. If a candidate surpassed the $350,000-dollar self-contribution limit, the amendment tripled the donor limits for his opponent. Thus, the amendment tried to level the political battlefield by providing a disincentive for the wealthy to use their own funds.

Jack Davis, a Democrat from New York, unsuccessfully ran for the House of Representatives in 2004 and 2006. After contributing over $2.2 million of his own money to his 2006 campaign, Davis, and his attorney Andrew Herman, sued the FEC because they believed that the Millionaire's Amendment "[makes] it easier for your opponent to beat you."[30] Davis argued that the amendment violates the First Amendment because it chills his speech by hindering the efforts of self-financing candidates during an election. Davis also contended that the amendment contradicted the precedent set in *Buckley v. Valeo* (1976),[31] which struck down limits on campaign expenditures and upheld the right of individuals to contribute to their own campaigns without limits.

Oral argument in *Davis v. FEC* was heard at the Supreme Court on April 22, 2008, and the decision was announced on June 26, 2008. Ultimately the Court struck down the Millionaire's Amendment because it violated Davis's First Amendment rights. Despite minor disagreements among the Court's conservative faction (which prompted Thomas to write a dissenting opinion on the second part of the ruling), Roberts, Scalia, and Kennedy joined Alito's opinion.

Justice Alito's ruling in *Davis v. FEC* shed light on Alito's rhetorical framing as well as his judicial philosophy regarding issues of political contributions. Alito began his ruling on Davis's claims of First Amendment erosion by declaring:

> [The Millionaire's Amendment] raises the limits only for the non-self-financing candidate and does so only when the self-financing candidate's expenditure of personal funds causes the OPFA threshold to be exceeded. We have never upheld the constitutionality of a law that imposes different contribution limits for candidates who are competing against each other, and we agree with Davis that this scheme impermissibly burdens his First Amendment right to spend his own money for campaign speech. . . . *Buckley*'s emphasis on the fundamental nature of the right to spend personal funds for campaign speech is instructive. While BCRA does not impose a cap on a candidate's expenditure of personal funds, it imposes an unprecedented penalty on any candidate who robustly exercises that First Amendment right.[32]

Justice Alito resorted to his doctrinal modality to begin his assessment of this case. Using precedent set in *Buckley*, Alito acknowledged that there were unequal electoral rules facing candidates who surpassed the OPFA threshold in comparison to those who do not. He explained that the FEC's arguments had "no constitutional basis," and that "[the Millionaire's Amendment] imposes a substantial burden on the exercise of the First Amendment right to use personal funds for campaign speech, that provision cannot stand unless it is 'justified by a compelling state interest.'"[33] Clearly, one basis for his decision was the violation of precedent by the Congress in passing and by the FEC in enforcing the amendment. Alito's willingness to use the doctrinal modality solidified what had been observed both in his confirmation hearings and in other court cases; he typically bases his decisions on a strict prognosis of precedent. However, the doctrinal modality was not the only one utilized by Alito in this opinion.

Alito employed a historical-prudential hybrid modality to conclude his ruling. He declared:

> The argument that a candidate's speech may be restricted in order to "level electoral opportunities" has ominous implications because it would permit Congress to arrogate the voters' authority to evaluate the strengths of candidates competing for office. . . . Different candidates have different strengths. Some are wealthy; others have wealthy supporters who are willing to make large contributions. Some are celebrities; some have the benefit of a well-known family name. Leveling electoral opportunities means making and implementing judgments about which strengths should be permitted to contribute to the outcome of an election. The Constitution, however, confers upon voters, not Congress, the power to choose the Members of the House of Representatives, Art. I, §2, and it is a dangerous business for Congress to use the election laws to influence the voters' choices.[34]

Justice Alito uses the framers' constitutional intent as a foundation for his logic, which stems from the historical modality that "relies on the intentions of the framers of the Constitution and the ratifiers of its subsequent amendments."[35] By using historical intent to explain his doctrinal reasoning, Alito fortified the legitimacy of his decision. From his introduction of historically charged framing, we note that Alito acknowledges the importance of what the Founders intended in their legal doctrine.

It is clear that Alito frequently used certain modalities when adjudicating. However, a more recent case involving Alito presented a problem of contradicting modalities and, more importantly, gave advocates insight into his prioritization of modalities. *Citizens United v. Federal Election Commission* (2010)[36] was a landmark five to four decision that overturned the parts of the 2002 McCain–Feingold Bipartisan Campaign Reform Act (BCRA) that restricted corporations' ability to fund independent political commercials. Justice Kennedy wrote the majority opinion, but many of the justices filed concurring and dissenting opinions, indicating how controversial the five to four decision was. The ruling lists the following lineup:

KENNEDY, J., delivered the opinion of the Court, in which ROBERTS, C. J., and SCALIA and ALITO, JJ., joined, in which THOMAS, J., joined as to all but Part IV, and in which STEVENS, GINSBURG, BREYER, and SOTO-MAYOR, JJ., joined as to Part IV. ROBERTS, C. J., filed a concurring opinion, in which ALITO, J., joined. SCALIA, J., filed a concurring opinion, in which ALITO, J., joined, and in which THOMAS, J., joined in part. STEVENS, J., filed an opinion concurring in part and dissenting in part, in which GINSBURG, BREYER, and SOTOMAYOR, JJ., joined. THOMAS, J., filed an opinion concurring in part and dissenting in part.

Thus, Alito let others do the talking for him in this case until he found his voice in a unique venue. Alito made his opinion on these legal questions very well known during the State of the Union Address delivered on January 27, 2010, when he mouthed the words "not true" in response to President Obama's criticism of the majority's opinion. As a member of the majority in *Citizens United v. Federal Election Commission* (2010),[37] Alito believed that components of BRCA challenged his bedrock constitutional principles and thus deserved to be struck down. In this case, Alito was willing to overturn over a century of precedent to reestablish the political voices of corporations and unions. In other words, his reliance in this case on original intent trumped his concern for precedent, leading some to conclude that dubbing him Scalito may not have been so far off the mark after all.

CONCLUSIONS

My application of Bobbitt's modalities to Justice Alito's confirmation hearings and important Supreme Court decisions revealed Alito's judicial conscience.[38] Initially, we learned through Alito's confirmation hearings that he presented himself as a strict doctrinal adjudicator who would use a structural rationale to buttress his opinions. However, in examining his opinions in First Amendment cases, it is clear that Alito's judicial philosophy is based on other modalities as well.

Justice Alito also has a tendency to incorporate prudential logic as a substitute for doctrinal logic, but in many cases, he employed the prudential modality to reinforce his stance. The introduction of a supporting modality is noteworthy because Alito did not utilize this rhetorical frame during his confirmation process. Additionally, an argument can be made that Alito used this rhetorical strategy as a way of functioning outside of legal precedent while still acknowledging the precedential nature of his overall contention.

First and foremost, advocates before the Court should frame arguments in terms of precedent in order to persuade Justice Alito. Catering to Alito's preference for the doctrinal modality would require an advocate to ground an argument in precedent before using prudential or structural strategies for reinforcement. Should an advocate seek to overturn precedent, the best modality to use would be the historical, much in the way Alito did in joining various opinions in the *Citizens United* case in his break with precedent. If original intent is used as a supplement or warrant for various arguments, Justice Alito will most likely react favorably. Evidence for this thesis was provided recently in his dissenting opinion in the *Hastings* ruling; Alito argued that original intent prevented the campus from prohibiting a group simply because it disagreed with the group's exclusion of certain potential members.[39]

Finally, it is important for advocates to remember that Alito has shown himself to be partial to the combination of modalities. *Hein v. Freedom from Religion Foundation* (2007)[40] and *Davis v. Federal Election Commission* (2008)[41] both demonstrated that he is very willing to strengthen his opinions by using several modalities. Justice Alito's opinions consequentially suggest that advocates should be prepared to combine modalities in order to effectively frame their rhetorical messages.

NOTES

1. *Confirmation Hearing on the Nomination of Samuel A. Alito, Jr., to Be an Associate Justice of the Supreme Court of the United States: Hearing before the Committee on the Judiciary, United States Senate, 109th Congress, 2nd session, January 9–13* (Washington, DC: Government Printing Office, 2006).

2. Charles Babington, "Alito Is Sworn in on High Court," *Washington Post*, February 1, 2006: A1.

3. David D. Kirkpatrick, "Kerry Gets Cool Response to Call to Filibuster Alito," *New York Times*, January 27, 2006, http://www.nytimes.com/2006/01/27/politics/politicsspecial1/27alito.html (accessed September 2, 2009).

4. John Dickerson, "Ready to Rumble: The Supreme Court Battle We Have All Been Waiting For," *Slate*, October 31, 2005, http://www.slate.com/id/2129101/ (accessed September 11, 2009).

5. Ilya Somin, "Alito's Libertarian Streak," *Spectator*, November 10, 2005, http://www.cato.org/pub_display.php?pub_id=5188 (accessed September 16, 2009).

6. Smith, chapter 1 of this book

7. Hein v. Freedom from Religion Foundation (Hein), 551 U.S. 587 (2007).

8. Davis v. FEC (Davis), 554 U.S. ___ (2008), slip. op. 06-01185 (2008).

9. *Confirmation Hearing on the Nomination of Samuel A. Alito, Jr.*, 14.

10. *Confirmation Hearing on the Nomination of Samuel A. Alito, Jr.*, 403.

11. . Bobbitt, *Constitutional Interpretation*, 12–13.

12. Ginsberg v. New York, 390 U.S. 629 (1968). Alito's tendency toward the ethical in ambiguous situations was recently reflected in his lone dissent in Snyder v. Phelps (562 U.S. ___ (2011) Slip. Op. Alito argued that when the difference between private and public speech was difficult to determine, and the lower court had awarded a tort judgment based on the speech being private, it was best to sustain the lower court's award.

13. Janice Schuetz, *Communicating the Law—Lessons from Landmark Legal Cases* (Long Grove, IL: Waveland Press, 2007).

14. *Confirmation Hearing on the Nomination of Samuel A. Alito, Jr.*, 439.

15. Bobbitt, "Constitutional Fate," *Texas Law Review*, 58 (1980), 7.

16. Smith, "Introduction, Methodology, and Overview."

17. Smith, "Introduction, Methodology, and Overview."

18. "Senate Begins Final Debate on Alito," Associated Press, January 25, 2006, http://www.msnbc.msn.com/id/10993560/ (accessed September 6, 2009).

19. Kathy Kiely, "Alito Joins High Court After 58–42 Vote," *USA Today*, January 1, 2006, http://www.usatoday.com/news/washington/judicial/2006-01-31-alito_x.htm (accessed September 6, 2009).

20. Hein v. Freedom from Religion Foundation, 551 U.S. 587 (2007).

21. William Branigan, "Justices Quash Suit over Funds for Faith Groups," *Washington Post*, June 26, 2007: 6.

22. Flast v. Cohen, 392 U.S. 83 (1968). This decision allows taxpayers to sue the government if government funds are being used to encourage and promote religion.

23. Hein v. Freedom from Religion Foundation, 551 U.S. 587, 593 (2007).

24. Bobbitt, *Fate*, 7.

25. Flast v. Cohen, 392 U.S. 83 (1968).

26. Hein v. Freedom from Religion Foundation, 551 U.S. 587, 607 (2007).

27. Linda Greenhouse, "Justices Reject Suit on Federal Money for Faith-Based Office," *New York Times*, June 26, 2007, http://www.nytimes.com/2007/06/26/washington/26faith.html?_r=1 (accessed September 11, 2009).

28. Hein v. Freedom from Religion Foundation (Hein), 551 U.S. 587, 604 (2007). Alito was referring to the precedent set by Lujan v. Defenders of Wildlife, 504 U.S. 555, 573–74 (1992).

29. Davis v. Federal Election Commission, 554 U.S. slip. op. 06-01185 (2008).

30. "Justices Dissect 'Millionaire's Amendment,'" Associated Press, April 22, 2008, http://www.firstamendmentcenter.org/news.aspx?id=19952 (accessed September 2, 2009).

31. Buckley v. Valeo, 424 U.S. 1 (1976).

32. Davis v. Federal Election Commission, 554 U.S. ___ (2008), slip. op. 06-01185, 336.

33. Davis v. Federal Election Commission (2008). This argument relies on precedent established in Buckley v. Valeo, 424 U.S. 1 (1976).

34. Davis v. Federal Election Commission (2008).

35. Smith, "Introduction, Methodology, and Overview."

36. Citizens United v. Federal Election Commission, 558 U. S. ___ (2010), slip. op. 50.

37. Citizens United v. Federal Election Commission, 558 U. S. ___ (2010), slip. op. 50.

38. Bobbitt, *Constitutional Interpretation*, 163.

39. Hastings College of Law v. Martinez, 561 U. S. ___ (2010), slip. op.

40. Hein v. Freedom from Religion Foundation, 551 U.S. 587 (2007).

41. Davis v. Federal Election Commission (2008).

Chapter Twelve

Conclusion

Craig R. Smith

Cicero would be proud of the foregoing chapters by budding and brilliant scholars because they reveal that simple categorization of sitting justices is unreliable as a guide to their decision making. Like Cicero, these authors understand that a useful profile for rhetorical adaptation can only be formed from a close reading of the testimony and opinions of the justices instead of reliance primarily on secondary sources. That primary source approach combined with a guiding methodology that is leavened by rhetorical criticism has produced a nuanced profile of each justice that better differentiates him or her from colleagues than such unsophisticated labels as "conservative," "liberal," "originalist," or "strict constructionist."

Table 12.1 presents a profile of the justices of the Supreme Court based on the foregoing chapters.

Justice Thomas, for example, has a healthy respect for the originalist tradition, but he means originalist in the historic sense. And he undergirds that historic sense with textual, prudential, and precedential arguments that advance his respect for the historic tradition of the Supreme Court, not just the Founders of the nation. He is also capable of justifying his decision by relying on higher laws and rights embodied in the Declaration of Independence, a trait he shares on occasion with Justice Kennedy, but not necessarily in First Amendment opinions.

Justice Kennedy grounds his decisions in an almost subliminal ethicism that respects the involvement of the public in democratic discourse. He draws this ethical stance from Enlightenment thinkers who influenced Jefferson's version of the Declaration of Independence. More overtly, he then uses close reading of the Constitution's text, and precedential and prudential arguments,

Table 12.1.   The Justices and Their Preferred Modalities

Modalities	Historical	Textual	Structural	Doctrinal	Ethical	Prudential
Roberts		Foundation	Support	Support		Support
Alito	Support		Support	Foundation		Support
Scalia	Foundation	Foundation	Support	Support		
Kennedy	Support	Support		Support	Foundation	Support
Thomas	Foundation	Support		Support	Support	Support
Ginsburg				Support	Foundation	
Breyer				Support	Support	Foundation
Souter/ Sotomayor	Support			Support		Foundation
Stevens/ Kagan	Support			Support		Foundation

Notes: (1) The historical incorporates original intent and the subcategory of higher laws as derived natural law as "inalienable rights" in the Declaration of Independence; (2) the textual modality is better known as strict constructionalist reading; (3) the structural infers "rules from relationships that the Constitution mandates"; (4) the doctrinal applies rules derived from precedent (stare decisis); (5) the ethical reflects "moral commitments of the American ethos"; (6) the prudential balances "costs and benefits."

to advance his agenda. It is his textualist approach that causes many writers to place him in the conservative camp. But Professor Johnson's analysis reveals why Kennedy is better seen as the swing vote on the Court.

Justice Scalia sailed through his confirmation hearings because he was terribly knowledgeable about case law and about as affable a witness as the Senate Judiciary Committee had ever seen. However, once seated on the bench, Scalia revealed a feisty streak that at times has offended his colleagues. His opinions are as much fun to read as his questions during oral arguments before the Court are to hear. Professor Asenas has discovered in her analysis that Scalia is much more complicated than any of us may have suspected. He is an originalist and a textualist who advances his readings of the Constitution with precedential and structural arguments. He also relishes *ornatus*, the art of fashioning a statement with tropes and figures.

Chief Justice Roberts made clear during his nomination hearings that he was a knowledgeable conservative, which pleased the Republican majority on the Senate Judiciary Committee and the president who nominated him to the Court. He might be seen as a "kinder, gentler" Scalia. As Research Fellow Tim West makes clear, Roberts relies on precedent to affirm his plain reading of the Constitution. When he faces conflicting precedents, as he did in *Morse v. Frederick* (2007), he raises prudential arguments to decide the case. Roberts also lends credence to a thesis I have developed in another book, *Silencing the Opposition: Government Strategies of Suppression.*[1] I argue in that study that in times of crisis, the Supreme Court tends to restrict

First Amendment rights. On June 21, 2010, Roberts wrote for a six to three majority that ruled that a 1996 antiterrorism law covered giving advice about legal strategies and venues to groups that the secretary of state listed as terrorist supporters. In this particular case, professors who gave advice to the Kurdistan Workers' Party on how to take grievances to the United Nations, or gave legal advice to Tamil separatists in Sri Lanka, had violated the law, according to Roberts and his majority.[2] The communication under investigation in this case did not concern action; it concerned ideas and legal aid. Therefore, we see that Roberts will overturn precedent and original intent when he perceives a threat to the nation's interests.

After a controversial nomination process, Justice Alito not unexpectedly aligned himself with Scalia and Roberts, but as time goes by he may become a more independent thinker. As Tim West reveals in his analysis, Alito is more libertarian than his conservative colleagues when it comes to First Amendment issues. Though he relies heavily on stare decisis, Alito erects a historical altar, which has been tempered by his prudential and structuralist bent. It should be noted that Alito is a member of the Catholic majority on the Court, which, with the addition of Justice Sotomayor, is rather disproportional, at two-thirds of the composition of the Court.[3]

Justice Breyer, normally seen as a "liberal" who endorses a "living Constitution," is really a pragmatist at heart, closely examining how the law affects everyday citizens in the contemporary world. However, he is not a pragmatist who argues that if it works, keep it, regardless of its virtue. As Professor Heyse makes clear, he has a strong ethical bent, as do most liberals on the Court, in that he seeks to be guided by and to contribute to a "web" of good law. Thus, Breyer has respect for precedent and often relies on it to ground his ethical approach.

Justice Stevens has long quarreled with his conservative counterparts. He was so upset with President Reagan's agenda for the Court that he publicly took on Attorney General Edwin Meese over the issue of original intent, as we have seen. In First Amendment law, Stevens has sought to extend rights, except when it comes to symbolic speech. He often clashed with Chief Justice Rehnquist when the latter achieved a majority in support of cutting back on advertisers' rights. Stevens eventually prevailed by reversing Rehnquist's *Posadas* ruling of 1986 with the *44 Liquormart* decision of 1996. In that ruling, Stevens renewed his criticism of Rehnquist's attempts to curtail advertisers' rights. Stevens quoted from newspapers at the time of the passage of the First Amendment in 1791 to show that free press meant freedom to advertise. Professor Brandon Anderson reveals that Stevens, who was one of the few swing votes on the Court, often relied on history to support his decisions. He did this in several cases. In *44 Liquormart*, for example, he relied on the historical context at the time the First Amendment was approved. In other cases, he examined the historical context at the time of the case. And finally, he showed great respect for the history and traditions of the Court as they have evolved. He also examined the original intent of the Founders but does not believe it is the be-all and end-all for his decisions.

These factors all came together rather dramatically in *Texas v. Johnson* when Stevens dissented from a narrow liberal majority that saw flag burning as protected symbolic speech. Eighteen years later, Stevens would join the liberals in dissent in *Morse v. Frederick*, arguing that student speech was protected unless some compelling government interest could be established to justify censorship. What seems to have emerged in Stevens's case is a healthy dose of pragmatism that often undercuts his respect for precedent. This is true particularly in campaign spending cases, where he has been a regular critic of the *Buckley* compromise wherein contributions can be limited but expenditures cannot. However, in one of his final decisions, released June 21, 2010, Stevens sided with the conservative majority to support a restriction of First Amendment rights in *Holder, Attorney General, et al., v. Humanitarian Law Project, et al.*, proving once again that he is fundamentally a pragmatist.

Justice Ginsburg is probably the most consistently liberal voice on the Court, but is not one often heard on First Amendment issues. They do not seem to be an interest of hers. As Professor Katie Gibson makes clear, Ginsburg uses precedential and ethical modalities to advance her liberal view that the Constitution can be adapted to contemporary times. Her view of constitutional dynamism often puts her in the minority, as with her dissents in establishment clause cases and *FCC v. Fox*, in which she chastised the majority for upholding government censorship of the airwaves. However, her endorsement of some "play in the joints" of the First Amendment clauses has led to a majority opinion in which she protected the rights of prisoners to exercise their religion. She did write the majority opinion in the case that upheld Hastings Law School's restriction on clubs that excluded minorities,[4] an ethicist ruling that seems to contradict the *Hurley* (1995) and *Boy Scouts of America* (2000) cases in which the courts ruled that private parades and clubs could exclude members that did not embrace their values.

Justice Souter, who left the Court as we were writing this study, was appointed by President George H. W. Bush, who had heard good things about the judge from associates. Souter was considered a safe, conservative addition to the Court and was easily confirmed. However, within a few decisions of his appointment, it became clear that he was one more case of a judge changing his spots once he was appoint to the high court for life. Befriended by Justice Breyer, Souter soon felt no obligation to the Republicans who had helped him get appointed. As Research Fellow Megan Loden points out, Souter became known for his First Amendment dissents. Like his conservative colleagues, Souter respected the history of the Constitution and the Court and buttressed that respect with a doctrinal reading of the law.

However, he moved toward the liberal end of the spectrum when he engaged in prudential balancing of the interests involved. One of the landmark moments for Souter came with the crisis of the election of 2000, in which the Supreme Court intervened to stop a recount in Florida and ensure that George W. Bush would become president. Souter was deeply disturbed by the decision, in which he joined Breyer in dissent. Many report it was this crisis that first led a disillusioned Souter to consider leaving the Court.

He was replaced the lively judge Sonia Sotomayor, who has positioned herself as the Scalia of the left. Smartly, during her confirmation hearings, she refused to answer questions concerning specific decisions. Her decision in an affirmative action case, which was only one paragraph, caused only mild controversy. More troubling was her comment that her life, gender, and ethnicity would not only inform her decisions but make them better than those issued by white men. Megan Loden's analysis predicts that Justice Sotomayor will be a pragmatic justice who has little use for the original intent of the Founders. In the *Holder* ruling (see above), she sided with Breyer and Ginsberg, coming down on the side of protecting speech that was not action in the case of advising foreign political groups with terrorist ties.

Once one understands just how complex these profiles of the justices are, one realizes how difficult it is for advocates to make arguments that create a consensus of support on the Court. However, an analysis of these profiles indicates that the number-one preference among the justices would be for arguments based on precedent. These arguments not only play to justices like Thomas, who respects the Founders and the history of the Court, they also share common ground with every other justice seeking a way to decide a case under the cloak of objectivity.

The problem with precedents is at least twofold. First, they are essentially used as support for other modalities, not as a foundation, for most of the justices on the Supreme Court. Second, many precedents exist, and they often exist on both sides of an issue. This phenomenon is particularly true in First Amendment case law. For example, while the Court cut back on the freedom of expression of high school students in such cases as *Fraser* and *Haseltine*, the landmark decision of *Tinker* still promises that students do not lose their First Amendment rights at the schoolhouse door. Private groups may exclude members under the freedom of assembly clause, while groups that take federal money may have more difficulty doing so.

The second-most-used modality is the prudential. Because it is foundational in the rhetoric of three justices, it is the most potent modality of all those listed. It is the prudential modality that is used by both liberals and conservatives when they justify a shift from their normal bases of argument. To take a non–First Amendment case as an example, look at the rationale used by the majority in *Bush v. Gore* to justify moving away from states' rights and embracing judicial activism. In almost every concurrence and in the per curiam itself, a prudential argument limits the impact of the ruling to the specific case at bar.

The third-most-used modality is the historical, but its high ranking results from the fact that Bobbitt included what we have discovered to be three submodalities in this category. The category not only includes those who appeal to original intent, making the modality foundational for them, but those who appeal to higher laws embodied in the Declaration of Independence, such as Thomas and Kennedy, and those who use history to contextualize cases, such as Stevens. Thus, in the future, it may be wise to break this modality into three different categories: (1) those who employ original intent as a guide, (2) those who appeal to higher laws based on Enlightenment thinking in the Declaration of Independence, and (3) those who use history to create a context and/or tradition.

It may surprise some readers that the plain reading of the Constitution or its strict construction is not as highly used as other modalities. However, there is an explanation for this. If a law can be found to clearly violate the First Amendment, it is normally struck down *before* it reaches the Court. Laws that violate a plain reading of the Constitution are usually dealt with in the lower courts. Laws that reach the Supreme Court for adjudication do not usually evoke a plain reading of the Constitution or may call conflicting clauses in the First Amendment into play. Thus, other methods of argument must be employed. However, from the analysis performed by the scholars in this study, it is clear that when certain members of the Court have an agenda that offends a plain reading of the Constitution, they advance it nonetheless. Two strong precedents stand out. The first is *Buckley v. Valeo*, in which the Court ruled that a "perception" of corruption was enough to justify curtailing freedom of expression. The alleged influence of contributions on the political system compromised it by giving the appearance of corruption. In this case, there is a presumption of guilt rather than innocence, shifting the burden of proof onto the defenders of freedom of expression. Worse yet, the case fell into self-contradiction: money is not speech when it is contributed to a campaign; therefore, it can be restricted. However, money is speech when spent by a campaign; therefore, it cannot be restricted in that form!

The second case is *Pacifica v. FCC* (1978), in which the Supreme Court held that indecent speech, kind of obscenity light, could be regulated by the Federal Communications Commission. The Court ruled that George Carlin's semantic lesson regarding "seven dirty words" that were not allowed to be uttered during the day on radio and television was without redeeming social value. Despite many efforts to overturn a decision which advanced no provable compelling government interest, it remains precedent to this day.

Based on our analysis, advocates may wish to look at some of the subtler points in the justices' profiles. For example, Justice Kennedy is a swing voter and thus crucial to creating a majority in favor of a position. If one appealed to an ethical standard embedded in the American consciousness, Kennedy might find it appealing, as would justices Ginsburg and Sotomayor. So would Justice Breyer, particularly if an advocate could show a beneficial pragmatic impact. The combinations of consensus building that can be created from the profiles laid out here are myriad.

I believe the successful advocate will understand that each judge should be treated as a different audience and then similarities among those nine audiences should be examined to find out how to build consensus. The danger is that in appealing to one audience, an advocate might offend another. And, of course, the details of the case at bar will restrict the kind of appeals an advocate is allowed to make. Properly trained advocates who set out the full array of arguments available to them within the realm of linguistic possibilities in any given case, and examine the full array of arguments the other side, are more likely to gain adherence before the Court. They can tailor their arguments to the nine audiences in their briefs and in their oral arguments. Arguments before the Court are often stylized for clarity; metaphors abound, from the "chilling effect" of arbitrary and capricious restrictions to the "pig" of obscenity invited into the "parlor." In each case, arguments need to be framed in the hopes of building consensus. If a justice accepts one advocate's framing of the case at bar, the justice is much more likely to render a favorable ruling for that advocate. It is not a far step from those strategies of audience analysis to building a consensus by appealing to each justice's more nuanced criteria for decision making. By educating advocates about such criteria, we hope to level the playing field before the Supreme Court and thus give the truth and the better ruling a good chance at emerging in First Amendment law.

The analyses performed by the contributing authors to this study also indicate that even Philip Bobbitt's approach to judicial modalities can be made subtler by a close reading of the rhetoric of the justices. I have already discussed the possible three-part nature of Bobbitt's historical modality. The ethical modality is also more complex rhetorically than Bobbitt revealed. He rather vaguely claimed that it relies on an American ethos, but America's diversity clearly divides that ethos into many subsets. Thus, it is not surprising that justices use the ethical modality in different ways. Justices Kennedy and Thomas use it to connect with higher law through the historical modality, which is based on natural rights. Justice Stevens used it to find an evolving ethos based in the Constitution and the tradition of the Court. Justice Ginsburg uses it to ground her view that the Constitution is dynamic.

Therefore, the best way to build on Bobbitt's model is to reveal how these modalities are used for rhetorical ends. To what end is a given justice trying to persuade his or her colleagues? If we begin by discovering the telos of the justice, I believe we better understand which modalities will be used and why justices shift between modalities. The modalities are not after all an end in themselves; they are rhetorical strategies to achieve an end. Justice Scalia may be a textualist because he believes it is the right way to read the Constitution. However, he is not above using other modalities to achieve his vision of how a case should be decided to contribute to his vision of a perfect society.

In the end, I believe we have proven that, like many other governmental agencies and branches, the Supreme Court is essentially a rhetorical venue, not simply a logical one.

NOTES

1. Craig R. Smith, *Silencing the Opposition: Government Strategies of Suppression* (Albany: State University of New York Press, 2011).

2. Holder, Attorney General, et al. v. Humanitarian Law Project et al. (CERTIORARI TO THE UNITED STATES COURT OF APPEALS FOR THE NINTH CIRCUIT), no. 08–1498, argued February 23, 2010, decided June 21, 2010.

3. By way of full disclosure, the editor of this book and this chapter is a Catholic existentialist. The Catholics on the Court include Alito, Kennedy, Roberts, Scalia, Thomas, and Sotomayor, constituting a two-thirds majority.

4. Hastings Christian Fellowship Society v. Martinez, et al, 561 U.S. ___ (2010).

Index of Major First Amendment Supreme Court Cases Cited in this Study

About the Editor and Contributors

EDITOR

Craig R. Smith is director of the Center for First Amendment Studies and professor of communication studies at California State University, Long Beach. He is the author of several articles and books on freedom of expression, including *The Four Freedoms of the First Amendment* (2004) and *Silencing the Opposition: Government Strategies of Suppression* (second edition, 2011). In 2010, he won the Douglas Ehninger Award from the National Communication Association for his work in rhetorical studies.

CONTRIBUTORS

R. Brandon Anderson is a graduate student at the University of Texas. He received his master's degree from California State University, Long Beach. He was also a graduate research fellow of the Center for First Amendment Studies and has published a university press book chapter on the government restrictions following the attacks of 9/11.

Jennifer J. Asenas is an assistant professor in the Department of Communication Studies at California State University, Long Beach. She is the lead author of a forthcoming chapter, "Saving Kenneth Foster: Speaking with 'Others in the Belly of the Beast,'" in *Communication Activism*, volume 3.

Katie L. Gibson is an associate professor in the Department of Communication Studies at California State University, Long Beach. She recently completed a university press book chapter on the suffrage movement. Her work focuses on public address and freedom of expression.

Amy L. Heyse is an assistant professor in the Department of Communication Studies at California State University, Long Beach. She recently completed a university press book chapter on the suffrage movement. Her research focuses on political and gender rhetoric, engaging issues of collective memory and subjectivity.

Kevin A. Johnson is the director of research for the Center for First Amendment Studies and director of communication for the NAACP of Long Beach, California. He is author of numerous articles on political rhetoric, mass media, and the psychoanalysis of culture.

Megan Loden received her master's degree in 2010 from California State University, Long Beach, where she also coached the forensics team. Her thesis concerned a rhetorical restructuring of the Republican Party.

Tim West was a graduate research fellow for the Center for First Amendment Studies at California State University, Long Beach. He completed his master's degree in communication studies in 2010, and served as a coach for the debate team. He is currently pursuing a law degree.